Women Writing Plays

THREE DECADES OF *The Susan Smith Blackburn Prize*

EDITED BY ALEXIS GREENE

FOREWORD BY EMILIE S. KILGORE

INTRODUCTION BY MARSHA NORMAN

UNIVERSITY OF TEXAS PRESS

AUSTIN

BOOK THIRTEEN
LOUANN ATKINS TEMPLE WOMEN & CULTURE SERIES

See the permissions section at the back of this volume
for information on individual copyright holders.

Requests for permission to reproduce material from this work
should be sent to: Permissions, University of Texas Press,
P.O. Box 7819, Austin, TX 78713-7819
www.utexas.edu/utpress/about/bpermission.html

⊗ The paper used in this book meets the minimum requirements
of ANSI/NISO Z39.48-1992 (R1997) (Permanence of Paper).

LIBRARY OF CONGRESS CATALOGING-IN-PUBLICATION DATA
Women writing plays : three decades of the Susan Smith Blackburn
Prize / edited by Alexis Greene ; foreword by Emilie S. Kilgore ;
introduction by Marsha Norman. — 1st ed.
p. cm. — (Louann Atkins Temple women & culture series ; bk. 13)
Includes bibliographical references and index.
ISBN-13: 978-0-292-71325-3 (alk. paper)
ISBN-10: 0-292-71325-8
ISBN-13: 978-0-292-71329-1 (pbk. : alk. paper)
ISBN-10: 0-292-71329-0
1. American drama — Women authors — History and criticism.
2. English drama — Women authors — History and criticism.
3. American drama — 20th century — History and criticism.
4. American drama — 21st century — History and criticism. 5. English
drama — 20th century — History and criticism. 6. English drama —
21st century — History and criticism. 7. Feminism and theater —
English-speaking countries. 8. Women in literature. 9. Susan Smith
Blackburn Prize. I. Greene, Alexis. II. Series.
PS338.W6W66 2006
812'.54099287 — dc22
2006000656

To Susan

Contents

✾

Foreword

EMILIE S. KILGORE

❦

When I heard that I won the prize, I decided one thing: that this prize was going to make me more daring. I think "daring" means to write about the great issues of our time. And to write about them fully, deeply, without fear, and without timidity. Twenty years ago, I'm sure if there had been a contest of this nature, there probably wouldn't have been enough plays submitted by women to occupy the time of the judges. But I also believe that twenty years from now, the words "woman playwright" will seem to us entirely outmoded and completely unfashionable.

—BARBARA SCHNEIDER, ACCEPTING THE SECOND
SUSAN SMITH BLACKBURN PRIZE FOR *Details without a Map,*
THE PLAYERS, NEW YORK, FEBRUARY 13, 1980

The Susan Smith Blackburn Prize is awarded annually to women who deserve recognition for writing works of outstanding quality for the English-speaking theater. The aim of the prize is to extend the creative influence of women in the theater, to encourage them to write for the theater, and to recognize excellence in the works of those who do.

I remember when, nearly three decades ago, in 1977, the Susan Smith Blackburn Prize came into being. It was a week or so after my sister's death at the age of forty-two from breast cancer. Her husband, Bill Blackburn, and I met with Dee Wells, a dear friend of Susan's, at Dee's house in London. We talked for a long time about Susan, wanting and hoping to find a way to honor her and extend her memory—to find a tribute that reflected her life and embodied her great interests. Susan's own words had been, "I want to *matter.*"

We talked about her gift for writing and her lifelong love of the theater. As a child, Susan had written plays that we children performed for visiting guests and relatives. She directed and nearly always starred in these family productions. Later on, she acted in plays at the Alley Theatre and the Little Theater in Houston, where we grew up, and at Smith College in Massachusetts, where, after a year of study in Spain, she wrote her thesis on the plays of Federico García Lorca. After graduating with honors, she studied acting with Uta Hagen in New York and played several leading roles in productions on and off Broadway.

Susan and Bill were married in 1960 in New York, and two years later they moved to London, where Susan would spend the last fifteen years of her life. With the move, and with two small children, her acting stopped, but her writing blossomed; as a freelance journalist, she wrote beautifully observed and often very funny articles for national newspapers and magazines on both sides of the Atlantic.

At our meeting in 1977, Bill, Dee, and I talked about Susan's other interests. She had been a delegate to the Democratic National Convention in 1972 and had co-chaired George McGovern's presidential campaign in Europe. Always outraged by injustices, she had organized a large and successful benefit in London for Native Americans. Dee recalled the fun that many friends had had eating out as paid restaurant inspectors for Susan when she was writing a much-lauded connoisseur's guidebook to London, a book that she revised and updated the last year of her life. She had been active in the Women's Movement and believed that it wasn't a question of women needing help from society but rather of society urgently needing help from women. Everything she did, she did with energy and passion and intelligence. We had witnessed these qualities in the last months of her life, when she devoted her characteristic energy to a search for a way to conquer her illness. It was one of the few efforts in which she was not successful.

So there we were, meeting after Susan's much-too-early death, because it was impossible *not* to do something, impossible *not* to want to perpetuate the vitality, the creativity, and the reaching-out that characterized her life. We put together her love of the theater, her gift for writing, and her desire to foster women's influence in the world. At the same time, looking at the playwriting landscape, we recognized that, despite the growing Women's Movement, a dire situation faced women writing for the stage in the male-dominated theater world of the 1970s. And thus the Susan Smith Blackburn Prize was born. The fact that Susan was an American living in London and that New York–London was the obvious axis of the English-speaking theater world led us naturally to establish our prize as a transatlantic one, in contrast to such prizes as America's Pulitzer and Britain's Booker.

As we began to build the organization, we got in touch with the American playwright Lillian Hellman, whom Susan had greatly admired, and asked her to join us as a director. She did so, thinking it was an inspired, much-needed idea. We realized from the beginning that if the prize was to be a significant one, the judges chosen by the directors must be persons whose views would be taken seriously and whose decisions would carry the weight we intended the prize to carry. We determined that we would call on the finest theater directors, critics, playwrights, actors, and other artists—distinguished men and women on both sides of the Atlantic—to serve on the panels, which each year would consist of six judges: three from the United States and three from the United Kingdom and Ireland. We were fortunate that there was instant recognition of a good idea whose time had come. The playwrights Edward Albee (U.S.A.), Tony Kushner (U.S.A.), and Tom Stoppard (U.K), as well as the actors Meryl Streep (U.S.A.), Fiona Shaw (U.K.), and Glenn Close (U.S.A.), are among those who have served. (A complete listing of judges grouped both alphabetically and by year can be found in the Appendix.)

The insistence on quality applied also to the system whereby winners and finalists would be chosen. After a brief period of experimentation, the process emerged that has proven equitable and efficient and has never had to change. To begin with, plays are submitted not by agents or individuals but by a wide variety of professional theaters that produce new plays. In September of each year, artistic directors and literary managers of theaters throughout the English-speaking world are invited to submit full-length plays for consideration. Although entries from the United States, the United Kingdom, and Ireland still predominate, we have extended the reach of the prize and now receive scripts from Australia, Canada, India, New Zealand, and South Africa. A play is accepted whether or not it has been produced, but any first production must have taken place within the preceding twelve months. Each script is read by at least three members of an international reading committee—a network of knowledgeable, perceptive readers who devote a tremendous amount of time to assessing individual works. In conferences that take place in both the United States and the United Kingdom, the top ten to twelve finalists are selected, and these scripts are then submitted to the panel of judges, each of whom reads every play.

The finalists are notified in January, and the awards ceremony takes place in February or March in New York, London, or Houston. The prize currently awards $25,000 annually to the finalists. The winner receives $10,000 and a

Willem de Kooning with Emilie S. Kilgore in the artist's studio at Springs, New York, 1977, signing his prints created especially for the Susan Smith Blackburn Prize. (Photograph: Cal Norris, courtesy Susan Smith Blackburn Prize)

signed, limited-edition print made especially for the Susan Smith Blackburn Prize by the abstract expressionist Willem de Kooning, who was a friend and admirer of Susan's. In addition, there are Special Commendations of $2,000, and each of the other finalists receives $1,000.

During the prize's first three decades, several thousand plays have been submitted to the competition. To date, 309 have become finalists, among which 195 were from the United States; 105 from England, Scotland, and Ireland; 3 each from Australia and Canada; and 1 each from India, Pakistan, and New Zealand. (A listing of finalists arranged both alphabetically and by year appears in the Appendix.) In many cases, the prize has anticipated later recognition. For example, to date, six plays recognized by the Susan Smith Blackburn Prize were subsequently awarded the Pulitzer Prize in drama, the only plays by women to have won that award since the Blackburn Prize was established. The prize has also fostered the interchange of plays between the United States, the United Kingdom, and Ireland. This often happens through judges' networking. For instance, when the London playwright Shirley Gee won the prize for *Never in My*

Lifetime in 1985, one of the judges, the American playwright John Guare, sent the script to a colleague—a director—which led to a U.S. premiere.

We give formal recognition to all the finalists. For many playwrights, this has proven to be a source of encouragement and has led to benefits, including productions, grants, and public recognition. When the *New York Times* announced that Sarah Ruhl's unproduced play, *The Clean House,* had won in 2004, the writer received four offers from major theaters to produce the play. It is rewarding to those connected with the prize to know that the lists of finalists have become an important resource for theaters interested in new plays. In Houston where I live, more than sixty Blackburn Prize finalists have been produced.

When the prize was established in 1978, only about 7 percent of the plays produced across the United States were written by women. A similar situation existed in Great Britain and Ireland. We know from various reports on the status of women in theater that there has been progress since then but that it has been inconsistent and extremely slow in coming, and some backsliding is unfortunately evident. According to the *Report on the Status of Women in Theatre: A Limited Engagement?* published by the New York State Council on the Arts, productions of plays by women stood at approximately 17 percent as of 2002. It is clear that the prize is still needed. Its goals may not be achieved in my lifetime.

There is something about reaching milestones that makes us want to look back. As we approach the end of our third decade, we felt it was an opportune time to mark this milestone in a significant way. A book emerged as the most appropriate project—one centered on a thoughtful investigation of women's playwriting throughout the English-speaking theater from the late 1970s until today. We are fortunate that Alexis Greene accepted the challenging job of serving as editor for this volume, and we appreciate all the contributors whom she engaged.

Looking back over these past decades of administering the prize, I remember the judges' stimulating, often heated, always surprising transatlantic discussions in their search for an Anglo-American consensus. And I remember the excitement and the spirit of every awards ceremony, when new voices were discovered. The playwrights who are honored each year have great scope and imagination, as Susan herself had. The prize reaches out as Susan would certainly have done with her own creations had she lived. The prize, therefore, is not only a tribute to her. It is the fulfillment of her promise.

Acknowledgments and Note to Readers

※

The editor would like to thank the board of the Susan Smith Blackburn Prize for its support, particularly Emilie S. Kilgore, who has been the guiding spirit behind the prize since its founding; Edwin Wilson, for his sage editorial suggestions; and Bill Blackburn, Michael Attenborough, and Mel Gussow, who generously contributed their time and advice. The editor would also like to thank Tim Staley and the University of Texas Press for their editorial expertise.

The support of The Brown Foundation, Inc. is gratefully acknowledged.

A special word of gratitude goes to Caroline Keeley, Meg Poole, Phyllis Hattis, Alex Kilgore, and Tanya Lovetro, who never tired of answering questions, making telephone calls, or helping in the preparation of this book.

Readers should note that the dates in parentheses after a play title refer to the first public production or, absent a production, the copyright date. An asterisk (*) after a title indicates that the play was a finalist for the Susan Smith Blackburn Prize.

WOMEN WRITING PLAYS

Introduction

Women Writing Plays

MARSHA NORMAN

Wendy Wasserstein recalls that when she was a drama student at Yale University, the only woman dramatist ever mentioned in class was Hrosvitha of Gander-sheim, a tenth-century canoness whose plays, it was said, were never produced. In her foreword to Yvonne Shafer's anthology, *American Women Playwrights, 1900 to 1950* (1995), Wendy remembers wishing for a book like this when she was a student. She would have turned nightly to the examples of Rose Franken, Dorothy Parker, and Clare Boothe Luce for comfort and guidance. "I didn't want to be a tenth-century canoness," she writes. "I wanted to be a working woman playwright."

Many women writing for the stage still feel the same way: they want to be working women playwrights, with the emphasis on *working,* where "working" means *produced.* To my mind, the Susan Smith Blackburn Prize has done more than any other single force or festival to make *working* a possibility for women playwrights by bringing attention to their plays. It has collected and publicized its finalists for nearly three decades, but it has given much more than the award. It has established a network of women, a network of readers, and a network of writers, who know one another through the work of the prize. It has made our lives visible to one another, has allowed us to act as mentors, role models, and colleagues, and in the process to become teachers, students, and friends. It has created a community, and in so doing, it has given us all a place to live and work in the world as women writers. And now I turn to the topic at hand.

In my lifetime, in America, women writing plays has gone from nearly un-heard of to nearly commonplace. Unfortunately, the producing of plays by women has not made the same leap. In its *Report on the Status of Women in Theatre: A Limited Engagement?*—a research initiative released in 2002—the New York State Council on the Arts (NYSCA) found "consistently low main stage

1

participation of women playwrights and directors, particularly among theatres with higher budgets." Even in theaters with the self-proclaimed mission of producing new American plays, "the number of plays by women produced on the main stage was extremely low; in some cases, none. More scarce still were female playwrights of color. Female directors were also absent on the main stages of many theatres."

The full report can be found on the web site of the Fund for Women Artists, www.womenarts.org. It is recommended reading for everyone who cares about women or theater or both—for everyone who is reading this book. But statistics are not my strong suit, or my subject here. I am charged with describing how women writing plays has changed in the nearly three decades I have been doing it.

When I was a teenager, Actors Theatre of Louisville opened its doors for the first time. The little stage was located up a set of rickety stairs in an old downtown building, the house lights were bare bulbs covered in peach baskets. Walking up those stairs was my introduction to the theater. The first plays I saw there—indeed, the first hundred plays I saw, probably—were all written by men: George Bernard Shaw and Arthur Miller, Sophocles and Eugene O'Neill, Shakespeare and Shakespeare. The central characters of those plays were mainly male, and the events were male as well—big and tragic. I knew of American women who wrote novels, short stories, and poetry, and I knew of English women who wrote novels, short stories, poems, *and* plays. But I knew of no American women who wrote plays except for Jean Kerr and Lillian Hellman, neither of whom I wanted to become. Still, I wanted to write for the theater.

When my work was first being done, new plays were largely a new idea. The old idea was that a handful of men would dominate a decade of theatrical writing and then pass their status on to the new members of the club. With few exceptions, these men lived in New York, and their contacts with their producers were social as well as professional. When Richard Rodgers had a new idea for a musical, he placed a call to his producer, and his producer called the theater owners and booked the theater. Clearly this is a gross oversimplification of the process, but it *was* a club, and to break in you had to be brought in by someone who was already a member. All was calm and orderly. Golden eras came and went.

Then in the sixties and seventies, things began to change. Not-for-profit regional theaters grew and prospered, founded by men and women who did not want their theaters to serve simply as venues for touring Broadway productions. They had gone to school with playwrights; some of them were playwrights themselves. Like the pioneering artistic directors who preceded them—Margo Jones in Dallas, Nina Vance at Houston's Alley Theatre, and Zelda Fichandler at the Arena Stage in Washington, D.C.—these founders wanted to program their theaters in a new way. They wanted to present *new plays* by unknown authors because they liked the plays, the authors, the process, and the hoopla. Also, plays like Howard Sackler's *The Great White Hope,* which premiered in 1967 at the Arena Stage, had shown that both fame and fortune could be made with a new play.

Many of the new plays were by women, and women were a hot new thing in the American theater. Where I was, in Louisville, we had plays by Beth Henley, Wendy Kesselman, Mary Gallagher, Enid Rudd, Heather McDonald, Shirley Lauro, and many other women, all produced during the Humana Festival at Actors Theatre of Louisville. Elsewhere in the country, other theaters were discovering their women playwrights, and a big article on women playwrights appeared in the magazine section of the *New York Times,* written by Mel Gussow, always a champion of women writers, and featuring yours truly on the cover. Things for women writers seemed to be looking up. Productions were everywhere, actors loved us, patrons loved us, and critics loved us. Women felt a part of the theater in a very real way. Major regional theaters performed our work. Even Broadway made some of us welcome. But then, as the seventies ended, it seemed that the hunt for the new playwright took a strange turn.

Instead of being a time when regional theaters developed deeper relationships with the writers they had discovered—men and women—the eighties saw theaters seem to jettison their new writers in favor of even newer writers. Experienced playwrights found it harder and harder to find productions. Theaters devised stranger and stranger schemes to find plays and playwrights, commissioning two-minute plays, ten-minute plays, plays on the beach, plays in a bottle, you name it. But these plays were not likely to endure, because they did not come from a writer's heart but rather from a marketing person's idea of what would attract the national press. These plays were exercises at best.

Playwrights, sensing that a new Competitive Era had begun, started frantically sending plays around, and plays arrived in stacks on the doorsteps of theaters. Artistic directors felt the need to direct in other theaters and thus remain viable as national players, and they began spending more and more time away from their theaters and reading fewer and fewer plays. The ultimate result was that local audiences lost their rooting interest in their new playwrights, or couldn't tell them apart, or couldn't tell the difference between the real writers and the wannabes. The theatergoer, who had felt challenged and inspired by a new generation of writers, now gave up and began to look for the regional version of the hot ticket. Playwrights lost their champions, and audiences lost their ability to judge for themselves. Suddenly, it seemed, there were too many new plays and too many new writers.

During this era, women directors were coming up, and a number of women assumed artistic control of major theaters. But this did not mean that more plays by women were chosen for production. Some theaters, sensing that wonderful writers were languishing, or fearing that they themselves had no real idea which plays to choose from among the hundreds of manuscripts piled in their offices, began to do readings. And thus began the really dangerous time for playwrights, where we find ourselves today: The Era of Readings. And since any time that is dangerous for playwrights is more dangerous for women playwrights (see the NYSCA report), The Era of Readings meant real trouble. Readings were not, and are not, the answer.

Women playwrights have little trouble today finding readings, even staged readings. But these are only minimally helpful at best and can be misleading, or worse. Real damage can accrue to plays as the result of the so-called development process. For instance, in addition to readings, women are regularly offered commissions for plays with the idea that the money is useful and "being at work" feels good to us. But however useful the commission money is, a commission for a play that fits a particular theater's thematic or grant-receiving needs may distract a playwright and interrupt the legitimate process already under way of writing a play of her own. Only a very open kind of commission is really helpful to a writer of substance. Imagine this ideal: When you have a play you want to write, and need some time, let us know, and we'll give you the money to take six months off from work, so you can write your first draft. Then we'll produce it. Because finally, the only thing that is really good for writers is production. A commission that does not guarantee the writer a chance to see the play on the stage does not help.

With Christopher Durang, I have been teaching at Juilliard since 1994. And although I have no statistical proof of this, it seems to me that women writers suffer more from readings than do men. The damage a play can incur as a result of even a well-intentioned reading is substantial. Maybe this is because women listen better than men, or because women writers feel more obligated to pay for their plane tickets with rewrites. I don't know. I do know that audience members, dramaturgs, literary managers, and artistic directors sometimes make comments and suggest rewrites out of genuine interest in the plays. But sometimes even well-intentioned people make comments out of a simple desire to participate, or to reassure the playwright that she has not come all this way for nothing. Sometimes theaters convey the impression that if the playwright makes the changes suggested in the talk-back, the play will be selected for production, or for a staged reading, or for advancement up the list toward consideration for a future season. And so the writer returns home and does the work but quite often finds she has simply arrived at the bottom of the next list.

How to get produced has become the problem, for both men and women. But as I said before, any problem is worse for women writers (see NYSCA).

So how can women writers get produced now and thus learn the rest of the craft, the things you cannot learn simply by writing? This is my new subject here. Enough history.

We may not like the truth, but here it is. Theaters choose plays for a variety of reasons, the main one being that they think they can sell tickets to them. Only rarely is a play produced because of an obligation to the writer. Plays are more likely to be scheduled if the director is known to the particular theater, if there is an actor whose presence will sell tickets, or if the resident company's actors can be cast in the show. Raising the odds of getting a production is one of the best things a writer can do for herself.

Gone are the days when all you needed was an agent. The first thing a woman writer needs to do now is make a list of the eight theaters most likely to produce her work, based on history, subject matter, and available slots for new plays—and make friends with them. A writer with an ethnic or political identity needs to seek out the theaters that have arisen in order to present that voice to the world. In other words, writers must look for the theaters that are looking for them. Don't send your work to the same ten theaters everybody else sends to. And don't worry about getting an agent. If you get yourself some good productions, the agents will find you.

Subject matter is another issue that women writers must think about now. Mel Gussow joked with me early on that my work was successful because all the women in my plays had guns. And while this was a joke, it was also right. I wasn't doing it on purpose, but the only plays of mine the critics have consistently liked are plays in which the women have guns. Plays about internal change, a topic that women often choose to write about, are generally perceived by male critics as "soft," lacking what male artistic directors would call "an event."

We do not yet have a theater where the problems of a female central character are seen as universal. A female character has a better chance of being admired if she is required to "fight" in the play, thus exhibiting more universal ("male") behavior. A female character accepting a loss, going through a life passage, responding to or easing the pain of another, risks being described by critics as passive. In other words, female characters face the same difficulties real women do in a world where being beautiful, weak, and tragic makes the headlines. (We're working on that, right?) Unfortunately, some of the greatest qualities often seen in real women—endurance, intelligence, compassion, tolerance, and strength—are very hard to dramatize. Plays that men write about us are usually about things that can be seen: abuse and victimization. Our task now is not to write about ourselves the way men write about us. It is to convey our inner lives in ways that are exciting to watch. We must find and tell stories that *show* who we are.

Another huge new problem for women writing plays is television's influence on the minds of writers, and on theaters and audiences. Writers who have grown up watching more television shows than plays often write plays that more closely resemble good television instead of good theater. They write plays that have a small domestic framework and feature characters who enter, sit, talk, and leave. These dramas involve furniture and other trappings of domestic life and only rarely take advantage of the scenic and narrative conventions that make a play truly theatrical. Given the current glut of entertainment options available to theater audiences, writers whose work can only be done in the theater stand a better chance of finding a production for it there.

But the primary way in which television has changed the world for women writers is the new desire of television producers and networks to hire us. When *Getting Out* had its initial production in 1977, I received an immediate offer for a production on the main stage of the Mark Taper Forum, and that production opened three months later (I promise this is true). I also received an offer for a feature film based on a Gay Talese book. Today, a well-received play in a regional theater is likely to generate offers to fly the author to Hollywood to meet with producers and story editors for television movies and series. There may be offers for publication and other regional productions, but the likelier scenario is that theatrical producers will fly in from all over, then wait to see who makes the first move. These days, most regional theaters prefer to wait until New York has had its chance to vet the play before they make their intentions known. That way, the New York press will work for them and help them sell tickets. Writers are also commonly advised now to hold back the regional rights for their plays until there has been a Broadway or Off-Broadway outing, or a production at one of New York's major not-for-profit theaters. All too often the result of this delay is that the play loses its momentum, and all too soon the attention of the theatrical producers, both regional and Broadway, has gone elsewhere. The play goes on top of the writer's stack of plays to be sent around for readings.

In the meantime, television offers will come in, and they will be attractive, because of the money these jobs pay and because access to an audience is guaranteed. Once people work for television, it is hard to come back to theater. Some writers regularly write for both but not without consequence, and I would include myself in this category. We find that more and more of our time is taken up by phone calls to producers, and the more we work, the more we become dependent on television money to pay the rent. The theater never will pay the rent; we know that now. But we had hoped that it would.

The real problem posed by television is one of our own making: the more time we spend there, the less leisure time we have, and leisure is where real work comes from. We become more likely to accept commissions and adaptations, and soon we find that it has been a long time since we even had an idea for a new play, much less wrote one.

When I began writing for the theater, the challenge was to get plays written and get them on. This is still the challenge for beginners. The opportunities exist, though they may be harder to find than they once were. Still, theaters are looking for new writers more than for new plays by writers they already know.

The challenge for established writers, and it is tougher than ever, is to find ways to support ourselves and still contribute to the vibrant art form that we love. To do this, we need to travel more, read more, rest more, and spend more time with our families and friends. For it is only in leisure that real stories come to us. It is only when we are rested that we become aware of the stories we must tell.

The theater will always be in some kind of crisis. As writers we must remain calm and still. We must be aware of the life around us and make ourselves available to record it. We must ask for favors when we need them and help each other without being asked. We must encourage young writers and pass along what we have learned. And we must remember that we are not here forever. We must get our work done and enjoy each other. And we must rid ourselves of anything that stands in the way of that simple plan. Get our work done and enjoy each other. Amen.

Rachel Roberts and Mia Dillon in the Broadway production of Once a Catholic *by Mary O'Malley, winner of the first Susan Smith Blackburn Prize, 1978–1979. (Photograph: Martha Swope, Billy Rose Theatre Collection, the New York Public Library for the Performing Arts, Astor, Lenox and Tilden Foundations)*

Remarks from Susan Smith Blackburn Prize Award Ceremonies

The actor Irene Worth, presenting the second Susan Smith Blackburn Prize to Barbara Schneider for Details without a Map, *the Players, New York, February 13, 1980:*

> This prize is like "tilling the arts," in that it may stimulate and encourage women to write for the theater who might otherwise have thought, "There's really no point, because nobody will see or care." This establishes that people do care, very much, and that there will be extra attention given to the effort of writing plays.

❧

The British director Michael Attenborough at the eighth presentation of the Susan Smith Blackburn Prize, to Anne Devlin for Ourselves Alone, *the Garrick Club, London, February 24, 1986:*

> I had three very good reasons for accepting the invitation eighteen months ago to be a director of the Susan Smith Blackburn Prize. The first reason was money for the playwrights. Many a good writer has drifted away from the theater and gone to write for the other media. Then, when they've been able to build up a reserve of capital, they've sometimes come back to the theater, often the medium they enjoy writing for most. So, anything which helps to support, foster, and enable those writers who want to create for the theater and are skilled at doing so, seemed to me eminently worthwhile and laudable.
>
> The second reason was that, certainly up until about ten years ago, few women wrote for the theater. It's a situation that's improving all the time. The last several years have seen many encouraging examples of new female playwrights. But the balance still needs to be better. The fact that this award was positive discrimination in favor of women writers again seemed to me to be an excellent reason for joining.
>
> And the third reason was that I have always been very interested in building bridges across the Atlantic, enabling a better understanding between our two theatrical traditions. The dialogue I have witnessed over the last two prizes has provided a channel through which we have exchanged, if you like, our cultural gifts.
>
> However, having articulated laudatory claims for cultural bridges, I can't help feeling proud that the winner this year is British!

PART ONE

Breaking the Silence

Breaking the Silence

Once upon a time in Western theater, there were no female playwrights—none, at least, whom history has revealed to us. We can imagine, as Virginia Woolf once fantasized in relation to Shakespeare, that Aeschylus or Sophocles or Euripides had a talented sister and that she desperately wanted to add her voice to the great tragedies performed each year in ancient Athens. But she exists only in our wishful imaginations. The truth is, from the fifth century B.C. to the seventeenth century A.D., the female playwright is a rarity. She is a tenth-century German canoness in Gandersheim named Hrosvitha; an Italian actor named Isabella Andreini, who belonged to a famous commedia dell'arte troupe, the Gelosi. She is, in other words, a longed-for but infrequently discovered occurrence.

Not until the seventeenth century do female playwrights emerge, finally to catch the ear of audiences but rarely the notice of historians. In Mexico her name is Sor Juana Inés de la Cruz, in Spain she is María de Zayas y Sotomayor, and in England, near the century's end, she is Aphra Behn, the first English woman to earn her living, however meager, as a writer, mainly of the theater. Soon, Behn is followed by a generation that includes Mary Pix, Jane Wiseman, Delariviere Manley, Catharine Trotter, Mary Davys, and Susannah Centlivre. The theater scholar Kathryn Kendall estimates that these six women contributed more than one-third of the plays performed in London between 1695 and 1706 (and made money from their work, what is more). As the eighteenth century progressed, additional women saw their plays take the commercial stage, particularly in England. There were Eliza Haywood, Penelope Aubin, and Charlotte Clarke; Frances Sheridan and Elizabeth Griffith; Hannah Cowley and Elizabeth Inchbald, among others.

But what a long time that is to wait for women to add their voices to the theater. From the fifth century B.C. to the seventeenth century A.D.—about two thousand years! And even so, the surge was momentary, historically speaking. After the eighteenth century, women would remain exceptions in Western drama—would almost disappear again in fact—until the beginning of the twentieth.

To what do we attribute these periods of theatrical silence? To women's fixed place in society, for one thing. Effectively owned by fathers and husbands, tied by biological destiny to their homes, women in western Europe, whether rich or poor, were cogs in rigidly operating economic and social systems.

In addition, for much of the Christian era, very few women could read or write. Those few who could often turned to poetry or, in the nineteenth century, when a rising middle class began educating its women in larger numbers, to novels. How much easier it was, after all, for a woman to sit at her desk of a morning and pen a romance than to risk the scandal of going to the theater and working side by side with "immoral" actors, or going to the theater even as a spectator. A woman who desired to write creatively could find models in published poetry and prose. But to write a play, she ultimately had to participate in theater itself.

And then, toward the end of the nineteenth century, women developed the will to change their world. A first wave of feminism spread across the British Empire and North America. Better educated than her mother and grandmother, the New Woman, as she was popularly called in England—and often caricatured on the stage—wanted to support herself financially, live independently, and hold the same political rights as men. Exiting the protective home in which she had been raised, she sought public forums in which to express herself, and one that she found was the theater.

Some women, notably Rachel Crothers in the United States, aimed successfully for the commercial theater. Many more wrote for what came to be known, on both sides of the Atlantic, as the Little Theatre movement. In England, playwrights such as Cicely Hamilton, Elizabeth Baker, Florence Bell, and Elizabeth Robins dramatized contemporary society's exploitation of women and called for women's suffrage. In the United States, Alice Gerstenberg and Susan Glaspell explored women's private lives and psychological frustrations. During a renaissance of black American writing, roughly from 1910 to 1940, women such as Georgia Douglas Johnson, Mary P. Burrill, Marita Bonner, and May Miller wrote plays about African American life that were produced in community theaters, churches, and other places where black Americans gathered.

The 1920s saw a rise in the number of white female playwrights produced commercially. The strong financial tide of Broadway and the road lifted women with it, among them Mae West, Sophie Treadwell, Zoë Akins, and Zona Gale, who, in 1921, became the first woman to win the Pulitzer Prize for Drama.

But there was never parity with men in terms of the number of plays produced, either in the United States or in England. And as these countries wound their ways through the Great Depression, a second world war, and a cold war against Communism, the spirit of feminism that had driven women to write plays at the beginning of the century lost its impetus.

The vitality of theater waned. By the end of the 1950s, a financially straitened commercial theater in both England and the United States was artistically conservative and, as in the past, controlled by men. An alternative theater, devoted to absurdism on the Continent and angry naturalism in England, seemed to allow little room for women. Women's voices, while not silent, diminished in volume.

Then, slowly, women once again began to make themselves heard. In the United States, a combination of artistic, societal, and political influences germinated America's own alternative theater, in which women participated, although in comparatively small numbers. Young American playwrights began to learn from the likes of Bertolt Brecht, Samuel Beckett, and Eugene Ionesco, who provided examples of new directions in form and content. The election of John F. Kennedy to the presidency in 1960 seemed to herald an open-minded intellectual climate, at least among the white, middle-class baby boomers who reacted positively to Kennedy's youthfulness and energy.

A fresh, largely anticommercial, generation of theater makers responded. Some formed companies, like Bread and Puppet Theatre in Vermont, the San Francisco Mime Troupe, and Joseph Chaikin's Open Theatre in New York City. These groups and others, plus an array of churches, coffeehouses, and lofts loosely defined as Off-Off Broadway, nourished enterprising and iconoclastic playwrights, including pioneering women such as Megan Terry, Joan Holden, and Julie Bovasso; Rosalyn Drexler and Adrienne Kennedy; and Rochelle Owens and Maria Irene Fornés.

In the United Kingdom during the 1960s, there was a similar spurt of what were called "fringe" theater groups and venues, which existed to counter the British theater's overreliance on classics and conventional dramas. And here, too, a few trailblazing women were slowly making themselves heard. But only a few.

By the end of the 1960s, in both the United States and the United Kingdom, theater and women were ripe for change.

At this point, the story of this book begins. As Charlotte Canning and Elizabeth Swain indicate in the opening chapter, "Social Change, Artistic Ferment," during the 1970s, a second wave of feminism encouraged women to write for the theater in significant numbers and to explore women on the stage with fresh purpose and intensity. Through what came to be called the Women's Movement, women on both sides of the Atlantic found strength in community and transferred that newfound awareness to both their personal lives and their art. In 1988, in her book *Writing a Woman's Life*, the feminist teacher and novelist Carolyn G. Heilbrun would state, "As long as women are isolated one from the other, not allowed to offer other women the most personal accounts of their lives, they will not be part of any narrative of their own." During the 1970s, after decades of largely silent isolation, women who wrote plays came together in consciousness-raising groups, in political demonstrations, in theater companies run by women for women—in all the varied causes and arenas that the Women's Movement engendered. They had many narratives to tell and now they had places to tell them and audiences eager to hear.

By the early 1980s, women were writing plays for many of the professional not-for-profit theaters that had been founded during the previous two decades. Several of these playwrights also broke into commercial theater, which had largely been a male province in both the United States and the United Kingdom. Mel Gussow, who covered Off Broadway as a theater critic for the *New York Times* during the years when female playwrights began their ascent and was a judge for the Susan Smith Blackburn Prize in 1982–1983, writes in "Entering the Mainstream" that three American women drew particular attention during the late 1970s and early 1980s: Beth Henley, Marsha Norman, and Wendy Wasserstein.

Similarly, in the United Kingdom, Timberlake Wertenbaker, who first gained attention in 1980 with her play *The Third,* established herself as one of Britain's most imaginative and intellectually challenging playwrights, and one who eventually would also find acclaim in the West End, London's equivalent of Broadway. In chapter 3, Michael Billington, the longtime theater critic for the *Guardian,* discusses Timberlake Wertenbaker's art and career with her and the esteemed British director Max Stafford-Clark, who was instrumental in developing Wertenbaker's plays. Timberlake Wertenbaker received Special Commendation from the Susan Smith Blackburn Prize in 1988–1989 for *Our Country's Good* and received the prize in 1991–1992 for *Three Birds Alighting on a Field.* Michael Billington was a judge in 1979–1980, Max Stafford-Clark in 1991–1992.

ONE

Social Change, Artistic Ferment

CHARLOTTE CANNING

ELIZABETH SWAIN

❧

The U.S.A.

CHARLOTTE CANNING

Urged by a friend to attend a meeting that had been called to found a new organization for women, Anselma Dell'Olio decided to go, even though she felt ambivalent about it. What kind of organization was this going to be? Even more important, why did women need one? Dell'Olio first went to the wrong address on that cold windy night in 1966. But she made it to the right place in time to hear Betty Friedan give an impassioned speech about the myriad ways women experience discrimination and injustice. As she took in the statistics, and Friedan's emotion, she remembers, "My mind was reeling." Dell'Olio had just found feminism, which, in the mid-1960s, was a politics that allowed women to feel that they were newly invented, that they existed as full-fledged human beings for the first time in history. That evening in New York City, at one of the first gatherings of the National Organization for Women (NOW), was the first step on a journey that was to reinvent Dell'Olio's life radically and, unexpectedly, to have profound implications for the theater.

Actress, journalist, and translator Anselma Dell'Olio is one of the thirty-seven women who provide first-person testimonies in a book edited by Rachel Blau DuPlessis and Ann Snitow, *The Feminist Memoir Project: Voices from Women's Liberation* (1998). Her narrative shares much with the others in the volume, especially the attempt to put into words the liberating experience of embracing feminism. Women newly introduced to feminism were applying this revelatory knowledge to all areas of their lives, and for Dell'Olio, one such area was the theater. Feminism, as a process-oriented politics that emphasizes the possibility of change, is perfectly suited to theater's aesthetic of conflict and transformation. Dell'Olio's decision to marry theater and feminism was to be a productive one indeed.

The scene shifts to 1969. Dell'Olio is making a television appearance on the *David Susskind Show* with fellow feminists Kate Millett, Rosalyn Baxandall, and Jacqui Ceballos (they were billed as "Four Angry Women"). She announces that she is founding a feminist theater and calls for written material.

For some of the women watching Susskind's show, this must have been another euphoric moment when the Women's Movement offered opportunities so liberating that hardly anyone had ever dared to dream about them. The call for writing generated an enormous response. Dell'Olio holed up in her apartment, turned off her phone, and winnowed a huge pile of material, ultimately crafting a cabaret-style evening of songs, sketches, and one-person performances. It was presented at a benefit for the National Organization for Women in March 1969, and its success was beyond what anyone involved had expected. "It was a triumph," Dell'Olio recalled. "TV news cameras and the pencil press were everywhere. With our shaky professionalism, we had zeroed in on the zeitgeist: we were trendy, we were a hit, we were the toast of the town. And merciful Minerva! we were funny. . . . We ended the show with a rousing parody of 'The Battle Hymn of the Republic,' written by Ruth Herschberger, and performed by the entire cast and crew, gathered onstage to ring down the curtain as we sang." Soon after, Dell'Olio founded the New Feminist Repertory theater group.

From writers to performers to audiences, the response to Dell'Olio's cabaret was ecstatically positive. After all, prior to that time, women had had few opportunities to see life represented in the ways they had experienced it. I once asked Patricia Van Kirk, who founded the Front Room Theater (FRT) in Seattle in 1980, why she had said that when she started FRT lesbians did not attend the theater in great numbers. "Why would you?" she had answered. "You don't see yourself up there. There's no reflection." Van Kirk's observations about theater were from the position of a lesbian spectator who rarely if ever saw herself or her community in any of the stories, images, or ideas onstage; but her words could have applied to the relationship between women and theater in the 1970s. Sue-Ellen Case, debating whether to start her groundbreaking book, *Feminism and Theatre* (1988), with an examination of works by men, wrote in her introduction: "I . . . finally decided that many of us originally adopted feminism because of the pain and anger we felt when we encountered the prejudices and omissions of the traditional theatre." It wasn't that women were absent from the stage, or that no women worked in the theater, but that women were not typically finding their realities — their experiences as they lived them — on that stage, because there was no concerted effort, on the part of producers, directors, playwrights, or audiences, to see women's personal and political realities represented there.

As early as 1955, women had attempted to explore women's realities through theater in light of social and political liberation struggles. Gerda Lerner, a community activist and political organizer who would later help to establish women's history as an influential field of study, collaborated with the playwright Eve Merriam to create the musical *Singing of Women,* which enjoyed a brief run Off Broadway. In a 1979 autobiographical essay published in *The Majority Finds Its Past* (2005), Lerner notes that she and Merriam were trying to "revive some of the heroic figures among American women and to celebrate their existence, their actuality." Their effort anticipated many of the elements of feminist theater still more than a decade away: it emphasized women through their particular experiences, it emerged out of collaboration among women, and it was intended to provide women in the audience with a sense of empowerment, inspiration, and belonging.

The experimental theater scene that exploded in the exploratory and permissive atmosphere of the 1960s brought with it a concomitant liberation of possibility for playwrights, including women. While not yet buoyed by the Women's Movement, these women found that the openness of alternative theaters provided possibilities for them as well. Maria Irene Fornés was a Cuban-born painter who came to the theater after being inspired by the Paris production of Beckett's *Waiting for Godot.* Her imaginative, whimsical plays of the 1960s, including *Tango Palace* (1963), the lightly satiric *The Successful Life of Three* (1965), and the poignant *Molly's Dream* (1968), quickly found people eager to produce them. Her best-known play, *Fefu and Her Friends* (1977), about a group of white, middle-class women in the 1930s who gather over the weekend to plan a symposium on education, focuses on how the women are connected to one another and on the tensions that undergird their relationships with each other, as well as with the men in their lives. The play's terrain is the various emotional undercurrents of the women's lives and the truths and hallucinations those emotions produce. The play was not well received initially, because Fornés dispensed with an easily understood structure for the work; the middle section comprises four scenes that the audience, itself divided into four groups, sees in four different sequences, as they move from setting to setting. But *Fefu* is usually positioned as Fornés's contribution to the Women's Movement, coinciding as it did with an especially productive time for women's theater.

Adrienne Kennedy was another woman whose plays in the 1960s were inspired by the artistic and political changes happening around her. Her first play,

Funnyhouse of a Negro (1964), about a young black woman's tormented sense of identity and subsequent suicide, proved typical of Kennedy's work: it drew heavily on the traditions of the twentieth-century European avant-garde, including symbolism, surrealism, and absurdism; the narrative logic of plot is subordinated to the narrative illogic of emotions, images, and dreams. Kennedy's unconventional approach would put her outside the typical work of both the Black Arts Movement and feminist theater, although her concerns resonated with the implications of both. As bell hooks, an African American theorist who has looked at the troubled intersection of race, gender, and class, commented in 1992, the search in Kennedy's plays by female characters for ways to express and understand their experiences "can be read as linked to a growing political concern in the fifties and sixties . . . with women's effort to come to voice." Kennedy may not have been directly involved with women's theater groups per se (and would not later be), but her plays were essential to making women's theatrical work possible.

For some other women in the 1960s, it was less their individual work that helped to pave the way for women's theater than the work they did with the major experimental groups. Playwrights emerged from the various male-dominated avant-garde theater companies. Megan Terry, for example, came to prominence through the Open Theatre, which was founded by Joseph Chaikin in 1962. She is usually credited with bringing a socially conscious form of inquiry to the company, notably through *Viet Rock* (1966), a musical that protested U.S. involvement in the Vietnam War. But her one-act play *Calm Down Mother* (1964) looked at the intricacies of women's relationships with one another, as well as the ways in which social and cultural pressures shape how women relate among themselves. An especially important element of *Calm Down Mother,* which would anticipate Terry's later feminist work such as *Approaching Simone* (1970) and *Babes in the Bighouse* (1974), was her insistence on emphasizing the tools women possess to improve and change their lives. The feminist critic and historian Helene Keyssar would later dub Terry "the Mother of American Feminist Drama."

Rosalyn Drexler's work was first produced at the Judson Poets' Theatre in Greenwich Village, which was started in 1961 as part of a larger effort by the Judson Church to support alternative and avant-garde art—dance, painting, poetry, and what would be later called performance art—in New York. Under the guidance of the composer Al Carmines, Judson's dedication to experimental work provided venues for many of the women playwrights trying to get started in the 1960s. Drexler's first play, *Home Movies* (1964), is an open-ended romp that experiments humorously with language. The play, as the historian Stephen Bottoms has it, "transforms a banal, bourgeois domestic situation into a three-ring circus of zany absurdity." With its explicit, if comic, exploration of sexual issues, including rape and incest, Drexler's play would have been unlikely to find a home anywhere else.

But even in the liberated sixties, there was the sense that women's work was still happening in isolation, still being received and evaluated according to norms set by a sexist, patriarchal society. Women in groups like the Open Theatre or Judson Poets' Theatre, the San Francisco Mime Troupe or the Firehouse Theater in Minneapolis had found their theatrical experiences enormously productive; they had gained valuable practical knowledge, as well as the ability to challenge and strengthen their commitments to a radical intersection of art and politics. But many women left these theater groups when the companies refused to deal with their inherent contradictions. Ostensibly committed to radical change and ending oppression, they were often unwilling or unable to face the oppressive gender dynamics in their own midst. Women found themselves in the odd position of being told that theirs was not an oppression that merited any real attention.

So, like Anselma Dell'Olio, they struck out on their own. Theater became one way women could try on and experiment with the liberation and validation they so urgently sought. During the 1970s, women came together in every region of the country to convey women's experience both collectively and individually. American theater had never witnessed a grassroots theater movement quite like it. It was decentralized and local, responsive to the particular conditions and issues pressing on women in a specific city or region. Each theater group defined for itself what feminism meant and what women's theater should include (some groups included men; others did not). Every women's theater company was uncompromisingly committed to representing women's experience, but there was no consensus as to what that meant or how to stage it. No single figure set an agenda, no national organization suggested guidelines. The only universal article of belief was that women's theater opposed definitive models, centralized or hierarchical organizational structures, and dogmatic manifestoes that limited what a group could do or how it could do it.

For many women in the theater, the commitment was to a group that would work together to create original pieces that they would then perform. The politically radical company Lilith, in San Francisco, began in 1974 much the way Dell'Olio's company had: a group of artists came together to create a cabaret, and out of that emerged a core of women who continued to work together. Until 1979, Lilith was informally under the artistic guidance of the playwright Terry Baum, who collaborated with company members Carolyn Meyers, Michele Linfante, and Resnais Winter to create the group's most popular work, *Sacrifices* (1977)—a feminist fairy tale. Lilith performed plays the women devised through improvisation—*Good Food* (1975), *Moonlighting* (1976), and *Exit the Maids* (1981)—although a member of the group would often serve as a writer and help to craft the material into a script. The company's artists also performed already existing work, like Dacia Maraini's *Manifesto* in 1977 and *Trespaso* by Martha Boesing in 1980. Lilith lasted until 1986, with many of the former members gathering to create a ritual to end the group formally.

Boesing was a member of a well-known company called At the Foot of the Mountain (AFOM), which was founded in Minneapolis in 1974 and survived until 1991. *The Story of a Mother* (1978, revised 1987) was its best-known piece— perhaps even the most well known original work to come from a feminist theater group in the United States during this period. A ritualized piece of theater, it looked at the many facets of the mother-daughter relationship; at the end of the performance, what one observer described as a "giant figure[,] a kind of totem of the mother" was brought out, and women in the audience were invited to take ribbons and put them on this "mega mother" and speak to her.

Women also created organizations that were intended to provide space, support, and productions for women making theater. Women's Interart, which was founded in New York by Margot Lewitin in 1969 and had its own space by 1971, provided a home base at one time or another for several important theater groups including Women's Experimental Theater (WET) and Split Britches, as well as many individual artists. In 1978 Julia Miles started the more mainstream Women's Project at the American Place Theatre in New York, to provide what the Project termed "a home for women playwrights." There it offered productions and readings of plays by a generation of pioneering dramatists, including Joan Schenkar, Emily Mann, Lavonne Mueller, Paula Cizmar, and Kathleen Collins. Now called Women's Project and Productions and long separated from the American Place, the organization has its own theater and produces an Off-Broadway season every year—one of the few women's companies to survive from the 1970s.

Responding to the same need to be supportive, in 1978 the Susan Smith Blackburn Prize was founded by Susan Blackburn's sister, Emilie S. Kilgore, and Blackburn's husband. It was created to provide recognition to women playwrights and to encourage them to flourish as dramatists. The first play to win the award, the British playwright Mary O'Malley's *Once a Catholic*, dramatized the experiences that made women feminists.

Whether their politics were radical or mainstream, women's groups were heavily invested in serving the larger feminist concerns. Groups as radical as Lilith or Split Britches, or as middle-of-the-road as the Women's Project, took their mandate to serve the feminist community very seriously. Few groups performed solely for all-women audiences, but many would set aside special performances for women only. There were also shows to benefit local feminist causes that had few if any men in the audience.

But performances were usually less a tool for proselytizing or conversion than a way to support those whose commitment to feminism made them feel isolated or embattled. Performances served to remind women about the bonds of community. Just as they had come to feminism through the realization that the personal is political, the experience of being in the audience helped to remind women viscerally and visually that they were not alone in that realization. Women's theater reminded its audiences that women struggled to live their feminist politics in the face of hostility or derision and that those experiences were not unique to any one woman.

Of course, there were lively, even rancorous, debates about definitions of feminism and about issues raised by the performances. While the absence of centralized goals may have been liberating and inclusive, both artistically and politically, it could often lead to harsh recriminations. No aspect of feminism or feminists was off limits or untouchable. This meant that discussions after shows could be as dramatic and influential as what had just been seen onstage.

The idea that theater had previously represented women through the lens of male experience and that the Women's Movement could help women to represent their experiences without filtering them through male norms was an empowering and liberating notion for women in and outside theater. This new idea was enormously indebted to consciousness-raising, or C-R, a technique for personal and political exploration that emerged around 1970 from the feminist political group New York Radical Women. They had agreed that one of the reasons women often felt they were fighting such an uphill battle was that most sources of information reinforced the sexist, patriarchal, and/or misogynist attitudes feminism was seeking to dismantle. If most historical sources—books, magazines, newspapers, and so-called experts—were not to be trusted, where could women turn for information? Even women themselves had so internalized their oppression that they were often the most vehement in defending it.

In response to this problem, C-R became a bedrock feminist tool of research, ideas, and action. Not only did most feminists in the 1970s belong to such a group, and credit it with life-saving support, but the insights gained through C-R were responsible in part or in whole for several important founding texts: Shulamith Firestone's *The Dialectic of Sex* (1970), Kate Millett's *Sexual Politics* (1970), and Anne Koedt's 1973 article, "The Myth of the Vaginal Orgasm."

There are two crucial ideas embedded in the theory and practice of C-R. The first is that all previous information on women, no matter what the source, should be distrusted. Authoritative pronouncements on women's limitations were, as the Women's Movement came to realize, more about reinforcing existing power structures than articulating accurate information. The other crucial idea was that resistance would come from women themselves. Women would become the new sources of expertise, truth, and action. By sharing her experiences with other women, a woman could analyze and compare her experiences with theirs. This would allow women to work against the ways in which society traditionally isolated them from one another. Through structured discussion sessions, C-R brought women together so they might see how connected they really were, the commonality of their experience, and how their isolation strengthened the illusion that their experiences were personal failings. An individual woman's frustrations, and her inability to conform to some model of womanhood, became evidence instead of a larger pattern of oppression. Women came to be politicized through powerful and revealing encounters with their own lives. Their own experiences were no longer irrelevant but a source of truth, power, and political vision.

C-R had its limitations, however. The theory and action that emerged from its processes tended to mimic the larger cultural and social positions of the participants. Women of color and lesbians were quick to point out that although C-R may have been invaluable in articulating the ways in which experience is related to gender, it was far less adept at recognizing the ways women were embedded in race, class, and sexuality. C-R's legacy is mixed; it was an invaluable tool for changing women's lives, but it was one that needed to be examined as rigorously as the oppression it challenged.

Women's theater often embodied the beliefs of C-R. Its work emerged from the sense that there were stories not being told and ways of seeing the world that were not being staged. A woman seeing women's theater for the first time usually experienced the same sense of revelation described in C-R groups. Clare Coss of WET recalled seeing It's All Right to Be Woman Theater, a group founded in New York in 1969: "I remember feeling totally affirmed as a woman, that it was the first time I had really seen a positive image of a woman onstage that made me think this is what my life is about." The playwright Karen Malpede had a similar reaction: "I had never been in a room with three hundred women before and it was the most exhilarating experience." These moments did not just work as affirmations or support; they also worked as catalysts for creativity.

But women's theater also struggled with the limitations of C-R-based ideas. Lesbians left women's theater groups because the heterosexuals in the companies were reluctant to explore lesbian characters or themes. Terry Baum notes that her frustration with Lilith began around the time the group refused to make a protagonist a lesbian, because they were afraid that people would think the performers were lesbians. Women of color had similar experiences. Marga

Gomez left Lilith because she felt that the white women were not committed to overcoming their racism, and Bernadette Cha experienced similar frustrations with both Lilith and AFOM. Perhaps because the Women's Movement was often seen, although not entirely accurately, as a white woman's movement, there were few women's theater groups entirely composed of women of color. The short-lived Valentina Productions produced only one show, the 1981 *Voz de la Mujer* in San Francisco. Las Cucarachas, also of San Francisco, was a 1974 effort to support individual creative work. The Onyx Women's Theater in New York was founded for African American women only, but there is no record of their productions. Spiderwoman Theatre was originally a mixed-race group whose work took up a variety of feminist ideas, but with the departure of Lois Weaver and Peggy Shaw to set up Split Britches in 1981, the group reorganized to focus more intently on its Native American identity.

An example of an emphasis inherited from C-R was the powerful complexity of mother-daughter relationships. Women's groups and individual playwrights both focused on the issue, although there was no single approach or consensus. WET's play *Daughters* (1980) called on the audience to join the performers in reciting a ritual chant that traced a woman's line of descent through her mother as far back as she could. This play, while it looked at the stresses of the relationship as well as the rewards, ultimately valorized the bond as an essentially feminist and positive one. At the Foot of the Mountain's *Story of a Mother* also focused on the mother-daughter bond as a source of power and strength for women.

Individual playwrights often preferred to look at the contradictions in the relationship between mothers and daughters. Pearl Cleage took up the mother-daughter tie as the subject for one of her earliest plays, *Hospice** (1983), which was a finalist for the Susan Smith Blackburn Prize in 1983–1984. Here, Alice, a poet who long ago abandoned her ten-year-old daughter, Jenny, for the greater freedom of the expatriate life, has returned home to Detroit and the house she inherited from her own mother. Jenny, now a grown woman and pregnant, is also living in the house and throughout the play is in the early stages of labor. Alice is dying from cancer, and Jenny desperately recognizes that this is her last chance to reach out to her and to find out why Alice abandoned her.

Alice resists Jenny's attempts to establish a connection between them. Despite her success at both writing poetry and avoiding domesticity—the two reasons she fled her daughter—Alice knows that her bargain was a Faustian one, without the possibility of redemption. As both women work through their individual physical pain—Alice's from dying and Jenny's from childbirth—they try to work out their mutual emotional pain and establish some kind of relationship in the little time they have left.

The mutual pain of adult mothers and daughters is also the subject of Marsha Norman's *'night, Mother** (1982), which won the Blackburn Prize in 1982–1983. The play has a very simple premise: one night, Jessie announces to her mother, Thelma, that she will kill herself at the end of the evening. The resulting struggle between mother and daughter comes as Thelma does everything she can to prevent Jessie from fulfilling her plan. Together they revisit old wounds, and Thelma reveals secrets about Jessie's father, Jessie's husband, and their lives together—part of a desperate strategy to convince Jessie not to kill herself. In this play about miscommunication and crisis, Norman never flinches from the incredible pain she reveals in the dissection of failed hopes and dreams. Although men are mentioned, they are peripheral to the drama (and never appear onstage). The tragedy of the play ultimately is not Jessie's suicide but that her suicide is largely the result of the failed mother-daughter relationship. Had Jessie and Thelma ever managed to have an honest and loving relationship, Norman implies, Jessie would not have seen suicide as the only logical solution to her problems.

Tina Howe, in her play *Birth and Afterbirth* (1973), took up the subject from a different perspective. She was interested in the isolation of mothers and in the cultural silence about what she calls the "savagery" of being a mother. The nuclear family in this purposely grotesque comedy includes a mother, a father, and a four-year-old son, who is played by an adult male actor to signal the potential monstrousness of children. The play is set during the son's birthday party, which veers between family arguments and sentimental expressions of love that only exist, it seems, to convince the family members of their supposedly special bond. The play's starkest image is the isolation the mother, Sandy, experiences. Her husband cannot hear her expressions of anguish, for he is too wrapped up in his problems at work. She is sometimes loving, sometimes hostile to her child, because she cannot balance the demands of being a mother and being her own woman. Howe's play makes an argument for the importance of relationships among women. There is another woman in the play, but she is no more responsive to Sandy's needs than anyone else. The play serves as a cautionary tale about the toll that conventional family structure takes on women. The feminist idea that Howe takes up, which owes a debt to C-R, is not so much the mother-child bond as it is the need women have for one another and the necessity of having a community that can understand one's struggles.

That women serve themselves well when they bond into a community existed in mother-daughter plays but was also explored through other plots and themes. Ntozake Shange credited feminism and its community with the inspiration for her choreopoem, *for colored girls who have considered suicide/when the rainbow is enuf* (1974), which she modeled on a cycle poem by Judy Grahn titled *The Work of the Common Woman,* a collection of poems written between 1964 and 1977. Shange's seven female characters are named for colors: brown, yellow, purple, red, green, blue, and orange. Each recounts her experience of gender, race, or sexuality. Stories of losing one's virginity, of date rape, prostitution, discovering black history, and the death of a child are woven together with dance and music. The women also express their suspicion of and alienation from a world that often works to destroy them: "Bein alive & bein a woman & bein colored is a metaphysical dilemma/ i haven't conquered yet," says the Lady in Yellow. The play ends with all seven women speaking different lines of a communal poem, finally singing in unison, "I found god in myself & i loved her/ i loved her fiercely." The women of the play have experiences not in isolation or individually but in relation to one another, as a community. They are subjects with the power to act, and they use that power in relationships with one another.

Ultimately, it may be that relationships among women—whether those within a family or those within the larger world, those that provide power and joy or those delivering frustration and pain—are the most important focus that emerged from the intersection of feminism and theater during the 1970s and early 1980s.

Women have kept writing plays. They have continued to insist upon the messy and difficult experiences of women's lives as rich and productive inspiration for dramatic exploration. They still interrogate the power structures that oppress women, even when women themselves are complicit with those structures. The current fearlessness of women's plays owes everything to the feminist interventions in theater of the 1970s and early 1980s. Reflecting on those days, Anselma Dell'Olio mused, "There was an outpouring of ideas, brains, wit and talent, the likes of which I have never experienced again." The historical moment in which she produced one of the first instances of second-wave feminist theater is certainly past, and the initial euphoria has worn off. But "brains, wit and talent" are still to be found in the women creating for the theater.

At the end of Dell'Olio's 1969 cabaret, the revised "Battle Hymn" resounded through the theater. "Our eyes have seen the future and rejoice at what's to be;/ Every woman in position to achieve equality." Feminists in the theater still have that future to invoke and anticipate. The next line's promise, "We will vote ourselves to power with our own majority," has not actually yet occurred. But since 1969 a new possibility has been added. "Our eyes have seen" the past as well as the future. That past offers many instances for rejoicing, as well as for rejecting, but in its mixed legacy it is very much an inspiration.

The U.K.

ELIZABETH SWAIN

The opening of John Osborne's *Look Back in Anger* at the Royal Court Theatre in May 1956 heralded a new and vital era in British theater. The Royal Court soon became known as a "playwrights' theatre" because of its introduction of new British, American, and European writers and its encouragement of unusual subject matter, character types, stage settings, and themes.

But a quick look at the roster of playwrights during the Royal Court's first two decades shows a remarkable scarcity of women. The list of British entries includes the pioneers Shelagh Delaney (*A Taste of Honey*, 1958) and Ann Jellicoe (*The Sport of My Mad Mother*, 1958; *The Knack*, 1961), as well as Kathleen Sully, Alison MacLeod, Doris Lessing, Gillian Richards, Gwyn Thomas, Mary McCormick, Edna O'Brien, and Caryl Churchill. Two Americans appear, Carson McCullers and Adrienne Kennedy; and Marguerite Duras from France. The male roster runs to over two hundred. Conditions for women in other areas of the theater were not much better. Directors and designers were predominantly male, and plays always offered far more roles for men than for women. What conditions finally opened new doors to women in theater? And what conditions enabled their successes, particularly as playwrights? The beginnings perhaps lay outside the theater.

The Women's Liberation Movement in Britain held its first official conference in 1970 at Ruskin College, Oxford. The same year, Germaine Greer published her groundbreaking feminist book, *The Female Eunuch*, which she declared was part of a second phase of feminism. The suffragette era had been the first and inspirational phase, but their methods were far too genteel for contemporary needs, which, she thought, demanded outright revolution against the patriarchy. The year 1968 had seen the Abortion Act and the Family Planning Act; 1969, the Divorce Reform Act; and 1970, the Matrimonial Property and Equal Pay Acts. All of this legislation edged women out of the Victorian era and on the way, albeit slowly, toward public recognition of their rights — sexually, domestically, and in the workplace.

Another piece of legislation was to have profound effects on the nature, content, and conduct of theater: the Theatres Act of 1968, which ended stage censorship. Since the Theatres Act of 1843, the Lord Chamberlain had possessed the authority to decide what could or could not be put on any stage in Great Britain. He had the power to delete what he deemed offending passages and scenes; he could even ban entire plays. What's more, since a play had to be

Meryl Streep, actor, SSBP judge, and presenter, sits beside Caryl Churchill, who won the sixth Susan Smith Blackburn Prize for Fen. *The Players, New York, February 24, 1984. (Photograph: Nancy Crampton)*

approved before rehearsal, the effect was to ban anything in the professional theater except a scripted performance. Improvisational theater was impossible. The new Theatres Act opened up immeasurable possibilities for subject matter, language, and dramatic treatment and created a favorable climate for the highly political theater that was emerging.

There was much to be political about. Throughout the seventies, unemployment rose, industrial strikes were rampant, the economy worsened, and the schisms between the relatively stable south of England and the increasingly depressed north widened. Despite the 1966 and 1968 Race Relations Acts, designed to protect the rising number of immigrants against discrimination, the National Front Party, with its clear anti-immigrant bias, set down roots. Events elsewhere in 1968 contributed to a growing politicization of the war-baby generation: the Soviet invasion of Czechoslovakia; the Tet Offensive in Vietnam, and the ensuing surge of antiwar demonstrations in the United States and Europe; and student activism in the United States and on the European continent, particularly in Paris, where students joined forces with labor. In the United Kingdom, the Women's Liberation Movement was making its initial demands for meaningful equality in the workplace, for equal pay, equal education, equal opportunity, available child care, and free contraception and abortion. Not since the suffragettes demanded the right to vote in the decade before World War I had there been such political agitation by women.

And as in the suffragette era, the theater became a locus for this political activism. Politicized, largely socialist companies developed within the fringe, which could be defined as a number of small, low-budget theater groups that played in nontraditional theater spaces, presented new plays, and often experimented with form and style. The fringe movement had probably begun as early as 1963, when Jim Haynes founded the Traverse Theatre in Edinburgh. But now there was a new impetus. The 1968 lifting of censorship opened up performance possibilities for these companies as they professionalized, and Arts Council funding gave an added boost. Between 1964 and 1970 the Arts Council budget tripled to more than nine million pounds, and Jennie Lee, the Labour Party's minister for the arts, instituted grants to the new fringe companies and community arts programs, enabling their expansion. In addition to the Traverse in Edinburgh, fringe companies opened all over the United Kingdom, many of them set up as touring companies: the General Will in Bradford, Hull Truck in Hull, and the 7:84 Company established touring companies in England, Wales, and Scotland. Companies such as the Everyman in Liverpool were receptive to innovative and political work. Most of the innovative companies were in England, certainly in the early years—hence the focus of this essay. Later, alternative groups would spring up elsewhere in the United Kingdom, including Northern Ireland, where in 1983 five women in Belfast formed the Charabanc Theatre Company to address the concerns of women in their country.

Women's issues, typically based on the original demands formulated at the first Women's Liberation Conference in 1970, were part of the agendas of some of the new political groups. To further that agenda, separate women's companies were formed, some focusing on simply improving conditions and opportunities for women in the theater, others adopting an overtly feminist rationale. Additional companies sprang from street theater and political activism (the Women's Street Theatre Group, started in 1970, was one). Perhaps the best-known events—and true landmarks in feminist theater—were the 1970 disruption of the Miss World contest by demonstrators inside the Albert Hall and street demonstrations protesting the 1971 contest. These last included *The Flashing Nipple Show:* black-clad demonstrators outside the Albert Hall wore flashing lights on their breasts and crotches to point up the sexual objectification of women in beauty pageants.

The enormous growth in alternative theater in Britain in the seventies had not yet included a vital black theater ("Black British" was until quite recently an accepted, inclusive term for Britons of West Indian, African, and Asian descent), although a few separate black companies, notably Carib, Temba, Tara Arts, and the Black Theatre Cooperative (now known as Nitro) were forming to address issues specific to the Black British experience. Many more would follow in the 1980s and 1990s and would include women-focused and feminist companies. But black women playwrights would not have a real base of support until their own companies started to form, again in the 1980s and 1990s.

In her invaluable book *Carry on Understudies: Theatre and Sexual Politics* (1986), the feminist critic and playwright Michelene Wandor usefully divides feminist theater in the United Kingdom into four phases. The first, from 1969 to 1973, covers a time of heightened political activism in response to the key social and political conditions touched on earlier (industrial disputes, a worsening economy, slow application of the new legislation on equal pay).

This was the period of street theater as well as of touring companies, which went all over the country, playing in workingmen's clubs, upstairs rooms in pubs, community centers—wherever a space could be had. Issue-based agit-prop pieces dominated, featuring cartoon-style visual imagery and music, often with a naturalistically presented story at the center. The scripts were typically created collectively. Influenced by consciousness-raising groups, discussions would often follow performances. Pub theaters were also opening up at this time, especially for lunchtime shows, and provided new venues for political pieces, including feminist work.

The second phase of feminist theater, from 1973 until 1977, was initiated by the first Women's Theatre Festival, held at the Almost Free Theatre run by Inter-Action, a group founded by an American named Ed Berman. There were workshops, readings, and meetings leading to a season of four lunchtime programs of plays by women. The women who participated soon called themselves the Women's Theatre Group (WTG) and were the founding members of what would become a long-enduring company. The playwrights were Jennifer Phillips, Pam Gems, Dinah Brooke, Jane Wibberley, and Michelene Wandor and the American writer Sally Ordway. That scripted feminist plays were being performed in a professional fringe theater suggested the start of a new phase of recognition for women playwrights, although collective work on scripts still remained the norm for most companies. The second Women's Theatre Festival was held at the Haymarket Theatre in London in 1975, featuring the playwrights Nancy Posener, Olwen Wymark, Pam Gems, Caryl Churchill, Jennifer Phillips, Dinah Brooke, Liane Aukin, and Michelene Wandor; and the third festival was held in 1977 at London's Drill Hall, spearheaded by the director Nancy Diuguid.

Wandor sees the third phase of feminist theater as beginning in 1977 and as being generally marked by a stronger dependence on commissioned scripts. The companies were moving away from the agitprop/documentary approaches of the earlier collective work. Workshops encouraging new writers and other theater artists had been a feature of many companies, and now there were identifiable women playwrights to be found. Since Arts Council funding to political companies began to diminish after 1975, commissioning a proven playwright was perhaps seen as wise planning.

A fourth phase of feminist theater is marked by what Wandor calls "the numerous new voices of playwrights, women and male gays, whose work has been written and produced since 1979." This phase could also include solo performance, performance art, and cabaret.

Among the many feminist companies that emerged during the 1970s, three stand out and span all of Wandor's "four phases": WTG, Gay Sweatshop, and Monstrous Regiment. Many women whose plays would later be produced in the mainstream began writing for these and similar companies, pioneering radical subject matter and experimenting with form.

In 1975 WTG established an outreach policy of taking its productions to teenage audiences, beginning with a collectively created piece, *My Mother Says*, about teenage sex and contraception, followed by *Work to Role* (1976), about teenage job possibilities and sexism in the trade unions. Their next play, *Out! On the Costa Del Trico* (1977), was about a topical industrial dispute involving women striking because they were paid less than men for the same job. WTG—one of the first avowedly feminist companies to gain national recognition—has been guided by the basic principle that the personal is political, that home and family and work are inextricably linked. The company has also taken part in retrieving and rethinking women's history. Between 1980 and 1982, for instance, they performed Timberlake Wertenbaker's *New Anatomies*, about Isabelle Eberhardt, who in the late nineteenth century dressed as an Arab man to gain the freedom to explore the Middle East. Before 1978 WTG's performances were collaboratively created, but the company then moved generally to scripted plays, working with several playwrights who were to become known for their successes in mainstream venues: Wertenbaker, Bryony Lavery, and the South African–born Deborah Levy. In 1991 the company changed its name to the Sphinx Theatre and is still active in production, still running educational workshops and conferences.

Inspired by the success of the Women's Theatre Festival in 1973, Ed Berman suggested a Gay Theatre Festival for spring 1975, also at Inter-Action's Almost Free Theatre and also a first. The plays dramatized such subjects as gay parenthood, gay identity, heterosexual bigotry, and gay love stories. Because Berman had not approved the one woman's entry, Nancy Posener's *Any Woman Can*, which was eventually performed at the second Women's Theatre Festival in 1975, the season was entirely about male homosexual relationships. Still, out of this event, and the earlier Women's Theatre Festival, emerged a company of gay men and women called Gay Sweatshop. Men and women worked together on several projects, but as Wandor points out in *Carry On, Understudies,* because of fundamental differences in performance styles—the men favored the camp/drag tradition, the women were more comfortable with agit-prop/docudrama—and a growing sense that gay women had more in common with other women than with gay men, the women broke away in 1977 and functioned separately as the Sweatshop Women's Company until the mid-eighties. (Power struggles were also a problem in politically based companies; that men tended to end up with the power positions in the mixed companies often led the women to separate and form their own groups.)

The first production of the Sweatshop Women's Company was *Care and Control* (1977), about the rights of mothers, especially lesbian mothers, to the care and control of their children. The issue was topical because of recent court decisions against women who did not conform to traditional norms of motherhood and family. Scripted by Michelene Wandor, the play evolved from research and company workshops, a method common to many of the politically oriented companies that worked with established playwrights. In the mid-eighties, the men and women joined forces again, and the company, now mainly a touring group, functioned until 1997, when the Arts Council cut off all funding, possibly because of the increasingly controversial nature of its plays.

Monstrous Regiment was formed in 1975 by the director Gillian Hanna and a group of performers dissatisfied with women's underrepresentation in theater, particularly in political and fringe companies. The company's archival history states that the aims were "discovering and encouraging new women writers, exploring the theory of feminist culture, reasserting the 'hidden history of women,' creating non-stereotyped images of women, acting as a consciousness-raising group, attempting the theorizing and practice of collectivity and finding a new audience." The company included men and women until 1980, when by a process of evolution rather than conscious decision, it became an all-female company. Scripts were both commissioned and worked on collaboratively.

The first production in 1976 was of a play by Claire Luckham and her husband, the director Chris Bond, called *Scum: Death, Destruction and Dirty Washing,* an examination of sexual and socialist politics set in a laundry at the time of the Paris Commune. The second production that year was Caryl Churchill's *Vinegar Tom,* a drama that would have ongoing popularity, and the third entry was *Kiss and Kill** (1977) by Susan Todd and Ann Mitchell, about political and domestic violence. Churchill would continue writing for the company, as would Bryony Lavery, Michelene Wandor, and the Americans Wendy Kesselman and Susan Yankowitz. The company functioned successfully until 1993, when diminished Arts Council funding and lack of continuity in membership made production difficult to sustain. With its commitment to women administering the company and to providing many strong roles for women, with its theatrical activism and its touring, Monstrous Regiment was one of the most influential feminist companies and boasted an especially impressive roster of playwrights.

The work of feminist theater has been defined by a sense of community, so it is perhaps unsurprising to find one of the pioneers of women's writing turning to writing what came to be known as community plays. In 1979 Ann Jellicoe started work on the first of her community plays. These were plays specific to a community, often exploring its history and involving hundreds of local men and women as performers, researchers, costumers, and location managers. Her community play *The Tide** (1980), for Axminster, Devon, is set during the Napoleonic Wars and examines how a community coped economically. There were press gangs, smugglers, hunger, and loss of jobs to threshing machines, but the final victory occurs when the carpet industry, for which the area would become famous, was established through great community effort.

The collaborative spirit that marked the community plays and the early women's companies inspired and nurtured many of the playwrights who would soon find mainstream recognition. Among those who came to notice in the 1970s, the best known are Pam Gems and Caryl Churchill.

Pam Gems was born in Bransgrove, Hampshire, in 1925, of working-class parents. She studied psychology at Manchester University, married, raised four children, and moved to London with her family in the early 1970s to continue her playwriting career. She wrote two pieces for the Almost Free Theatre, which prompted the Women's Theatre Season and the founding of the Women's Theatre Group. Although some of her early work with this company and with the Women's Playhouse Trust was collaborative, in a 1994 interview with Lizbeth Goodman, published in Goodman's book *Feminist Stages* (1996), Gems expressed her misgivings about collaborative writing:

> I used to find, partly because I was older than everybody else, that people love to throw in all their ideas but in the end you the writer have to find a structure, and the reason, and a subtext, a text. This can be hard. If you're doing something like a play about abortion, and you've got one good strong theme, you need all the contributing ideas you can get, so that you can't be second-guessed. But there's another side to writing, and it's the side which is mysterious in all arts—painting or music or writing—and that tends to be disregarded in collaborative work . . . that deep, passionate energy which comes from one head.

Gems's passionate energy imbues the strong female characters at the core of the plays that won her mainstream recognition: *Queen Christina** (1974), *Dusa, Fish, Stas and Vi* (1976), *Piaf* (1980), and *Camille** (1984). Other plays include *Aunt Mary* (1982), an affectionate portrait of a transvestite couple, their lives, work, and endangerment by the commercial media; *Loving Women* (1984), about a triangular relationship between a man and two women; and the commercially successful *Stanley** (1996), a character study of the British painter Stanley Spencer.

Dusa, Fish, Stas and Vi was Gems's first commercial success: first performed as *Dead Fish* in Edinburgh, it then went to London's Hampstead Theatre Club before transferring to the West End. It concerns four women from different backgrounds sharing a flat in London: Dusa is battling to get custody of her children, who have been kidnapped by their father; Fish is trying to accommodate her upper-middle-class background to her socialist political activism, in the workplace and sexually; Stas, a country girl, works by day as a physiotherapist and by night as a high-class "hostess," to earn money for an education in marine biology (a situation that evokes Shaw's defense of prostitution as a viable activity for a woman denied education); and Vi is a seemingly hopeless young anorexic. At the play's end, Vi gets medical help and ultimately finds both hope and work; Dusa retrieves her children; and Stas will go to Hawaii to fulfill her dream of being a scientist. Only Fish, rejected by her lover, cannot go on, and she commits suicide.

Gems's play explores issues of women and work, class, and a woman's relationship to her body and to motherhood and children. In her afterword to the published edition of the play, Gems notes that *Fish* was inspired by Rosa Luxemburg, the Polish intellectual and revolutionary who was murdered in 1919 and becomes in turn a political inspiration for the character of Fish in the play. Fish's speech about Luxemburg is, for Gems, the crux of the drama:

> It's not just a matter of equal pay[,] . . . equal opportunity. For the first time in history we have the opportunity to investigate ourselves. . . . The nature of the social and political contribution of women is, at this moment, wholly in question.

Fish observes that Rosa never had the child she longed for, and in her suicide note she says that she, too, feels cheated of the motherhood she dreamed of.

Gems raises the issues of motherhood and its place in the life of an ambitious, intelligent woman in other plays. In *Camille,* the title character sacrifices her relationship with her son in order to get him an education and a future.

Queen Christina, brought up and educated as a man, lives the life of an independent intellectual, and only when it is too late does she realize that motherhood
might have brought her rewards.

Queen Christina was written in 1974 but not produced until 1977, largely
because it was turned down by the National Theatre and by the Royal Court,
which wrote a rejection letter asserting that the play would appeal mainly to
women. Fortunately the Royal Shakespeare Company (RSC) was wiser, and
Queen Christina became the first play by a woman to be presented at the RSC's
studio theater, the Other Place, in Stratford. Later it transferred to the Warehouse, the RSC's studio theater in London.

In Queen Christina, Gems explores many of the themes of Dusa, Fish, Stas
and Vi. But the play is also an example of her ongoing interest in revisionist
history. Hollywood has left us with the image of the exquisite Greta Garbo as
Christina; Gems gives us the historically accurate picture of a physically unat-
tractive woman with "a swivelled, crooked appearance." Educated as a man and
as the last hope of an heir to her father's throne, Christina is trained to ride,
fight, lead an army, and run a country. She also becomes the intellectual equal
of the greatest minds in Europe, including Descartes and the pope. She is sexually liberated, enjoying both men and women, but aware that it is her privileged
position that allows her to choose her lovers, not her looks or charm. When she
finally ascends to the throne, she rebels against marriage and the possibility of
an heir, knowing it would erode her power and deny her a life of the mind.

Queen Christina is constructed as a chronicle play, spanning thirty years.
But Gems subverts traditional expectations of the form by giving us a female
protagonist who is always the focus and the only complex character. The play
examines the nature of being male and female, and of what is lost when gender
is constructed artificially. Christina is a woman biologically, but her education
and training all but destroy her female impulses. She acts and thinks like a man,
often dresses as one. At the beginning of the play, motherhood is portrayed as a
nightmare when Christina's mother, screaming in agony, loses yet another baby
in childbirth. And throughout, women are described as "weak," the "wrong
sex," "breeders," "ignored" with age, and "hysterical."

But at the end, the female is seen differently. Refusing to claim the throne
of Poland, Christina declares, "half the world rapes and destroys—must the
women, the other half, join in?" She adds, "How wrong I have been to condemn
women for their weakness . . . they have kept us alive!" She is moved by the
smell of babies, of bread baking, and rushes to save a child choking. The final
scene contains an extended debate on the nature of woman, between Christina
and the cardinal she loves. She is, finally, aware of the gains and losses of her

gender-confused life. We see her exit to her library, to enjoy what she has left — her mind.

Piaf also provides a stark, unsentimental version of a life often romanticized. At the beginning of the play, the diminutive Edith Piaf is a powerless, impoverished, working-class streetwalker at the mercy of her pimps. Her talent as a singer brings her newfound status, power, and independence but does not tame or refine her; she remains sexually voracious, cruel, selfish, irresponsible, and utterly vulgar — a lush and a drug addict. But she is also cheery, funny, indefatigable, and vital, and she loves her power. People try to use her for it, as they do Christina, and like Christina, Piaf lashes out, sometimes cruelly and with a certain relish.

Similar in structure to *Queen Christina*, *Piaf* presents nineteen episodes in the singer's life and career. She drives every scene and is, like Christina, the only fully realized character. Lovers and passing strangers, managers and fellow singers, criminals and resistance fighters — they all parade through her life, creating an uncompromising picture of a life lived dangerously but joyously. At the end, she is in a nursing home and, in a final act of generosity, rejects the young man who takes care of her, releasing him to pursue the singing career he could only have away from her. While many scenes are punctuated by songs, only at the end does Gems give Piaf one of her famous signature ballads, and appropriately it is "Non, je ne regrette rien."

Piaf was first produced at the Other Place in Stratford, a year after *Queen Christina*, transferring later to the West End and then to Broadway. Few British women writers in the 1970s had achieved such commercial recognition, and more successful plays would follow. Gems's early visibility in the mainstream undoubtedly encouraged women playwrights to submit their work, and companies and producers began to be less dismissive of them.

Caryl Churchill is thirteen years younger than Pam Gems, but like Gems she went to university, married, raised children, and wrote radio plays before connecting with political theater companies in the seventies. Her first plays were produced at Oxford while she was a student, and in 1958 she was a prize winner in the Sunday *Times* National Union of Students Drama Festival. Like Gems, she has received ongoing commercial success, especially with such plays as *Cloud Nine** (1978–1979), *Top Girls** (1982), *Fen** (1983), and *Serious Money** (1987). She is one of her generation's most prolific writers and is still highly productive; her recent work includes *The Skriker* (1994), *Blue Heart* (1997), *Far Away* (2000), and *A Number* (2002). Her plays are marked by groundbreaking experiments with form, structure, and language, by a political concern for the effects of capitalism and class structure on human relationships, and by a guiding feminist

Burt Caesar, Daniel Webb, and Paul Moriarty in the Public Theater's New York production of Caryl Churchill's Serious Money, *winner of the tenth Susan Smith Blackburn Prize in 1988. (Photograph: Martha Swope, Billy Rose Theatre Collection, the New York Public Library for the Performing Arts, Astor, Lenox, and Tilden Foundations)*

viewpoint. The serious content of her plays is frequently presented with a keen eye for humor and irony, exemplified in her first professionally produced play, *Owners* (1972).

Owners was presented at the Royal Court, a theater to which Churchill would return several times in the seventies. The play examines the nature of power and powerlessness, economic privilege and ownership. Marion, an aggressive property owner and real estate developer, is married to the neglected, passive Clegg, reversing female and male stereotypes and creating, in the antiheroine Marion, a precursor to Marlene in *Top Girls*. Indeed, Marion is so dehumanized by her acquisitiveness that she not only evicts her tenants from a new property but, childless herself, takes their baby too, though she then has no use for it. In this play, every human life is something to be owned, an idea reinforced humorously by two running jokes: Clegg's many plots to murder Marion, whom he sees as his wifely property; and Marion's assistant, Worsley's, repeated suicide attempts and growing number of self-inflicted injuries, justified by his claim to ownership of his own body. The play is a macabre, sometimes funny, examination of the acquisitive spirit run amok, perhaps foreshadowing the cupidity of *Serious Money* (1987).

In 1976 Churchill embarked on a collaborative approach to playwriting with *Light Shining in Buckinghamshire*, which she created with the Joint Stock Company. Max Stafford-Clark founded the company in 1974 and would continue his support of women playwrights when he was artistic director of the Royal Court from 1979 to 1993. Stafford-Clark, the company, and Churchill participated in a three-week workshop, improvising, talking, reading, sharing research. Then Churchill wrote the script before returning to work with the company during its six-week rehearsal period.

In her introduction to the published edition of the play, Churchill acknowledges that "many of the characters and scenes were based on ideas that came from improvisation at the workshop or during rehearsal" and that "just as important, though harder to define, was the effect on the writing, of the way the actors worked." They researched the Civil War and the failed revolution in seventeenth-century England, drawing on original documents from the period to create a picture of the crushed hopes for a new society. The workshop phase also produced an unexpected approach to casting, in which the same character was played by different actors in different scenes. The result was to diminish psychological involvement with the characters, allowing for an intellectual reaction to events. This Brechtian approach would continue to be a hallmark of Churchill's writing.

Churchill would return to a collaborative or workshop approach to playwriting in such plays as *Vinegar Tom, Cloud Nine, Fen,* and, in 1990, *Mad Forest.* Such close work with actors and directors has clearly made her plays, workshopped or not, particularly actor friendly. She understands the process. The overlapping dialogue found first in *Top Girls* and then in *Fen* guides an actor's focus; the double casting or multiple role-playing in *Cloud Nine, Top Girls, Fen,* and *Light Shining in Buckinghamshire* deepens the meanings of the plays while providing actors with wonderful challenges. Perhaps the assurance of her experiments with form and time, language and character, evolved from workshop processes that allowed her to see and hear the possibilities.

Just before she started the workshops with Joint Stock, Churchill had been approached by Monstrous Regiment to work on a play about witches. She met with the company, and they discussed and shared background reading, although they did not workshop the material. *Vinegar Tom,* the play that resulted, opened in Hull, England, in October 1976, one month after *Light Shining in Buckinghamshire* opened at Edinburgh's Traverse Theatre (both plays would eventually be presented in London).

Churchill's subject in *Vinegar Tom* is the scapegoating of women as witches in the seventeenth century and their marginalization in society for such crimes as not being married, being sexual, being healers, being abortionists, and being old. In a series of twenty-one scenes, Churchill paints a vivid portrait of a community embracing superstition and enduring poverty and a community in which women constantly feared unwanted pregnancies. It becomes clear that there are no witches, just women trying to grasp some autonomy in a misogynistic society, one that demands that a woman be either a virgin or a wife and mother. Between scenes, again using a device similar to Brecht's alienation effect, a series of seven songs, explicitly performed in modern dress, suggest that the problems of seventeenth-century England have not disappeared from today's world.

This was Churchill's most overtly feminist play to date in its exploration of the marginalization of women at a time of huge social upheaval. Already, familiar Churchill themes recur: women seeking autonomy; the economic and psychological ownership of others, especially women; social and class violence; and sexual politics. In her next plays, particularly *Traps* (1977), *Cloud Nine*, and *Top Girls*, she would maintain her feminist outlook and would increasingly pose challenges to realism, an even stronger feature of her more recent plays.

Cloud Nine was her second play to be developed with Max Stafford-Clark and Joint Stock Company, in 1978 and 1979. As with *Light Shining*, there was first a three-week workshop, then scriptwriting, which took twelve weeks in this case, followed by a six-week rehearsal period. The workshop was about sexual politics, and Churchill notes in her introduction to the published play, "Though the play's situations and characters were not developed in the workshop, it draws deeply on this material, and I wouldn't have written the same play without it." They explored sexual stereotypes and also did what were called status exercises, which helped to further explore class and gender relationships. The script's two acts took final form when Churchill settled on an idea that had come out of the workshop: "the parallel between colonial and sexual oppression." Churchill made changes to the script during rehearsals, during early performances, and during later productions, including the New York premiere.

Churchill reaches a new level of playwriting confidence and originality in *Cloud Nine*. Cross-dressing is a familiar device in British popular theater but usually used for comic effect (as in the British pantomime) or to titillate (the breeches role tradition going back to the Restoration), and drag performance has its own set of conventions. Here, Churchill uses the device thematically and politically. In the first act, set in colonial Africa, Betty, the colonial wife, is to be played by a man because, as she tells us, "[I am] a man's creation . . . what men want is what I want to be." Her daughter, Victoria, is played by a "dummy," suggesting the young Victorian female is something to be looked at and played with but lacks any voice of her own. The son is played by a woman whose strongest desires, to his father's horror, are not for "masculine" pursuits but for playing with dolls and having illicit sex with Harry Bagley, an "explorer." Joshua, the African servant, who also has sex with Harry, is played by a white man, since he has seemingly erased his roots to serve his oppressor. The second act is set in London in 1979, but the characters age only twenty-five years, suggesting that progress is slow.

The sexual confusions of the first act are brilliantly and farcically comic. Clive, the colonial administrator, tries to run everything. He introduces us to the family and household he "owns" but does not know. He sees his wife as a symbol of feminine purity, but in fact she, like her son, lusts after the explorer. Preaching Victorian morality to all, Clive is nonetheless happy to have adulterous sex with Mrs. Sanders, a neighboring widow. He glorifies the friendship of men but is horrified when Harry responds sexually. He solves that problem by marrying Harry off to his son's governess, Ellen, who happens to have lesbian longings for his wife, a situation that, onstage, is doubly amusing and confusing since Ellen is played by a man. Harry and Ellen's wedding is the culmination of Act 1: Clive makes a speech and toasts the British Empire, only to expire when Joshua, a man whose family has recently been massacred in a native revolt, shoots him.

Act 2 is written in an utterly different, realistic mode. Again, it is only twenty-five years later for the characters from Act 1, most of whom reappear in Act 2. The same actors may now take different roles. In contemporary London, there is a new freedom to experiment sexually, to find one's identity in a slowly evolving society, a familiar Churchill theme. There is a raw frankness to the characters' dialogue and sexual experimentation. But ironically, the array of possibilities creates new confusions, challenges, and fears for most of the characters. Only Betty, who has a remarkable monologue about self-discovery and sexual awakening, provides a powerful symbol of a better future. The linked themes of colonial and sexual repression emerge again, in a scene where the ghost of a soldier killed in Northern Ireland, an ongoing locus of colonization, expresses the uselessness of the fight there: all the soldier kept thinking about was sex, and then he got shot, rather like Clive in Act 1.

The double casting of characters from Act 1 to Act 2 resonates thematically, although Churchill expressly leaves the doubling choices to her directors. *Cloud Nine* is a gift to the transformative power of the actor.

Similarly effective double casting guides *Top Girls* (1982), which was written for the Royal Court and a cast of seven women playing sixteen roles. In the tantalizing first scene, we meet Marlene, a young woman celebrating a major promotion in the employment agency where she works. Significantly, her fellow celebrants are neither friends nor coworkers but a group of historical and mythical women spanning the centuries: Isabella Bird, a nineteenth-century traveler; Lady Nijo, a Japanese courtesan and later a Buddhist nun; Joan, believed to have been a ninth-century pope; Patient Griselda from Chaucer's *Canterbury Tales;* and Dull Gret, who led a charge of women through hell to fight the devils in the Breughel painting, *Dulle Griet.* The actors playing these roles double as other characters in the rest of the play, which is set in the employment agency and in the home of Marlene's sister, Joyce.

The women seem to have nothing in common, given their origins and times, yet each tells a tale of rebellion against her society's restraints, of forging her own original path. All but the childless Isabella lost children; each found solace in art, poetry, or learning; Joan and Gret dressed as men to invade the male territories of learning and warfare; Griselda and Lady Nijo dressed to entice their men; Isabella dressed practically but always as a woman, a decision echoed later by Marlene's avowal, "I don't wear trousers to the office." All of these women rose above the restraints of their societies, and Marlene's success would suggest she is doing the same. But the political questions posed by the play are pointed: How long do women have to keep trying to rise above society's restraints? How do they break through? And what is the cost?

It is in this play that Churchill introduces overlapping dialogue, a technique used again in *Fen* and other plays. The effect, particularly in the first scene, is to point up the lack of community among the women, despite their commonalities. They speak over each other. In the second part of the play, the lack of support of women for women is demonstrated in the handling of the office interviews, in the dismissive attitude toward the wife of the man who expected Marlene's promotion, and in the insensitivity to the woman who had watched men be paid more and promoted over her. The issues examined are about work and marriage, job and pay discrimination, and the nature of male and female identity. Essentially the play is an indictment of the capitalistic policies practiced by Prime Minister Margaret Thatcher and bourgeois feminism's "if-you-can't-beat-'em,-join-'em" approach, suggesting that women must listen to and support each other, despite individual achievements, if real change is to happen. A "top girl" can be very lonely.

Marlene's success does come at a price. She is male-identified and cut off from other women, including her sister, who is raising Marlene's child as her own and also takes on responsibility for the care of their ailing mother. Politically, Marlene has embraced Thatcherism, alienating herself from her class and socialist roots. Angie, her daughter, has the last and telling line in the play when she stumbles in, half waking from a dream, and mutters, "Frightening."

The play is open ended. We do not know what will happen to Marlene and her child. The last scene is a long and emotional confrontation between the sisters, raising such issues as the economics of unpaid housework, child rearing, class, and politics. Churchill seems to be commenting on the future of feminism in a Thatcheresque world, suggesting that it will be frightening unless women reassess goals, work together, and bridge class and politics.

Churchill's plays have burst the doors wide open on subject matter, form, and use of the actor, and she is one of the most influential of her generation of playwrights, male or female. But she was not alone. When she and Pam Gems were making their marks in the seventies, several other, mostly younger, women were forging paths in their wake. Mary O'Malley broke ground for women playwrights with her *Once a Catholic** (1977), which is less a feminist play than a scathing satire on the Catholic church. It transferred from the Royal Court, where O'Malley had a residency, to an award-winning three-year run in the West End, thus opening yet another door for women playwrights in the commercial theater. It would win the first Susan Smith Blackburn Prize during the 1978–1979 season.

Maureen Duffy, Louise Page, Sue Townsend, Olwen Wymark, and Claire Luckham—these are only a few of the many women playwrights who followed the examples that Gems and Churchill were setting. Subject matter often broke taboos: in *Rites* (1969), one of the first overtly feminist plays to be produced professionally, Duffy set a modern-day *Bacchae* in a ladies' lavatory. Louise Page, who says the first play she saw that was written by a woman was Gems's *Dusa, Fish, Stas and Vi,* wrote about breast cancer in *Tissue* (1978). Form was malleable: Wymark, an American who lived in London, wrote about a child's mental illness in *Find Me** (1977); the lead character, Verity, is played by five actresses, and there is fluid and changing casting in other roles too, a technique that keeps the audience at some emotional distance, thus allowing them to grasp the complexity of the issues. In *Trafford Tanzi* (1980), Claire Luckham experiments with both content and form. Taking a dominantly male environment, the world of wrestling, she places a woman at its center and presents a play in ten "rounds," requiring that her six actors really wrestle; she uses the idiom of popular theater by having the referee function as a music hall emcee, addressing and involving the audience directly.

In the eighties, Nell Dunn, Sarah Daniels, Bryony Lavery, Andrea Dunbar, Deborah Levy, Catherine Hayes, and Timberlake Wertenbaker, again to name but a few, continued the march, addressing such topics as pornography (Daniels's *Masterpieces,* 1983), disaffected youth and teenage sexuality (Dunbar's *The Arbor,* 1980), and *Rita, Sue and Bob Too* (1982). Wertenbaker's *The Love of the Nightingale* (1988) dealt with rape—sexual and political—and the silencing of women.

As I am writing this essay, a British Sikh woman, Gurpreet Kaur Bhatti, has been awarded the 2005 Susan Smith Blackburn Prize for her controversial play *Behzti (Dishonour)* (2004). She is the first British woman of color to receive the prize. She continues the tradition, firmly established in the seventies, of women playwrights breaking boundaries and making the personal political.

Pam Gems sums it up in her notes in the 1982 Methuen edition of her play *Dusa, Fish, Stas and Vi:*

Art is of necessity. Which is why we need women playwrights just now very badly. We have our own history to create, and to write. Personally I think there will be brilliant women playwrights. I think the form suits us. Women are very funny, coarse, subversive. All good qualities for drama, and for the achievement of progress by the deployment, not of violence, but of subtlety, love and imagination.

TWO

Entering the Mainstream

The Plays of Beth Henley, Marsha Norman, and Wendy Wasserstein

MEL GUSSOW

✻

For many decades, women held a secondary position as playwrights in the American theater. Early in the twentieth century, Zona Gale, Susan Glaspell, and Zoë Akins were all Pulitzer Prize winners, but during the midcentury, the heyday of Tennessee Williams and Arthur Miller, only Lillian Hellman was a consistent presence on Broadway—and she never won a Pulitzer or a Tony Award. The others who had occasional successes were generally writing the stage equivalent of television situation comedies, or adaptations of previously published material. One rare Broadway exception was Lorraine Hansberry in 1959 with *A Raisin in the Sun.*

Away from the mainstream and outside the commercial spotlight, women were, of course, writing plays, and in 1972 six of America's leading female playwrights—Julie Bovasso, Rosalyn Drexler, Rochelle Owens, Megan Terry, Adrienne Kennedy, and Maria Irene Fornés—created a theater collective called the Women's Theater Council. The idea was to produce their own work and that of their colleagues and to increase opportunities for women in other areas of the theater—as directors, designers, and actors. In the *New York Times,* I said that, at moments, the first meeting of the council seemed like a caucus of revolutionaries. Unfortunately, the group soon disbanded, and the writers went on to their individual careers. But other collectives and theaters for women took its place. Somehow their impact was felt. In the late 1970s and the 1980s, there was a seismic shift, as rewarding plays by women appeared both on Broadway and Off Broadway and in regional theater.

Leading the movement into the mainstream were three talented playwrights of the same postwar generation: Beth Henley, Marsha Norman, and Wendy Wasserstein. Each wrote with a different and original voice, and it was their difference in subject matter, as well as style, that was to open doors for others who followed (including, many years later, Paula Vogel, Margaret Edson, and Suzan-Lori Parks). They demonstrated that varied approaches were possible, that one did not have to follow a formula or a predictable path in order to succeed. All three won other prestigious awards, had long runs of their plays on Broadway, and saw them turned into films.

Henley and Norman share southern roots—Henley from Jackson, Mississippi; Norman from Louisville, Kentucky—and in the late 1970s both had their work first done at the Actors Theatre of Louisville, which the artistic director, Jon Jory, was to make a primary source of new plays. As playwrights, Henley and Norman were studies in contrast.

In *Crimes of the Heart** (1979), *The Miss Firecracker Contest* (1980), and other plays, Henley found universality in small-town life, offering warmhearted but probing studies of families under stress. The mother of the three Magrath sisters in *Crimes of the Heart,* unseen in the play, killed herself after having "a bad day," words that were to become the playwright's signature. Despite those bad days—and the mother's death—Henley's characters, here and in other plays, buoyed themselves with humor. It is as if they were taking to heart that classic Beckett statement, "Nothing is funnier than unhappiness, I grant you that."

Beneath the dysfunction, Henley uncovered a congeniality and a feeling of community among the Magrath sisters. Congeniality was not Norman's mode. In *Getting Out** (1977) and *'night, Mother** (1982) she focused on women embattled in repressive and even oppressive situations. The plays were relentless and searing indictments about women entrapped in lives with no release. Although Norman's work has had glimmers of humor, she is far more earnest and unforgiving about life's desperation. Jessie, the daughter in *'night, Mother,* is forced to confront not simply a bad day but an irrevocably sad life.

Because of her irrepressible humor, the third playwright, Wendy Wasserstein, could easily be categorized as a kind of clown or class cut-up, a label that would shortchange her standing as a wise and witty observer of women who shatter the glass ceiling of societal expectations. In *The Heidi Chronicles** (1988) and *The Sisters Rosensweig* (1993), her characters repeatedly surprise us with their insights into their lives and with their understanding of the need for individuality.

Eventually the three playwrights were recognized as significant and influential artists. Each won a Pulitzer, and Norman and Wasserstein won the Susan Smith Blackburn Prize; Henley's *Crimes of the Heart* was the runner-up for the prize in 1979–1980 to Barbara Schneider's *Details without a Map** (1982). And Wasserstein became the first woman to win a Tony Award for an original play, *The Heidi Chronicles.*

As one sign of the diversity of the playwrights, each emerged in the spotlight

Lee Anne Fahey, Kathy Bates, and Susan Kingsley make a contemporary portrait of three sisters in the Actors Theatre of Louisville production of Crimes of the Heart *by Beth Henley, which received Special Commendation the second year of the Susan Smith Blackburn Prize, in 1980. (Photograph: David S. Talbott, courtesy Actors Theatre of Louisville)*

in a distinct fashion. On a weekend in February 1979, I was in Louisville at the Actors Theatre for the third annual Humana Festival of New American Plays. During two days of nonstop theatergoing, the outstanding play was *Crimes of the Heart,* a world premiere by a new young playwright. It was immediately evident that this was a fresh, exuberant, and high-spirited play and that Henley, at twenty-six, was fully formed as a writer for the theater. As acted by Susan Kingsley, Kathy Bates, and Lee Ann Fahey (playing three indomitable sisters in the small Mississippi town of Hazlehurst) and as directed by Jon Jory, it added a euphoric note to a breathless weekend.

During the festival, there was a general feeling of openness and spontaneity, onstage and off, as critics met at the downstairs bar between plays and—in direct contrast to New York—informally discussed the work that they had just seen. After the performance of *Crimes of the Heart,* I had an encounter—really an argument—with another New York critic who dismissed the play and the playwright, at least covertly expressing a view that seemed misogynist. Others, of course, agreed with me. I reviewed the play favorably in the *Times,* and the following year after it opened in New York, I was one of three jurors for the

Pulitzer Prize in drama when the play was awarded the prize. Later it was also named Best American Play by the New York Drama Critics Circle.

Ntozake Shange's *for colored girls who have considered suicide/when the rainbow is enuf* (1974) had opened Off Broadway in 1975 (and the following year moved successfully to Broadway), and in 1977 Marsha Norman had been introduced with *Getting Out* at the Louisville Humana Festival. But as provocative as those plays were, they did not have the same impact as *Crimes of the Heart.* It was a breakthrough for Henley and for women writing in the theater.

In her introduction to the published version of *Crimes of the Heart,* Henley said she wrote in 1978 in a breakfast nook in a rented house in West Hollywood, California. It was her first full-length play, a follow-up to her one-act *Am I Blue* (1973), which she had written as an undergraduate at Southern Methodist University. *Crimes of the Heart* (originally titled *Crimes of Passion*) was, in fact, a quintessential kitchen-table play. In common with Edward Albee, who wrote *The Zoo Story* (1959) at his kitchen table, it had a firsthand immediacy. Sitting at her table, and presumably thinking about herself and her own siblings, Henley had a vision of the Magrath sisters in their kitchen: poignant, unmarried Lenny; Babe, who rose to an act of violence against her husband; and Meg, a woman of wanderlust who returns to Hazlehurst and reawakens the ardor of her old boyfriend, Doc Porter. Each in her own way was suffused with loneliness, finding kinship and consolation only in their family bond. And, of course, there was Chick the Stick, the pushy cousin, the hypercritical outsider—a stand-in for Natasha in Chekhov's *Three Sisters* (1901), which shadowed this play.

Crimes of the Heart emerged from a deep southern tradition, more of novelists than playwrights. Watching Henley's play unfold, one thought about her progenitors, Eudora Welty and Flannery O'Connor, whose novels and stories chronicled the eccentricities of thwarted lives, and about Tennessee Williams and Carson McCullers, who doubled in fiction and theater. But Henley had her own special flavor, mixing compassion with dark humor, as the sisters squarely faced the violence within them (Babe's assault on her husband, their mother's suicide). In the final scene in *Crimes of the Heart,* the sisters come together to celebrate Lenny's birthday a day late. Lenny makes a wish or, rather, has a vision "of the three of us smiling and laughing together," not forever, just for this one time. Laughing joyously, she says, "Oh, how I do love having birthday cake for breakfast!" followed by a freeze-frame, as in a photograph of a shared memorable occasion.

The cast changed as the play moved to the Manhattan Theatre Club, then to Broadway, and eventually to the movies, with Diane Keaton, Jessica Lange, and Sissy Spacek—and Sam Shepard stepping into the role of Doc Porter. But that first encounter in Louisville remained foremost in my mind, a synchronicity of play, direction, and performance. Henley's success writing about home, family, and tradition inspired other playwrights, many of whom joined Jory's venturesome team in Louisville.

Both Henley and Norman were discovered by Jory, and Norman was his particular protégée. After majoring in philosophy at Agnes Scott College in Decatur, Georgia, and after marriage and divorce, Marsha Norman returned to her hometown, Louisville, where she worked with disturbed children at Kentucky Central State Hospital. Later she wrote and edited a column for young people in the *Louisville Times.* Attracted to the theater, she sent an idea for a musical to Jory, who encouraged her to write a play and suggested that she write about busing in Louisville. She soon had her own idea, remembering a teenager she had met at Central State, "a kid who was so violent and vicious that people would get bruises when she walked into a room." Eventually the girl had been convicted of murder. Trying to understand the nature of her strange character, Norman wrote *Getting Out.* After opening at the Actors Theatre, it had a long Off-Broadway run.

Several plays later, she wrote *'night, Mother,* a direct confrontation with a woman's despair and eventual suicide. As the playwright said, "I thought this was a play that no one would ever want to see, so there were no compromises to be made. Just write it for you, get it straight, get the score settled." Moving from the American Repertory Theatre in Cambridge, Massachusetts, to Broadway (with Anne Pitoniak and Kathy Bates as mother and daughter), it won the 1983 Pulitzer Prize, the second time in three years that it had been awarded to a woman. Later the play was filmed with Anne Bancroft and Sissy Spacek.

In May 1983 I wrote a cover story on Norman for the *New York Times Magazine.* It was both a profile of her and her whirlwind success and an essay about women who were making their mark as playwrights: Henley, Tina Howe, Mary Gallagher, Emily Mann, Wasserstein, Wendy Kesselman, and Lavonne Mueller. The piece emphasized their differences as well as their common bonds. In *Crimes of the Heart,* Henley wrote about a homecoming. In *Getting Out* and *'night, Mother,* Norman wrote about leave-taking, women forcibly severing ties of blood, marriage, family, the past.

Primarily the playwrights were writing about women of their generation, but the plays also dealt with mothers, fathers, and husbands resolving their own attitudes toward the newly liberated women in their lives. There was also a reevaluation of tradition, an attempt to understand the effect of formative influences and to redirect one's place in a future generation. Analyzing the work of Norman and other writers, Jory said, "With women today, there is a kind of directness and toughness, a lack of fragility. The characters in their plays very often seem more emotionally affecting to the audience than characters men have been writing about. While men are dissecting characters and detecting flaws, women are creating characters you can love. That says something about women's new, positive sense of self."

At the core of the profile was *'night, Mother*. About it, I wrote, "A spare but lyrical dialogue, *'night, Mother* probes deeply into the mother-daughter relationship while making a disturbing statement about responsibility and courage. It is as artfully designed as a sonata, rising in each dramatic movement until it arrives at its inevitable destination, a conclusion that asserts one's right to control one's life even to the point of suicide. In common with *Getting Out*, which dealt with a young woman on her release from prison, *'night, Mother* is as tough-minded as it is sensitive. The play stands out as one of the season's major dramatic events."

In a spare, intermissionless ninety minutes, Jessie, the daughter, tries to convince her mother that her choice to die is her only choice. In the play's pivotal scene, her mother issues a vain cry of protest, "You are my child!" Jessie can only answer, "I am what became of your child." Looking at baby pictures, she realizes, "That's who I started out and this is who is left." Her only reason to remain alive would be to keep her mother company, but, she says, "That's not reason enough because I'm not . . . very good company."

In speaking about her play and her approach to theater, Norman said that she had "terrible emotional ups and downs," but what kept her fighting was her conviction "that from that darkness comes an understanding." She quoted Theodore Roethke: "I learn by going where I have to go." As she said, "Writing plays is an act of faith"—faith in the validity of the art form, and also faith in one's talent and integrity.

Even at the rather early stage of her career, she was an articulate advocate for women in the theater and for tackling controversial subjects, in this case suicide. After Norman came Naomi Wallace, Margaret Edson, Suzan-Lori Parks, and others exploring questions of illness (emotional as well as physical), violence, and death. I remember once leading a panel discussion of playwrights for Women's Project and Productions and asking the participants if they thought there still were any taboos in terms of subject matter. Parks answered that there was nothing she could not write about and that she was limited only by her courage and her confidence in herself as a writer. But if she heard of a taboo, she added, that would provoke her to write about it.

Six years after *'night, Mother*, another woman, Wendy Wasserstein, won the Pulitzer Prize for drama for *The Heidi Chronicles*. Wasserstein was born in Brooklyn and grew up on Manhattan's Upper East Side, and the people who lived in that area—professional, economically advantaged—became the principal subjects of her plays, beginning with *Uncommon Women and Others*, submitted to the Susan Smith Blackburn Prize by the director Harold Clurman and a finalist for the first award. Written in 1976, produced Off Broadway by the Phoenix Theatre in 1977, it looked back on the playwright's identity-seeking days as an undergraduate at Mount Holyoke College. That was followed by *Isn't It Romantic* (1981), an equally autobiographical reflection about mothers and daughters and the rites of career and courtship.

With *The Heidi Chronicles*, she moved into deeper territory. It was a portrait of her generation, children of the 1960s confronting a quickly changing, often hostile world. More a humanist than a feminist, Heidi Holland (played by Joan Allen), an art historian, wants a banquet of possibilities: motherhood, sisterhood, and a career. Near the end of the play, Heidi gives a talk to alumnae at her high school on the subject, "Women, Where Are We Going." In it, she explains why she is unprepared for her speech. She attended an exercise class. Surrounded by twenty-seven-year-old "hotshots" and older women desperately trying to catch up with their times, including "a naked gray-haired woman extolling the virtues of brown rice and women's fiction," she feels alone and stranded. She says, "I thought the point was that we were all in this together."

Eventually Heidi finds a kind of self-fulfillment as a single mother and an independent woman, a route also followed by the playwright herself. Wasserstein's Heidi and the three sisters in *The Sisters Rosensweig*, along with Henley's three sisters, achieve a certain equilibrium—and they survive, with memories intact.

Directed by Dan Sullivan, *The Heidi Chronicles* benefited from a by-now-familiar route, from regional theater (the Seattle Repertory Theater) to Off Broadway (Playwrights Horizons), and, having proved its popularity and its award-winning prowess, it moved on to Broadway. Not that Broadway is an end-all, or even a desirable place for all plays, but it certainly widens an audience, and with *Crimes of the Heart, 'night, Mother,* and *The Heidi Chronicles,* Henley, Norman, and Wasserstein demonstrated—and it always needs demonstrating—that art can have a life in the marketplace.

Wasserstein learned early that "what mattered most . . . was having an interest in your own individual voice." In her case, that voice was resolutely comic, even in moments of greatest stress. Her work is defined by its humor—socially conscious as well as self-deprecating—and also by a kind of confessionalism. After her came Lisa Loomer, Gina Gionfriddo, and others with their wry commentaries on the roles of women today. In a sense, Wasserstein could also be regarded as an influence on playwright-performers who became the embodiment of their own stories, people like Claudia Shear, Lisa Kron, and Sarah Jones.

Subsequent plays by Henley, Norman, and Wasserstein have not yet equaled their initial success. The playwrights seem fated to be known primarily for the plays that brought them their first fame. But each has remained a leader and a role model for those who have followed them. It is extraordinarily difficult for playwrights to make theater a full-time career, and in each case, out of necessity they have also investigated other avenues of creativity (movies, television, musicals).

While still writing plays rooted in her home base—family life—as in *Impossible Marriage* (1998) and *Family Week* (2000), Beth Henley has occasionally reached into the world of fantasy. Of the three, she remains the most prolific as a playwright. At the same time, she has become a proficient screenwriter, writing *Nobody's Fool* (1986) and collaborating on *True Stories* (1986) as well as adapting her own plays.

Wendy Wasserstein has continued to study the roles of uncommon women and also moved into the wider world of politics (*An American Daughter,* 1997) and real estate and economics (*Old Money,* 2000). Increasingly, she has turned to nonfiction, writing amusing articles and essays (many of them appearing in the *New York Times*) about personal as well as social issues, and she has also written books for operas and musicals.

In recent years, Marsha Norman's plays have been intensely personal (*Trudy Blue,* 1994), as well as fanciful (*Last Dance,* 2003). She has also written screenplays for movies and television (*The Audrey Hepburn Story,* 2000) and books for musicals. In 1991 she won a Tony Award for the musical *The Secret Garden* and she has written the book for the musical version of Alice Walker's novel *The Color Purple* (2004). In addition, she has become a primary example of an accomplished artist who has helped emerging artists. As a teacher of playwriting (with Christopher Durang and, on occasion, other playwrights) at the Juilliard School in New York City, she has made a valuable contribution. Through her class, she has nurtured and encouraged a generation of writers for the theater, many of them women, including Jessica Goldberg, Kira Obolensky, Julia Jordan, and Brooke Berman.

As individual careers expanded, there seemed to be more opportunity for women as playwrights, at least on the workshop level. But the commercial theater and to a certain extent the institutional theater faced economic strictures and seemed less open to new work. Having entered the mainstream, even name playwrights do not always find it easy to have their plays produced. But with an intrepidness that is endemic to their talent, Henley, Norman, and Wasserstein never stop writing new plays, and in August Wilson's phrase, they continue "to test the limitations of their instrument."

In the *New York Times Magazine* profile, Norman said, "We are soldiers marching, and we must not step on the mines. We are trying to clear the path, to tell you what's out there." She wanted to warn herself and her colleagues to be daring but also to be watchful guardians of their creativity and their freedom. You learn by going where you have to go.

THREE

A Conversation

Timberlake Wertenbaker, Max Stafford-Clark, and Michael Billington

❦

The following conversation took place at Timberlake Wertenbaker's home in England in May 2004. Since 1980 Wertenbaker has contributed a versatile range of plays and translations to the canon of women's theatrical work, including Our Country's Good, *for which she received special commendation from the Susan Smith Blackburn Prize in 1989, and* Three Birds Alighting on a Field, *for which she won the prize in 1992. Here, with the British director Max Stafford-Clark and with Michael Billington, who has followed her career from his position as theater critic for the* Guardian, *Wertenbaker talks about her experiences writing and rehearsing plays, agreeing and disagreeing with a director, and living in England.*

MICHAEL BILLINGTON: Timberlake, could you tell us about your cosmopolitan upbringing, because I suspect it's highly relevant to your approach to drama and theater.

TIMBERLAKE WERTENBAKER: Well, I was brought up in the Basque country, in the southwest corner of France—brought up by a mixture of my parents and a Basque family. That upbringing was very influential, because it was at a time when the French authorities weren't allowing Basque to be spoken in the schools. And, although I didn't realize it at the time, that affected me deeply, because it was my first direct experience of not being allowed to speak a certain language. Growing up in a generation that could not talk to its parents in their native language started an obsession with language: what it means to have a language, what it means not to have a language, what it means to have a second language. Then I left the Basque country and went to lycées in France and America, and ultimately to university in the United States.

MB: When you realized you wanted to write, what made you choose drama rather than fiction or poetry?

TW: It happened by chance. I was in Greece teaching French and surrounded by people working in the theater, and for fun, we all sat down to start writing a play. It was like trying on a glove that fits. I thought, "This is something I love doing. I love being with other people. I love telling stories in dialogue." I then went off and rewrote the play, and we put it on. It was pure amateur theater, but it was at a time when the Greek colonels had burned the libraries, and there was little professional theater. So we did some plays for children and some plays for ourselves. It was a very happy experience, because I didn't fully appreciate the technical difficulties of writing a play.

MAX STAFFORD-CLARK: What language did you write in?

TW: Partly Greek and partly English.

MB: And how old were you at that time?

TW: In my early twenties.

MB: But it was an instant feeling of coming home?

TW: It was. I'd obviously seen a lot of theater and read a lot of French plays, but I hadn't separated this experience from other kinds of writing. I thought I was going to be a novelist. But since I hate descriptions and am rather impatient, fiction was obviously the wrong form for me. I can't explain it, but drama just felt right. It was crazy to embark on it, but I didn't know that then.

MB: You had a number of plays done on the London fringe in the 1980s, and you wrote some very fine Marivaux translations for Shared Experience, an experimental theater company that often employs a storytelling technique. But it was when you started working at the Royal Court that you achieved a higher profile: *Abel's Sister* at the Royal Court Upstairs in 1983 and *The Grace of Mary Traverse* at the Royal Court Downstairs in 1985. Did you see the Royal Court as a spiritual home?

TW: It was a home I wanted to enter. From the time Max took over in 1979, I just remember going to see everything there. It was a very exciting place, and I was just desperate to have a play put on there. I can't say it was a spiritual home, but it was the theater I wanted to write for without any question.

MB: Max, how did Timberlake come to your attention?

MS-C: Well, I became aware of Timberlake through *Abel's Sister,* which we put on at the Royal Court Upstairs and over which I had to try and resolve some knotty contractual problem. Then came *Mary Traverse,* which was commissioned for Upstairs but, although I didn't direct it, I decided to put on Downstairs in the larger space, partly because Janet McTeer was in it, and it's always a help when you're graced by up-market casting. I thought the play showed a fine command of history and language.

MB: *The Grace of Mary Traverse* is a fascinating play. It's about an eighteenth-century politician's daughter who crosses the accepted sexual frontiers — hence her name — and learns that if you play by masculine rules in a patriarchal world, you end up bruised and battered. But what made you choose an eighteenth-century setting?

TW: I didn't know the English side that well, but I knew the French eighteenth century. The whole play sprang, oddly enough, from the fact that I was living in South London in the 1980s at the time of the Brixton Riots, which were a protest by the local black population against white authority figures. Someone said to me that riots weren't new in England and mentioned the Gordon Riots, which happened in 1780; these were antipopery riots directed against the government and led by a certain Lord Gordon. As with most riots, they went out of control, and there were huge fires. Researching them, I became fascinated by the period and conceived of this character crossing the accepted sexual frontiers. I wanted her to be in the midst of the riots, to be where everything gets out of control. That is the ultimate symbol of her transition from private to political power, and of the destructiveness she experiences. But as often happens with plays, it had a slightly haphazard origin.

MB: Max, you said you decided to do the play Downstairs. Was that because it was a big, epic play?

MS-C: It wasn't big in terms of cast, but it was epic in terms of ideas and the sweep of history. One should perhaps explain that the Royal Court Upstairs seats only sixty-five and the Downstairs space four hundred, so deciding to do a play by a relatively unknown writer in the main theater is a big decision; you have to work out where the box office is going to come from. It depends on the notices, and the casting is absolutely crucial. I thought the play had breadth and depth and command of that period. It got good notices, did respectable business, and was a gamble that paid off.

MB: I read one interview, Timberlake, where you said that it had to be done Downstairs, because Janet McTeer was an extremely tall actress who wouldn't easily fit into a studio space. Was that a joke, or does it have a measure of truth?

TW: It's kind of a joke. But Janet, who wasn't that well known at the time, is a wonderful actress and a big personality in every sense. So perhaps the moral is that you should always write for tall people if you want to get the best spaces!

MB: You said, Max, that *Mary Traverse* did well. Did that lead you to commission Timberlake to adapt Thomas Keneally's novel *The Playmaker* (1987) for the stage? That, too, is set in the eighteenth century, although it deals with a group of English convicts who are deported to Australia and discover their identity in the process.

MS-C: Yes. Absolutely. I knew Timberlake had a feel for the period that was obviously right. She also understood the changes taking place in Georgian society at that time. Also, if you adapt any book for the stage, you have to choose the themes you are going to discard and those you are going to amplify. And one of the things that interested me was that while the male convicts were downwardly mobile once they arrived in New South Wales, the women were upwardly mobile. They either became wives or concubines of the English officers and were often deposited in token sheds in their gardens before moving into their houses and becoming part of a new society. So the men became very dependent on the women in ways that the authorities hadn't anticipated, and that made me think it would be good to have a woman writer tackling Keneally's novel.

MB: Because the play is about a group of convicts staging Farquhar's *The Recruiting Officer* (1706) in Botany Bay, and discovering a form of language and identity in the process, it inevitably seems a play about the redemptive possibility of drama. Did either of you set out with that intention in mind, or did it just emerge organically?

TW: That was very much something I detected in the book, and I told Max at the very first meeting that was what I wanted to write about. It was just an instinct that this was the way to give a forward thrust to the novel.

MB: And what was the process? Did the whole company engage in a long period of collective research?

MS-C: It was actually quite a brief period of research. But we'd all read Robert Hughes's book *The Fatal Shore* (1987), about the founding of Australia. The violence that society begins with and the descriptions of the beatings and brutalization of the men and women—all described in the diaries of Ralph Clark, who was one of the officers in charge—became one of the areas we explored through improvisation. David Haig, who played Ralph Clark, arrived late for the improvisations and came in at a point where we had stripped the men down to their underpants and were beating them with newspapers. But he threw himself into this with extraordinary abandon and emerged pink all over.

The violence was something we concerned ourselves with in the workshops. The dreams, too, became very important. I suppose the starting point —as with David Hare's *Fanshen* (1975), where we had to ask, how do we play Chinese peasants?—was, how do we play starving, eighteenth-century con-

At the Hartford Stage in Connecticut, Amelia Campbell and Stephen Rowe in a scene from Timberlake Wertenbaker's Our Country's Good, *which received Special Commendation in 1989, the eleventh year of the Susan Smith Blackburn Prize. (Photograph: T. Charles Erickson)*

victs? How do we understand that world? And Timberlake's play, Keneally's novel, and Robert Hughes's book gave us an intellectual comprehension of that.

MB: Did the workshops Max is describing have an impact on the finished text?

TW: They had a huge impact. When you write a historical play, your first concern is to ask what its contemporary resonance is. We did a great deal of research into contemporary prisons, and that was really the key to the whole thing. We went to see a performance of a Howard Barker play, *The Love of a Good Man* (1978), in Wandsworth Prison, and that was extraordinary. *Our Country's Good** (1988) was not an illusion. Talking to the convicts doing the Howard Barker play, and discovering their passion for it, inspired all of us.

MS-C: It came at just the right point in rehearsal, so it confirmed where we were going rather than setting us off in a new direction. The prison actors we met were obsessed with the play they were doing. What do you do in prison? You become a born-again Christian. You become a gym queen pumping iron. Or you become—like these people—theater nuts. They'd rehearsed the Barker play for eight months, in two sessions a week of two hours each.

They knew they had to use every second of rehearsal. There were no women in the prison, so the women were professional actors brought in from outside. But the debate in *Our Country's Good* about whether convicts should be allowed to put on plays was absolutely paralleled by reality, because the prison authorities said that the Barker play wasn't suitable to be seen by other inmates. ILEA—the Inner London Education Authority—said, "You can't stop us doing the play, because it's part of the educational remit you've subscribed to." So what happened was, ILEA got an audience from outside that included the director Trevor Nunn one night and lots of agents and casting directors. What had been a fill-in job for the professional actors became a high-profile showcase. And one of the prison actors, Joe White, was really excellent and kept up a correspondence with Timberlake. I said to him, "There are a lot of casting directors here. How long are you going to be in for?" And he said "Ten to fifteen years." So you suddenly thought that maybe this was not going to be such an imperative after all.

MB: *Our Country's Good* is based on the redemptive power of drama. But does that become an illusion if you're confined to long-term imprisonment?

TW: It didn't for the prisoners we met. I corresponded with three or four of them, and a few years later they did *Our Country's Good,* so everything came full circle. For them to have done that play and the Howard Barker was a huge thing. I also mentioned their work when I accepted an Olivier Award on television. They suddenly felt that they'd achieved some recognition outside prison. And from their letters, which are published here and there, it became clear that it did change them. The whole experience did convince all of us that there was something in theater that offered a form of hope.

MB: That shows how research can confirm what you've already deduced. But were there cases when research might have changed the direction of the text?

MS-C: I can think of a couple of cases where research was instrumental in transforming scenes. It's not rocket science, but Mark Lambert, who played the Hangman, read a book by Albert Pierpoint, the last hangman in Britain, which explained how to hang someone: the importance of the weight, how the drop has to be so much to hang them but not so much to pull the head off, and the whole dynamic of hanging.

TW: In fact, that scene—the Science of Hanging—was one of the few taken directly from an improvisation. The scene hinges on the question of whether the character of Lizzie, who is about to be hanged for stealing food, will speak up in her own defense to the midshipman, Harry Brewer. Jim Broadbent and Linda Bassett had improvised that scene, and it was about whether Lizzie would decide to talk or not. One night Linda called me at about midnight and said, "I was about to talk." So something that the actors imaginatively explored, namely, Lizzie's sudden discovery of her voice, informed and shaped what I wrote. But what's interesting is that Linda had thought and thought about it and said, "I have to call you and tell you this." That's where a writer can get a sense of the emotional path an actor has followed in improvisation. I don't necessarily like to take the words from an improvisation, but an emotional truth that the actors have discovered can be immensely helpful.

MB: What actually is the chronology? Do you do a draft script that is subject to workshops, and then do you go back and rewrite accordingly?

TW: It depends. With *Our Country's Good* there was no draft script before the workshops. First there was the workshop. Then came a two- or three-month period in which I wrote and pursued my own research. For instance, a lot of the play is about the development of the officer Ralph Clark, who left behind his journals and letters. He is the second lieutenant, who is haunted by the sexual activity he has seen on the voyage out, sets up the production of *The Recruiting Officer,* and is torn between his love for his wife and for the convict, Mary Brenham, whom he appears opposite in the play. He is a deeply disturbed character, who elevates his absent wife into a sort of female icon and is tormented by sexual guilt. I went to a psychoanalyst friend in London, showed her some of Clark's journals, and discussed his behavior with her, and that was just as important in defining the character as anything we did in the workshop. What I am really saying is that however helpful workshops are, in the end the writer has to do his or her own research and get down to the play in comparative solitude. But then comes the rehearsal period, where the script undergoes further modifications.

MB: What happens when the play is subsequently produced elsewhere (and this play has had a wide circulation in Britain, America, and Australia)? Should the actors do their own research each time, or simply take the text as a given?

TW: Actors research anyway whenever they do a play. What makes it different the first time around is that the actors have been researching the play for as long as the author, and you don't have to explain things to them. But I've certainly encouraged people doing *Our Country's Good* to make their own explorations. They're just not as complete, which is why the first productions have a special kind of life to them. In fact, when Max's production was done in Australia, half the cast was different, but they got into the same spirit and started reading.

MS-C: The first actors in a play like this have an ownership of the text that is quite exciting, and you're involving them in skills that other productions don't, so there is a learning curve for them in which their critical faculties become engaged and much sharper.

MB: Can we move on to *Three Birds Alighting on a Field**, which was done at the Royal Court in 1991 and won the Susan Smith Blackburn Prize in 1991–1992. Briefly, it's about an upper-class Englishwoman, Biddy, who starts out as a trophy wife married to a Greek entrepreneur and gradually discovers a passion for art and for a neglected English landscape painter. Is it a natural successor to *Our Country's Good,* in that it's about the redemptive possibility of art, as opposed to drama?

TW: I think it's an area that interested me and that I hadn't quite finished with in *Our Country's Good.* It was also written straight after the 1980s, and I was interested in that society. But I was keeping that notion of the value of art — whether it has any value, and if so, what that value is. The difference was, the central character was upper-class, privileged, rather shallow, and not particularly alive at the beginning of the play.

MB: As you point out, it came after a decade of Thatcherite money worship. Rereading the play, I was struck that it's very much the work of a cosmopolitan observer like yourself, who suggests that England has to start loving itself again and overcome the dogmas of the eighties. Is that how you saw it?

TW: I think it's how I saw it at the time. I was horrified, like most of us, by the eighties and by Thatcherism. The play was an attempt to throw that off and get back to something I imagined England still had, which was a sense of value. I loved England then — probably more than I do now — and I felt there was a beauty in England that was being destroyed by Thatcherism. So, yes, it was about that.

MB: How much was this play shaped through improvisation?

MS-C: Not as much as *Our Country's Good.* There was a workshop in which we went to art auctions and met a couple of dealers from Bond Street, talked to painters. That contributed to the auction that begins the play and acquainted us with a particular world. I don't think the text changed much in rehearsal.

TW: I think I had longer to write it, so the play went through more drafts before rehearsal. It was in fairly finished shape when we started. But in this case, I came to Max and said that I'd like to do an exploratory workshop, and that was very good, because people from various art galleries came to talk to us. It's very helpful when you're doing research with actors alongside, because people feel very free. If I go to interview someone privately, he or she will often be defensive. But he or she will open up to a group. It was also very helpful going to an art auction. I had no idea that the tone was so rapid and that people just lifted a finger to make a bid.

MS-C: And it's so witty. The auctioneer is flirting with the crowd. He's saying, "The lady with the lovely haircut over there: two hundred thousand. Two hundred and fifty to the gentleman on my right. Are you just scratching your nose, madam, or are you bidding? Two hundred and sixty . . ." All that goes on. So it's a form of entertainment. And we went to one where the man we'd dealt with, Bernard Jacobson, bid for a Stanley Spencer triptych. He said beforehand, "My limit is going to be eighty thousand; I'm not going to go above that." In the event, the bidding went to a hundred and fifty, a hundred and sixty, and he was thrilled and said, "I got it!" We said, "But you said eighty thousand was your limit." He said, "No, I was thrilled and couldn't stop."

MB: The play is a satire on the intense commercialism of art but, like Caryl Churchill in *Serious Money** (1987), did you become engrossed in the world you were satirizing?

TW: Yes. You do, although it's such a bitchy world, it can't quite take you in. Unlike theater, where there is a sort of consensus, I discovered that in the art world some people will talk about a reputable painter and just hate him. There is no area of agreement or objectivity. And while in drama a play is judged by external criteria, such as how it was received or how many people went to see it, or how people remember it, in art you're dealing with privately owned objects to which people pin a subjective value. It's a very odd world.

MB: In the end, the heroine pairs off with an English landscape painter. Is the play meant to be a hymn to the English landscape?

TW: Very much so. I felt we should learn to love our country, particularly the physical aspect of it, which again was being destroyed.

MB: The controversial aspect of the play was the inclusion of certain scenes that paralleled the main action with Greek myth. What was the general purpose of those scenes?

TW: I wanted to experiment, and I wanted something coming in that was not satire, to give the play another dimension. It was the story of Philoctetes, who was abandoned by the Greeks on a desert island and then became vital to the fall of Troy because of a prophecy concerning his bow. I thought it would be interesting to have that as part of the play's texture. But it didn't work. We tried it, and Max directed it, but I think those scenes were written in a slightly arch fashion that destroyed them. I think this was one of the few cases where I wanted to cut something and you . . .

MS-C: . . . I wanted to keep working on it . . .

TW: . . . partly not to be accused of cutting it! And it didn't work.

MS-C: My recollection is, what was difficult about the play was that there were three plots—three stories going through it. There wasn't the simplicity of a single central character as in *Mary Traverse*. I think the central character, Biddy, was very well developed from the start of rehearsal, and it was a question of getting the other strands into focus. And those Greek scenes—

and there were only two—were like a pale residue of something that wasn't developed sufficiently to take its weight in the play.

MB: Timberlake, you talked about your reaction to Max's retention of those Greek scenes. That raises the larger question of your professional relationship. Are you as free to comment on Max's direction as he is to criticize your text?

TW: Yes. I think Max and I were always very stretched, which is why it was a very fruitful relationship. We were very different temperamentally and saw things very differently, which made the relationship a constant challenge. But I always felt I could trust him. I always felt free to say during rehearsals or previews, "I don't think this works" or "What about this?" I felt Max was very generous and would always listen, even if he didn't agree. We would sometimes argue over particular lines that I fought for, or argue over jokes that I liked and he didn't. But Max was brilliant at his ability to "see" a play and discover if there was something that stood outside the whole.

MB: How would you describe the relationship?

MS-C: "Argument is not a bad word: debate is a good word," to quote from *Our Country's Good*. I think rehearsal etiquette is very important. David Hare, when we were doing *The Permanent Way* (2003) for Out of Joint, disagreed with something an actor was doing in rehearsal. So I said, "Why don't you tell him?" David said, "You mean I can speak to the actors? Richard Eyre never lets me do that." Different directors work in different ways. But I don't pretend with actors that one always agrees with the writer. If we disagree, and there's a debate, we invite their opinion. The writer can feel you're all ganging up against him or her, so you have to beware of that, but a good part of rehearsal is debate about the script. There were a couple of examples I could quote. For instance, in *Three Birds* you wanted to cut the auction scene . . .

TW: That was after the first preview, because nobody laughed, and I panicked. I said, "Cut it, cut it, cut it." And Max said, "No, just keep it."

MS-C: And then it was triumphant at the second performance.

TW: It was terrific. But if I'd been directing the play myself, I would have cut it, which would have been a shame.

MS-C: Another example is the dream scenes in *Our Country's Good*.

TW: Oh, I couldn't stand them. I don't remember holding on to those.

MS-C: Oh, I remember you holding on to those. . . . [Laughter]

TW: No, but we did have endless arguments about the final scene in *Our Country's Good*.

MS-C: The final scene?

TW: You don't remember, but I was in tears.

MB: What was the source of the argument?

TW: There were various lines in what was a very big scene. Because there are a lot of people talking, it's very hard to focus, and that's where the direction of that last scene was so brilliant, because every single moment was clearly defined. But when Max was first directing it, I felt, "God, there are eight people all talking at the same time, and a million things going on. How am I going to focus this for the audience?" In fact, when watching it, it was as if the ball was being expertly passed from one character to another. But it took a while. And I remember saying, "Do you want me to change the text?" and you said, "Yes, I want you to change everything." But you never said what. The problem wasn't the text but the director wrestling with staging it and trying to make something work. We argued over individual lines. A couple of times I said, "This is just a joke," and Max would say, "But it's not funny." But in the end, everything worked.

MB: Max, when you get a script from Timberlake, what's your own process? Do you go through it in minute detail, offering line-by-line analysis?

MS-C: To begin with, I read it quite quickly. Particularly if it's good, I stop reading, digest it, and come back to it a day later. You know quite quickly with a play if it's something you want to do. There are exceptions; some plays creep up on you. But on the whole, you know pretty quickly. And with *Our Country's Good*, there was an idea suggested to Timberlake, and with *Three Birds*, there was an idea that came from Timberlake, both of which I bought. I thought, "Yes, the art world as metaphor—excellent." In those cases I wasn't responding to a written script but to an idea and a concept.

MB: You worked again together on *The Break of Day* (1995), which was staged by Max's company, Out of Joint, in 1995 and toured to the Royal Court. This was played as a companion piece to Chekhov's *Three Sisters* (1901) and dealt with gender and the extent to which female identity is tied up with children. The general criticism at the time was that the play shifted from a country-garden first half to a second act showing two of the three women attempting to fulfill their maternal needs—one through fertility treatment, another through adopting an East European child. The feeling was that the play was disjointed. Looking back, do you feel that criticism was unfair?

TW: I was very hurt by the criticism of it. Really hurt. Maybe because I felt quite exposed in the play. I wanted a play with two different kinds of acts. I'm not saying it works, but the brokenness of it was intentional and, I felt, represented the contemporary world and all that. We live in a world where four or five things are going on at the same time and we're constantly shifting our attention. So the play was a deliberate attempt to do something that finally didn't come off. It was very painful for the two of us. If *Our Country's Good* was the love affair and *Three Birds* was the marriage, this was the divorce. It was very sad. We never really talked about it. I don't think the actors were . . .

MS-C: . . . convinced.

TW: . . . convinced. Or committed. They were different kinds of actors. The situation was different. It wasn't a production coming out of the Royal Court . . .

MS-C: The actors were committed before they had the script. They bought into the general idea. But I always felt we were one draft behind where we should have been . . .

TW: . . . we were one draft behind. Yeah.

MS-C: It was one of those occasions when you commit to opening on October the first before you've got the play. And sometimes those are triumphant occasions, and sometimes you're caught short by them. And here I think we were exposed.

MB: I remember feeling that the best scenes were those showing Nina, a singer-writer, wrestling with the Kafkaesque bureaucracy of a post-Communist country when she's trying to adopt a child.

MS-C: Not having read the play for a while, those are the scenes that live in my memory.

MB: What is the play's final gesture? Of the three women, one is an academic who ends up childless and says, "I live with dignity and some grace." Is the play finally suggesting that each woman has to make her own choice, that there is no golden rule that says gender identity can only be achieved through children?

TW: Yes. I suggested it be paired with *Three Sisters,* because in that play they say, "In a hundred years' time we'll be happy and we will work." My play was trying to take three women who have worked and realized that that's not the answer either, and in the end the play says that there is no single thing that will bring happiness. Just as there is no political system that will bring us peace or fulfillment, there is no single decision that you make as a woman that will bring a sense of complete fulfillment. So it's a slightly sad conclusion, but it says that you have to live with as much dignity as possible. I was given a chance to rewrite the play for ACT in San Francisco, but I felt so unhappy about the whole thing, I didn't take it up. I always wished it had gone through a couple more drafts and become a complete play. At the time, it felt like something worth saying.

MB: Doesn't society now accept the argument that it's perfectly legitimate for women not to have children, if that's their choice?

TW: But women themselves go through agonies. I see it in my stepdaughter: the decision to have a child or not, the fear of time passing and not being able to have one. The question of whether work is finally fulfilling, whether taking on a male role is the right way of going about life, is still very problematic. And whatever you say—that women should or should not have children—it's going to upset somebody.

MB: How does having a child affect your working life?

MS-C: It broadens your experience. On a simple level, you meet people at parent-teacher associations you wouldn't otherwise meet. It means you see the world through different eyes.

MB: Your more recent plays, Timberlake, have been done in a variety of venues. *After Darwin* (1998) was done at Hampstead Theatre, *Credible Witness* (2001) at the Royal Court Upstairs, *The Ash Girl (A Cinderella Story)* (2000) at Birmingham Rep. Do you feel that you have lost, temporarily, that permanent home at the Royal Court?

TW: Yes. When I did *Credible Witness* there after Max had left, it was like being in a strange land. I had taken it for granted that I could walk into the theater, go and have a conversation with the artistic director, and just talk about anything. It's very valuable for a writer. When you are out on your own, always working in your own house—and the play might be directed by this person or that person, go to this theater or that theater—it does feel very different. It's less happy, I must say. I've got used to it now, but it was quite a shock when things changed.

MB: Max, do you feel that writers thrive if they have a permanent home and a place where they are constantly welcome?

MS-C: Yes, because they have a working relationship that breeds confidence and security. Writers gain enormously from feeling that they've got a home. But writer-director relationships, like marriages, don't always last for ever.

MB: But can't you have a separation as opposed to a divorce?

TW: Had that production of *The Break of Day* originated at the Royal Court, there would probably have been another play done with Max. Because if you're a writer in a permanent theater, you have more freedom to fail: the well-known "right to fail" that was part of the Royal Court ethos. If you are in a freelance situation, it is more precarious.

MB: You've said, Timberlake, that your early work was about discovery and your more recent work about threatened or troubled identity. Why that shift in theme or subject matter?

TW: Some of that may be personal. You discover a lot about yourself and the world at large when you're younger, and you try to discover what your identity is. But it's very much a theme of the moment, because everyone is either fighting for their identity or seeing it destroyed. The whole current situation with terrorism is about identity. *Credible Witness* is very much about broken identity. But as a writer, something catches your imagination, and you work at it and work at it and then you go on to something else. At the moment I am interested in the meeting place of the public and the private, which I am dealing with in my next play, *Galileo's Daughter* (2004). In a sense it's a historical play, but it's also about how you can maintain your individuality when you're under social and intellectual pressures. I've probably finished with identity now and am interested in where the human being is in the world at the moment. Yet identity's always been a big theme with me because I have no identity. I have no single identity.

MB: Do you really feel that?

TW: I really feel that, because of my mixed background.

MB: Do you always feel an outsider?

TW: Totally. Wherever I am. And I desperately try to grasp on to things.

MB: But you've lived in England a long time now. That hasn't given you an acquired Englishness?

MS-C: The irony is that Timberlake is in some ways more English than the English. A character like Biddy in *Three Birds* — since all plays are a mixture of autobiography and journalism — has strong elements of Timberlake. She's very English. Couldn't be more English. [Laughter]

TW: But I always feel that I can be shifted or discarded in a way that an English person can't. I don't have the security of the English. I feel I can be moved quickly.

MB: But aren't there great advantages to being a writer who lives in England but sees the country through critical, outsiderish eyes?

MS-C: Exactly, you can observe it. And you see this in all Timberlake's plays. When we took *Our Country's Good* to Australia, they at first hailed it as a play about Australian history and then said, "Oh, no, it's really a play about England." So questions of identity pervade all three of the plays we've been discussing today.

TW: But when I write about foreign cultures, I don't see them as an English person would. *Credible Witness*, which is written from the viewpoint of two foreigners, is very un-English in a way. And that removes it from what the English want. It's a big question, whether you write only about one country or whether you should be free to wander geographically about the globe.

MB: What you say, though, is based on a dubious premise, which is that the English have a built-in security. I'm not aware of this, as someone who is totally English.

MS-C: Class is part of this . . .

TW: . . . class and where you went to school . . .

MS-C: . . . there is a smugness in Britain — let's not use the word "security."

There is a certain sense that the English know who they are and don't want anything to do with Europe.

TW: That's where I feel completely stretched, because I love Europe and feel more European than English.

MB: But surely we're living through a period when England is going through its own identity crisis and doesn't know whether it's meant to be a European power or cling to the coattails of America. At this of all times, it's the nation that is having an identity crisis, rather than individuals. We don't know if we're European or American, whether we want to be a monarchy or a republic. We don't know who we are anymore, do we?

TW: I think the English know who they are, but the country doesn't want to move with history. It doesn't want to be part of history anymore. It is apprehensive of Europe, yet has this strangely unexamined relationship with America.

MS-C: I think you're right. When I go to Ireland, I find they're much more relaxed about being part of Europe and have embraced it.

MB: But Max, you've been at the forefront of English theater for the last forty years. Isn't the very thing we're talking about the source of so much good writing in this country? This permanent questioning of who we are, where we belong, what is our identity, what is our place in the world? This anguish has fed into British—not just English—drama.

MS-C: Absolutely. The debate that constantly takes place contributes to the vigor and strength of English theater. Talent plus subsidy equals genius. And although Mrs. Thatcher made inroads into that equation, we assume the theater is going to be subsidized, and that has led to a strength and confidence and a will to examine what is going on. The theater, much more than fiction or visual art, has become where we debate who we are.

TW: But I'd say the theater is suffering from that Englishness we're talking about, suffering from an unwillingness to engage with Europe or more international subjects. There's a danger of English theater being primarily about English subjects. And that raises the bigger question of whether theater is best when it stays within its own country or when it reflects that, in the contemporary world, we have fewer borders.

MS-C: I'd say the theater thrives on being specific and local and examining the minutiae of Englishness. But it also thrives on the wider debate and has to embrace subjects beyond its own immediate concerns.

TW: And nationalities other than its own. That's very important for us to grapple with.

MS-C: Well, a play about the American connection, Timberlake, would be terrific. I'll commission you now! [Laughter]

PART TWO

Facing the World

Cheryl L. West, co-winner of the thirteenth Susan Smith Blackburn Prize for Before It Hits Home, *with playwright and presenter John Guare. The other co-winner was Rona Munro for* Bold Girls. *The Century Association, New York, February 26, 1991. (Courtesy Susan Smith Blackburn Prize)*

Remarks from the Susan Smith Blackburn Prize Award Ceremonies

The film and stage actor Meryl Streep, presenting the sixth Susan Smith Blackburn Prize to Caryl Churchill for Fen, *the Players, New York, February 24, 1984:*

I came to the competition with a funny feeling about its being just for women. I suppose I thought I would read plays that were obviously written by women, whatever that is. And there was a viewpoint that *was* different. But the scope and the range were totally unexpected, and interesting and thick. In *Fen,* I loved how Caryl Churchill's humor flew in, like Tarzan on a vine, to rescue these true, spare characters from the dead plain they inhabit. I loved the elliptical nature of the scenes, the way things were so felt and unforced — unsaid.

But each playwright had an idiosyncratic voice, and a vivid face. I realized I'd been reading screenplays for years, and they're so skeletal and bare, it was as if I'd been exposed only to sketches and drawings and prints, and then suddenly, after reading these plays, been invited into a room full of paintings, so colorful and rich was the experience.

❧

Cheryl L. West, accepting the thirteenth Susan Smith Blackburn Prize for Before It Hits Home, *the Century Association, New York, February 26, 1991:*

Thank you so much for this honor. As a woman, as the first black woman to win this most coveted prize, I am thrilled, I am honored, and I am humbled. This prize means a great deal to me because, so often, one gets discouraged as a writer. There are many women writing, but so few getting produced, and even fewer who are African American women. *Before It Hits Home* has had a long and arduous journey to production. The first version was presented in my hometown three years ago. Since then it has had readings and workshops, and finally its first professional production at Arena Stage in Washington, D.C., this year.

Before it found its home at Arena, I was reminded that there were dues to be paid; perhaps more because I was a young writer, a woman, and a black woman. I heard disparaging comments such as, "Our subscribers would be offended by the language"; "We have already done our black play and we don't want to exhaust our black audience." There were even threats of boycotts, outrage that I must be a white woman, because no responsible black woman could have written such a lie—after all, blacks don't get AIDS. As you can see, I'm not white; I am a very black woman who was afraid, who got discouraged about her play, a play that I wrote because I looked around and saw my people dying alone, without the comfort or the compassion of each other, estranged because of fear and ignorance. But my mother used to say, "If one door closes, another one will open." She was right for the most part, until I got into this thing called theater. So one day I said to her, "What if it never opens?" And she said, "Then you'll have to go and knock the damn thing down."

This is why this prize is so important to me. It is a signal and an answer back—that yes, we hear you knocking. It encourages me not to give up, to encourage other women not to give up, to keep on knocking at the door, politely at first, but then at all costs to persevere.

The first impulse of many of the playwrights who emerged during the Women's Movement was simply to put women at the center of their plays. Like the consciousness-raising groups that arose in the United States during the 1970s, American plays by women at first sought to investigate women's struggles and demonstrate women's strengths and to draw audiences that could share in as well as learn from the experiences being aired. And because the Women's Movement was largely a white, middle-class cause, the plays reflected that origin.

In the United Kingdom, the plays that emerged at the height of the Women's Movement embraced a wider spectrum, at least in terms of issues of class and politics. Caryl Churchill's *Cloud Nine** (1979) aggressively satirized the hypocrisies of the British Empire, and her *Fen** (1983) dramatized the economic and social entrapment of women who slogged for low wages in the fens of England, working for a capitalist system that did not care about them. Nell Dunn's *Steaming** (1981) celebrated female solidarity as a political tool.

Indeed, as the essays and memoirs in this part convey, many playwrights who drew sustenance from the Women's Movement wanted to do more than put women on pedestals. They wanted to examine subjects that traditionally had been considered outside the purview of women's playwriting: war, women's sexuality, social and political issues. To be sure, women writing for the theater before the 1970s and 1980s had approached these topics. Aphra Behn's comedies, for instance, dramatized women's sexual behavior in seventeenth-century England, where women were defined by men as either marriageable partners or prostitutes. The plays about suffrage that women wrote early in the twentieth century to support a woman's right to vote clearly had political intentions.

But as Charlotte Canning notes in chapter 1, one of the assumptions of the Women's Movement during the 1970s and early 1980s was that previous information about women should be questioned, no matter what the source. The second-wave feminists wanted to investigate politics and war and women's sexuality for themselves. They connected sexuality, for instance, to the contemporary issue of a woman's right to ownership of her body. In the United States in 1973, the Supreme Court had in effect defended this right with its ruling in *Roe v. Wade* that a woman could seek and receive an abortion if she chose.

As the playwright and director Emily Mann writes in the essay that follows, the dramatists who emerged with the Women's Movement believed that their female gaze could be turned on any subject in any way, so long as truth and artistry were the result. In fact, Mann states, perhaps the most important lesson she took from the Women's Movement was the freedom to write about anything she wished.

Part 2 demonstrates how a number of playwrights used this freedom and continue to do so. "Women and War" discusses six plays that tackle a topic that Western literature has conventionally believed was best served by male writers. Then, in a brief memoir, Sharman MacDonald revisits the territory of adolescent sexuality she dramatized in *When I Was a Girl I Used to Scream and Shout** (1984), and Susan Miller, writing just over twenty years later, celebrates being gay in an excerpt from her play *Sweeping the Nation* (2005). A woman's body can, unfortunately, be a repository for destruction and pain as well as pleasure, and Pearl Cleage, who has been a finalist for the Susan Smith Blackburn Prize for *Hospice** (1983), *Flyin' West** (1993), and *Blues for an Alabama Sky** (1995), writes a personal essay about the horrific battles waged on the bodies of African American women and their children.

Cleage has never shrunk from the issues that face African American women. In "Engaging Social Issues, Expressing a Political Outlook," the director Gwynn MacDonald discusses how a number of British and American playwrights have used their art to look into other areas that are frequently avoided, be it HIV in an African American community, in Cheryl L. West's *Before It Hits Home** (1998), or Rebecca Gilman's nightmarish drama of sexual stalking, *Boy Gets Girl** (2000).

As the 1980s progressed, the Women's Movement lost momentum in both the United States and the United Kingdom. Social and political conservatism swept into office with Ronald Reagan and Margaret Thatcher. In many quarters, "feminism" became a bad word; making money became the byword. In the United States, by the end of the 1980s, the number of theater companies dedicated to work by women had sharply declined, victims of decreased public funding for organizations that exuded any trace of a political outlook.

In response to their own questioning of feminism, some playwrights who had come up through the Women's Movement began to wonder whether they wanted to be identified as "women playwrights," and others believed that, to function in what was still a male-dominated profession, the description had become a liability. Still others watched the retreat from feminism, observed the increasingly conservative agenda being formulated by the U.S. and British governments, and wrote about it. In the United Kingdom, Louise Page's *Real Estate* (1984) painted an unflattering portrait of postfeminist women, and Kay Adshead's *Thatcher's Women** (1987) dramatized the ruinous effects on a wife of her husband's unemployment.

But at the same time that the Women's Movement seemed to be diminishing in political power, in and out of the theater, women's theater companies received a thrust from feminist women of color. In the United Kingdom, as Elizabeth Swain has written, "the Theatre of Black Women was founded in 1982.

The mixed company Black Mime Theatre engendered its own women's troop in 1 984; Talawa Theatre Company was created in 1985 by Yvonne Brewster, Mona Hammond, Carmen Monroe, and Inigo Espejel; and Kali Theatre Company was formed in 1990 by Rita Wolf and Rukhsana Ahmad, specifically to explore the perspectives and experiences of Asian women." In the United States, a thrust toward multiculturalism at universities and among arts organizations brought more women of color into the theater as dramatists during the late 1980s and early 1990s. In chapter 8, in a conversation called "Crossing Borders," four American playwrights—Bridget Carpenter, Lynn Nottage, Dael Orlandersmith, and Diana Son—talk about how they have wrestled with issues of race and gender in their own creative processes and in the business of theater.

FOUR

The Female Gaze

EMILY MANN

❦

In 1975 the filmmaker and critic Laura Mulvey wrote a landmark essay, "Visual Pleasure and Narrative Cinema," in which she concluded that in the majority of Hollywood movies the "male gaze" of the male filmmaker, male protagonist, and male spectator projected erotic fantasies onto a movie's female images. The result, Mulvey wrote, was that "women are simultaneously looked at and displayed, with their appearance coded for strong visual and erotic impact." In other words, women in these films were merely sexual objects. The phrase "male gaze" soon became almost a code for an attitude that objectified women, whether in the arts or in daily life. In the next essay, Emily Mann, the artistic director of McCarter Theatre Center in Princeton, New Jersey, and a finalist for the Susan Smith Blackburn Prize for her plays Still Life, Execution of Justice, Greensboro, a Requiem, *and* Meshugah, *discusses the possibilities and ambiguities of a female gaze. This essay was distilled from two conversations between Emily Mann and the editor.*

Do you know the brilliant Luis Buñuel movie called *That Obscure Object of Desire* (1977)? While Buñuel was making the movie, he decided to fire his leading lady—that object of desire. But instead of replacing her with one actress, he put two in the role. And what many found amazing was that male spectators rarely noticed there were two women playing the same part. The female spectators saw it immediately. I went once with male friends to see the film, and I asked each one if he had noticed anything about the woman in the title role. Both said, "No. She's beautiful." I said, "Did you notice that she didn't always look the same?" "No." "Did you perhaps notice that it's two different women?" And they said, "Oh, my God. You're kidding." Talk about the male gaze.

But this is film, you might say. Things are different on the stage, where there

Kathleen Chalfant is comforted by Helen Stenborg in MCC Theater's New York premiere of Margaret Edson's Wit, *a finalist for the sixteenth Susan Smith Blackburn Prize in 1994. (Photograph: Joan Marcus)*

is no camera, no editor, to predetermine an audience's focus or blur imagery. I would have to counter with, "Well, not always." The male gaze is an all-pervasive construct in our society. Sometimes women come up against it so forcefully that its presence is clear and we become aware and upset. At other times, the application of the gaze is very subtle.

The male gaze has been the controlling force in Western theater all the way back to the ancient Greeks, I should imagine, perhaps because men have mostly been the playwrights, producers, critics, directors, and historians. But where is the female gaze? There are periods when women came strongly to the fore in the English-speaking theater: in the United States, during the early twentieth century, there were playwrights like Rachel Crothers and Sophie Treadwell. Between 1902 and 1926, Crothers wrote a stream of successful Broadway comedies; she was the female Neil Simon of her day. Then, after the 1930s, she disappeared. Both Crothers and Treadwell were erased from people's consciousness. During the 1960s and 1970s, it was a different story: women began to break down barriers, and theater critics and producers supported them. Women broke through and began to be produced on a national level and to win national prizes, and their plays were placed on college reading lists. Now, if people are studying dramatic literature, they are reading plays written by women. But when I was coming up, I don't think I read a single play written by a woman, except for Lillian Hellman. Women so often get lost.

What is the female gaze? I'm not really sure, but when I was beginning to write plays, certain subjects were off limits to women. War was off limits. It didn't crystallize for me how off limits war was until *Still Life* (1980)—which involves a Vietnam veteran, his wife, and his mistress—was produced in London in 1981. I was interviewed by a journalist who assumed, as did everyone he was sure, that I had written this because I was having an affair with the soldier in the play. I was a naive young thing whose head was completely turned, and the play was my erotic fantasy. It was appalling. In his view, that was the only way I could talk about war: I was having an affair with a vet.

Still Life was my decision to look, not just at the violence on the field of battle, but also at the violence that was happening at home from a lot of the vets who came back—violence that was both conscious and unconscious. In the play, the wife has been physically abused and is afraid for her life. I decided to make the play a still life, a testimony, and have the characters tell their stories to us rather than act them out, because I thought there had been an eroticizing of domestic violence in media at the time. I was writing the play in the years after *The Godfather* (1972) had come out, a movie in which the character played by Talia Shire is beaten to a pulp in the kitchen by her husband. The scene was brilliantly acted, directed, and edited, and unfortunately, I thought, it was also wildly entertaining. There was something sexy about it. Often, when it came to abuse, the media seemed to be saying, "You know, if a man displays that much passion and violence over a woman, it's got to be love." So I decided that, rather than show the abuse onstage, I would show its result. I wanted the wife in *Still Life* to sit onstage, just sit—inert, pregnant, enraged, hiding her bruises and broken bones—and tell her story just as the vet's wife had told it to me. Mary McDonnell, who played the wife, was all over that part: she portrayed a bloated, angry, beaten-up woman talking about what she knows. I tried to show the cold truth of violence against women from the woman's point of view, rather than write that action-packed scene of a great-looking guy beating up on a lovestruck, beautiful, sobbing woman.

Perhaps that's what the Women's Movement did most for me, and for many of my fellow playwrights and directors. It enabled us to wrestle with assumed truths and question them—turn them on their heads. In that scene in *The Godfather*, we watch the violence from the outside. What about how the woman is receiving those blows? If you jump to a much later film—*Boys Don't Cry* (1999), which was directed by a woman, Kimberly Peirce—the horrific rape scene is shot, and experienced by us, from the victim's point of view. The women who grew up during the 1960s and came to theater in the 1970s and early 1980s were writing about war and politics and other societal issues. We had marched for the Equal Rights Amendment, we were turning our gaze outside the home. We had also come through a sexual revolution, which allowed us to look at our sexuality on the stage. We weren't sticking to the so-called domestic female issues. We felt that we didn't have to. And if we were, we were seeing them in new ways.

Quite consciously, I have used traditional female settings. I have set two plays in kitchens: *Annulla Allen: Autobiography of a Survivor* (1977), later retitled *Annulla: An Autobiography*, about a Jewish survivor of World War II; and *Having Our Say* (1995), about two African American sisters, both of whom are over one hundred years old. In each play, the characters cook and prepare food while talking to the audience.

I got the idea to set a play in a kitchen the first time I was going to use oral history as a jumping-off place for creating a play. My father was head of the American Jewish Committee's Oral History Project on Survivors of the Holocaust. The committee wanted to make oral histories of concentration camp survivors, and my father, who was a historian, felt that professional historians should not be conducting these studies. He thought the interviews should be conducted by family members or close friends, who could delve deeply into personal recollections. The oral history I happened upon was of a Czech woman who had been interviewed by her American-born daughter. They had talked in the mother's kitchen, and it was one of the most extraordinary mother-daughter scenes I had ever read. The daughter had finally found a way to ask how her mother had survived Treblinka, and the mother had told her about it for the first time.

I asked my father if I could use the interview as a one-act play, and he said, "No, it's the property of the young lady and it's going into the American Jewish Committee's archives. Why don't you do your own interview?" So I did. I went to Europe in 1974 and met Annulla Allen, the aunt of my best friend and a Jewish survivor of World War II, and as luck would have it, we interviewed her in her London kitchen while she was making chicken soup. The conversations were life-changing for me; the interviews became the basis for my first play.

Cooking in a kitchen, or watching someone cook and talking to them as they prepare food, is a familiar and often comforting activity. A kitchen is usually an unthreatening location to the people in it and, in a theater, to the audience watching. You can be talking about a whole lot of politics while dicing onions or making chicken soup. You can be talking, as Annulla does, about how the Gestapo came to her house on Kristallnacht, or what she had to do to get through the guards at Dachau in order to save her husband. In *Having Our Say,* which I also set in a kitchen, Bessie Delany tells how she was nearly raped by a white man in a colored-only waiting room at a Georgia train station. During much of the play, she tells why she doesn't like white people very much. She tells uncomfortable truths that are hard to hear. But she speaks these remembered truths in her kitchen, and this is familiar territory for an audience. Many of us have learned profound life lessons in a kitchen, our elbows propped up on a Formica table while we listened intently to the talk of our mothers, aunts, grandmothers, or neighbors as they prepared meals.

I find that audiences drink in the stories they are told this way, just as they once did when they were young. Rather than hear political truths assaulting us as polemic, we feel that we have had a long and informative talk with a dear friend or member of the family. Annulla Allen and Bessie Delany were funny, irreverent, and searingly honest. Bessie's sister, Sadie, was sweet, gentle, and equally candid. Through laughter and tears, audiences were often stunned by what they learned from these women, just as I was when I first heard their stories. By being welcomed into this traditional female space, our hearts opened; we heard and learned.

It hasn't always been easy telling these stories. *Betsey Brown* (1989), the rhythm and blues musical that Ntozake Shange, Baikida Carroll, and I collaborated on for eight years, is about a young girl's coming-of-age. It was very successful my first season at McCarter, but I remember a few male critics saying, "Well, she's such a passive central character. She doesn't *do* anything." At first I was baffled, and then I thought, "Oh, thank you. That's such a helpful (though idiotic) comment. Now I understand your problem: she is a girl!" When Betsey Brown got her first kiss, she didn't run after the guy and smack him on the lips; he ran after her. She *received* her first kiss. She received her first kiss, and her whole life changed—her world changed. Her insides turned upside down. This is huge, and she sings about it. She is not the pursuer in that event, but she plays a very active part. Several reviewers clearly wanted to follow the boy who ran up and kissed her; they wanted to know what happened to him. And we were saying, "Well, this time why don't we see what's happening to her?"

As a director, I told that story by focusing the audience on Betsey rather than the boy. Onstage, we were in a school yard; everyone was playing, and a boy came up to Betsey and gave her the kiss. She drew an enormous breath. He ran offstage, the lights isolated on her, and she sang about how she felt. It was like a film cut. As the director, and in this case also as coauthor, I controlled the audience's gaze. And I do that all the time. But still, the audience was watching a young girl's internal journey—her coming-of-age—which did not always interest some of the critics. I think, or, rather, hope, that this would be an easier story to tell now than it was in 1989.

Meshugah* (2002), which I adapted from a novel by Isaac Bashevis Singer, is about a writer named Aaron. He falls in love with an extraordinary, young, Jewish refugee named Miriam, who is having an affair with one of Aaron's friends, an elderly Jewish man.

To me, the center of the story was the young refugee. Singer adored women;

he couldn't live without women. And out of a lot of love and a lot of knowledge, he wrote absolutely thrilling female characters, like Miriam in his novel
Meshugah (1981). Miriam has survived the camps and survived World War II by
any means possible. Abandoned in Warsaw, she becomes a whore. Later, again
to survive, she becomes a Kapo in a concentration camp and the mistress of
the commandant. She is put in charge of the women's barracks, for many Jews
the worst possible sin. Better you should have died than collaborate in order to
survive. Miriam comes to the United States and falls deeply in love with Aaron,
and that spurs the central question and action of the play: At what point do
you draw a moral line between what you can or cannot accept in the behavior
of the one you love? What is and what is not forgivable?

When I directed the play at McCarter, Miriam was the center of the drama.
When the director Jason Slavik later staged *Meshugah* in Boston, the play became Aaron's. In part, that's because I wrote a new draft for the Boston production; I pared the script way down, and the play became more about the love
affair, and Aaron became more present. He now has a stronger through-line,
which is good, because Miriam is such a glorious character that Aaron can tend
to disappear.

But Jason also had a great personal investment in Aaron's role. In my staging
at McCarter, the character of Aaron came and went. In Jason's production, he
never left the stage. In my production, for example, when Miriam telephoned
Aaron, you saw her onstage; in one scene I had her reclining on her bed upstage
in a pool of light, with her hand between her legs, while Aaron was downstage,
talking to her on the phone. But where do you think the audience was looking?
In Boston, you saw him and only heard her; she was in voice-over. A director
could choose to do it either way, and I can't remember what has been published
for those scenes, Jason's stage directions or mine (shame on me). But both di-
rectorial approaches work. The story is the same, but the emphasis is different.
Perhaps that is a good example of the unconscious female gaze. I did not realize
until Jason's production that, even in Aaron's scenes, I was focusing on Miriam.

Sexuality is so complicated on the stage. You never know what baggage or experience an audience member brings to it. The most erotic scene I ever directed
involved a fully clothed woman alone onstage. In *Miss Julie* (1888), Strindberg
wrote an interlude that takes place between the time the servant, Jean, takes
Miss Julie into his room and seduces her and the time they come out. The play
calls for dancing and peasant jollity and antics, and in my 1994 production at
McCarter, I had two peasants come into the kitchen, drunk and happy, and
start to make love on the kitchen table. The peasants wake up Kristine, the cook,
who has fallen asleep alone in her room. Furious, she kicks them out and makes
herself a pot of coffee. Then she notices that Jean's door is closed and she's sus-

picious — after all, she knows him; they've been lovers for years. She sits down at the table with a cup of very black coffee, and on the table there's a bowl of hard sugar, and she just takes a hunk of sugar and dips it into her coffee and sucks on it. The lights slowly change, isolating her, and the music gets gradually louder and more erotic, and from her face, as she sucks on the piece of sugar, you see her picturing everything that Jean is doing in his room with Julie. It takes a very long time.

Kristine finishes her coffee and, enraged, goes into her own room and slams the door. Whomp — the lights change, and suddenly the long narrow room, which has been effulgent with midsummer trees and sky, becomes gray like a tomb. Now it is morning, and it's after Jean and Julie have made love. Jean has had his sexual fantasy fulfilled and is scared about the potential consequences, but Julie is completely besotted. Sexually awakened, drunk with it, she still can't get enough. She wants to hold him, she wants to touch him, she's willing to change her life for him. She's in postcoital throb. Another woman might stage the scene differently, but that's an absolutely female gaze on that play.

Many of us obviously operate from the female gaze, but we've trained ourselves not to label it, because if we label it, then we risk becoming dogmatic rather than creative. It's definitely a game I play with myself. I know the female gaze is operating, but I try to push that analysis aside and deal simply with the artistic truth. In other words, I just do my work — simply, instinctively, and very, very personally.

Recently, I was at a retreat with the playwright and actor Dael Orlandersmith, who writes brilliant multicharacter plays that she often performs herself. She stunned me with the new writing she was doing. It was very much in process, but she read some of it for me. Dael is African American; in this new play she became an Irish girl, a gay white man, an Italian American stud — all talking about race. Dael can write everyone, perform everyone, and it was thrilling to see all these people pass through her. Is the female gaze operating in this work? I don't know. What I do know is that the Dael Orlandersmith gaze is operating. At the end of the day, what makes great art, for me, is the individual artist unself-consciously speaking the truth as only she knows it.

Women and War

The Plays of Emily Mann, Lavonne Mueller, Shirley Lauro, Naomi Wallace, Shirley Gee, and Anne Devlin

ALEXIS GREENE

In Western culture, war has always been assumed to be a man's game. Men, after all, don the armor, crawl through the trenches, "man" the guns. In this scenario, women are the ones who stay at home. Mothers wave flags as their sons march through town on their way to the front. Wives and lovers wait patiently, if tearfully, for letters from the battle lines, and daughters grow up hearing about a father's patriotic exploits. Women serve in what history considers marginal roles: nurses, ambulance drivers, entertainers, and camp followers. Men and women, so the scenario goes, have separate domains in wartime. For men it is the battlefield, for women the hearth. "Keep the home-fires burning," went the first line of a popular song from World War I.

This narrative puts men and women on opposite sides of the war experience, for it places men in the thick of things and deems women ignorant of what men go through. Perhaps for that reason the literature of war has also been considered a man's province. From Homer to Hemingway, male writers have been considered the authorities, especially since many actually fought in the wars about which they sang. Women's war writing, although often vibrant and acute, was largely pushed aside and ignored, thought not to possess equal validity. Then, too, from the beginning women have largely disparaged war more than they have glorified it. The Greek poet Sappho, writing "To an Army Wife in Sardis" in the sixth century B.C., vows, in Mary Barnard's spare translation, that "The sound of your footstep and light glancing in your eyes/would move me more than glitter of Lydian horse or armored tread of mainland infantry."

Western theater, of course, was a male playwright's domain for so many centuries that men by default became war's primary storytellers on the stage. At times a playwright turned his gaze on the women in war. In *The Trojan Women* (415 B.C.), Euripides portrays Andromache, Cassandra, Hecuba, and the rest of the Trojan women as victims of a fight that men have waged over another woman — the beautiful but selfish Helen. These three Trojan women suffer the awful but traditional fate of captured wives and daughters: in defeat they become the property of the victors and are led off to be raped and enslaved. Watching the play as it has usually been interpreted by modern directors, we suffer with Hecuba as she lies weeping on the ground, we feel Andromache's wrenching pain when the Greeks take away her young son, to throw him from the parapets.

Still, placing *The Trojan Women* in the context of its time, one has the feeling that Euripides' tragedy is less a compassionate tribute to women in war than a passionate warning to Athens, which only a few years earlier had been battling Sparta and was on the brink of more fighting. "This is what will happen to your women," Euripides seems to be telling his city; "This is what will befall your men." Distraught though the Trojan women are, they praise the heroism of their murdered father and dead husbands and despise military cowardice. They hate the Greeks who defeated them, they hate the absurd reason for the war, but they do not hate soldiering.

Female playwrights came to dramatizing war slowly, perhaps because they simply came to theater many centuries after their male colleagues. Maybe they also took a while to realize that they had a right to tell war stories, that their experience of war was valid. Upending the assumption that only men fight wars, the pioneering seventeenth-century English playwright Aphra Behn wrote *The Widow Ranter* (1689), part comedy and part serious drama, in which the widow disguises herself as a man and ends up fighting a battle. In *The Rover* (1677), Behn writes about war indirectly, when the hero and his friends return from months abroad as mercenary soldiers; their sexual adventures on land, some of them fairly predatory, are, Behn suggests, the result of long periods of fighting when they were without female companionship. Similarly in Susannah Centlivre's *The Wonder; A Woman Keeps a Secret* (1714), Colonel Briton, on his way home after three years' warring in Spain, falls in love only to have his head turned by every woman he sees, so desperate is he to get a woman into bed.

But theater has never been the primary outlet for women's war writing. The women who lived through the American Civil War largely expressed their feelings and observations in diaries and journals, or through letters. World War I stimulated a surge of novels, pamphlets, and poetry, because women, while not in the trenches, saw the results of the action firsthand as nurses and ambulance drivers, and at home they stepped into jobs that men had left behind. World

War II brought sharp journalism and riveting personal accounts of the Holocaust. Plays were not women's literary form of choice for this subject. Sister M. Aloise Begley, in her 1948 master's thesis for Catholic University of America, "An Analysis of the Attitudes Toward War as Represented by Dramatic Works of the New York Stage from the World War to the Present Time," found that of the 147 "war plays" she studied, only 5 were by women.

With the rising tension about nuclear war during the 1950s and the intensifying of the Vietnam conflagration in the 1960s, women increasingly used theater as an outlet for their views. In England, the radical director Joan Littlewood and her Theatre Workshop created a satirical musical called *Oh What a Lovely War* (1963), ostensibly about World War I; and in the United States, Megan Terry, working with Joseph Chaikin's experimental Open Theatre, invented a fiercely antiwar musical, *Viet Rock* (1966). During the 1970s and 1980s, American playwrights like Emily Mann, Lavonne Mueller, and Shirley Lauro turned their gaze on Vietnam and its aftermath, while another American, Naomi Wallace, writing in the 1990s, saw a connection between Vietnam and the Gulf War. British playwrights such as Shirley Gee and Anne Devlin focused on the destructive battles between the English and the Northern Irish.

Why did women finally turn to theater to vocalize their experience of war? A confluence of events contributed to the shift. In the United States, the energy and ideas of the Women's Movement helped to birth a new generation of theater artists, who in turn received support from a burgeoning not-for-profit theater community. Spurred by the movement, women chose the flexibility that a playwriting career demanded. Largely liberal politically, these playwrights protested the war in Vietnam and questioned the assumptions that they believed had mired their country in a futile enterprise. They were liberated sexually as well as politically and, as a result of both the Women's Movement and the Antiwar Movement, saw a connection between domestic violence and violence on the battlefield. Finally, these women were writing about a confrontational period in American history, and theater is nothing if not a forum for the exposure of strong opinions, challenging ideas, and intense feelings.

The Women's Movement also affected English and Northern Irish playwrights. Women traditionally had been marginal players in the struggle between Catholics and Protestants, mostly suffering on the perimeters as their husbands, fathers, and sons died. Now, infused with a stronger sense of their abilities and private desires and more clear-eyed about the toll that the fighting was exacting on both sides, women took their reactions to the public by way of the theater.

This essay discusses how certain plays by women deconstruct the concept of wartime heroism, draw a connection between violence in battle and violence in the home, and further investigate the age-old connection between war and sex.

The canonized narrative of war extols heroism and the personal glory that war brings, accepts war's brutality, and sees the enemy's death and defeat as the apotheosis of victory. The plays under discussion here rewrite that narrative. They portray war as brutal, yes, but pointless and certainly without glory. Emily Mann's *Still Life** (1980), which Mann began to write in 1978 and is closest to the Vietnam War in time, is an example of what the playwright calls "Theater of Testimony." Distilled from interviews with a Vietnam veteran, his mistress, and the wife whom he has physically abused, *Still Life* offers a portrait of war in which soldiers, filled with hate and often seeking personal revenge, run amok. Mark, the Vietnam vet, recounts that he "killed three children, a mother and father in cold blood," a murder about which he feels no pride, only self-hatred.

In these plays, the goal of the individual in war is shown to be simply personal survival, especially in the face of a government's ludicrous demands. In Lavonne Mueller's *Five in the Killing Zone** (1985), five soldiers and medics work in an abandoned pagoda amid the constant threat of attack from both the enemy's forces and their own. Their assignment: to examine the tissue of dead soldiers in an attempt to discover a body they cannot identify, for that unidentified body, insists the government, will be taken back to the United States and buried in the grave of the Unknown Soldier. An African American named Yarde, adept at slithering through grass and avoiding snipers, frequently ventures forth and retrieves bodies or body parts for the microscope. When Yarde himself is killed, his fellow soldiers unanimously recognize both his anonymity and his heroism and declare him the Unknown Soldier. An empathic view of soldiers, Mueller's play is nonetheless an ironic and critical glimpse of war. What the men realize, but the distant U.S. government does not, is that on the battlefield every human being is equally small, equally unknown to the powers that send him there, and heroic simply by virtue of doing his job.

Heroism abounds in these dramas but not the sort that wins medals or makes headlines. In Shirley Lauro's *A Piece of My Heart** (1988), which is based on Keith Walker's volume of interviews with twenty-six American women who served in Vietnam, several nurses relate their experiences caring for the wounded, maimed, and dying. Through these nurses, we see that the frightened and suffering men they tend are heroic for withstanding indescribable pain and mutilation. The nurses themselves, as Lauro portrays them, are heroes every time they walk into a field hospital, itself possibly under attack, to care for the horrifically wounded.

Among these plays, probably the strongest challenge to conventional ideals of heroism occurs in Naomi Wallace's *In the Heart of America** (1994). Written in response to the Gulf War of 1991, *In the Heart* has a complex structure that melds the Gulf War with the Vietnam War and present reality with events in more than one past. In the present, a Gulf War veteran named Craver has returned to the United States, where he is visited by a Palestinian American woman named Fairouz, whose brother, Remzi, served with Craver in the desert. Scenes between Craver and Fairouz alternate with scenes between Craver and Remzi, who fall in love during the war, and with scenes from Fairouz and Remzi's difficult childhood. Weaving through the play is the image of a dead Vietnamese girl named Lue Ming, a spirit searching for an American soldier named Calley, who murdered her family.

In Wallace's drama, the so-called heroes of war are not human beings but weapons that fire incredibly destructive bullets incredibly efficiently: "Fishbeds, Floggers and Fulcrums, Stingers, Frogs, Silkworms, Vulcans, Beehives, and Bouncing Bettys." The heroes are bombs: "the GN-130" and the "GBU-10 Paveway II." And the heroes are airplanes: the "GR. M K-1 Jaguar with two Rolls-Royce Adour MK-102 turbofans." For Craver and Remzi, the names soothe like lullabies, and the men are in awe of the weapons' power and metallic grace. Killer weapons have replaced killer men. Once upon a time during the Vietnam War, Calley murdered the enemy, and before him came other men in other wars. War is endless, Wallace implies. Only the tools change.

As in Mueller's play, your average grunt is more victim than hero. Remzi and Craver have to pick up the pieces, literally, collecting and burying body parts after the elegant airplanes have dropped the smart bombs. Amid the horror, they fall in love, but their affair is discovered, and they are victimized by an army that does not tolerate homosexuality. Remzi is killed by men on his own side.

If these playwrights resist the traditional war narrative that confers glory on fighting men, they also resist the traditional separation between battlefront and home front. For Emily Mann writing *Still Life*, the battlefield stretches from Vietnam to the house where Mark, the vet, regularly beats up his wife. In Wallace's *In the Heart of America,* the battleground extends from the streets of America, where white kids once attacked the child Fairouz, to Vietnam and the Persian Gulf, where white Americans bomb Asians and Arabs. For these playwrights, it is all one war.

Mann establishes her continuum of violence at the outset, through her play's fractured structure. Sitting at a table, as though participating in a presentation, Mark and his wife, Cheryl, and his lover, Nadine, tell their stories, while Mark occasionally shows slides of his Vietnam experience on the wall behind them. Mann interlaces their comments and memories, so that Cheryl's remarks about her husband's abuse often come hard upon Mark's thoughts about combat. Mark himself makes the connection in the first act:

> I don't know what it would be for women.
> What war is for men.
> I've thought about it. A lot.
> I saw women brutalized in the war.
> I look at what I've done to my wife.

Throughout the play, Mann highlights the continuum. Mark describes how he and his fellow vet R. J., once they were back in the United States, got involved with heroin smuggling and at one point planned a nighttime attack on a car where the drugs were stashed. "We were doing the war all over again," says Mark. Nadine compares battle to her experience of childbirth, during which she almost died, and talks about daily life as "a jungle," about how she used to hit her husband and even might have killed him had they not divorced. And of course Cheryl, sitting bruised and broken, is prime evidence of a raging war. As Mark realizes:

> See, I see the war now through my wife.
> She's a casualty too.
> She doesn't get benefits for combat duties.
> The war busted me up, I busted up my wife . . .

Perhaps not surprisingly, of the three, Cheryl is the one who would most like to embrace the traditional dichotomy of military battleground and peaceful home. She wishes that Mark had left his war in Vietnam; she wants him to provide for her and their son. Unlike Mark and Nadine, she has difficulty recognizing the anger and violence in herself. Still, she knows that she is afraid of her husband. "And if I ever caught Mark hurting me/or that little boy again, I'd kill him," she says.

Mann draws a line that connects battle violence to domestic violence, but one has the sense from the play that war still begins at the front. In Naomi Wallace's *In the Heart of America,* there is the sense that war begins at home and is just a bigger, technologically more sophisticated brand of homegrown racial violence.

Like *Still Life, In the Heart of America* juxtaposes incidents and memories, drawing parallels between events in the past and actions in the present. Three plot strands interweave: Fairouz, as a child, attacked by white kids who smash one of her feet with a hammer and cripple her; Lue Ming searching for Calley; and the growing love between Remzi and Craver, which ends with Remzi beaten to death.

Wallace wraps these stories within a caul of racial prejudice. In this play, American aggression is always aimed at those of a different race or those who are, because of their sexual orientation, "other." Fairouz relates how children chanted, "Dirty Arab devil, you go home!" and assaulted her as she walked home from school. Remzi tells Craver, "On the streets of Atlanta I've been called every name you can think of: pimp, terrorist, half-nigger, mongrel . . ." And when Remzi and Craver are caught, officers beat them and taunt Remzi, calling him "sandnigger. Indian. Gook." Prejudice comes in all manner of ways, the play suggests — at the personal level and from miles above the earth. Killing Vietnamese and bombing Iraqis, Wallace implies, is just a continuation of a war already under way, just prejudice writ large. Fairouz and Remzi on the streets of Atlanta, Remzi and Craver in love — they are already combatants, fighting a war at the heart of America.

Both Mann and Wallace, in joining the military battlefield to a battlefield they perceive at home, aim to destroy a myth in which the United States used to take comfort — that war was always remote, "over there," far from its shores.

No such myth deludes Shirley Gee and Anne Devlin, who, in dramatizing the conflict between the English and the Northern Irish, show that war is on their doorsteps. Gee's *Never in My Lifetime** (1984) is the more conventional play. Like Romeo and Juliet, Tom and Tessie fall in love, only instead of coming from warring families, they come from warring political factions. Tom is an English soldier sent to Belfast to keep rebels in line; Tessie grew up in Belfast.

But despite the doomed romance at the play's center, *Never in My Lifetime* is hardly sentimental. The English soldiers cling stubbornly to a transparently thin concept of duty for queen and country, while the English and Irish women wrestle with a strained, centuries-old political tradition, which requires them to sacrifice their personal needs for a political end that never arrives. Few of the women have illusions about which is really more valuable, a man in bed or a hero shot to bits. In the end, Gee's play offers no hope for either side's success or indeed any resolution. Tom is dead, and Tessie has suffered a nervous breakdown. Tessie's best friend, Maire, a staunch supporter of Northern Ireland's cause, winds up in jail, raped and mutilated. Tessie's mother, whose own father preserves a bitter hatred of the English, gets the last line: "Someone will have to help us soon."

Gee gives equal stage time to the English and the Northern Irish, to the male and female characters. Anne Devlin's *Ourselves Alone** (1986), which takes place shortly after Bobby Sands and other Northern Irish activists went on hunger strikes and died in jail in 1981, focuses on three Belfast women. Frieda, who is in her early twenties, wants to sing and compose songs but to her frustration is only performing in a club used by the provisional Irish Republican Army (IRA). Josie, her older sister, works for the Republican cause and for a long time has had an affair with a married IRA leader; during the play, she falls in love with an Englishman who has supposedly come over to the Republican side. Donna is the common-law wife of the other women's brother, Liam, a jealous, abusive man who has spent the last several years in jail for political activity.

As in Gee's play, the war in *Ourselves Alone* hovers over Belfast's streets, invades living rooms and bedrooms. The front exists, not a country or a continent away, but in these people's homes. What's more, in *Ourselves Alone,* the Northern Irish not only fight the English, they also fight each other, for there is antagonism among various factions. One way or another, for as long as Devlin's three women can remember, these conflicts have been a presence in their lives: obsessing their men, upsetting their marriages and love affairs, interfering with work, and disrupting families.

Devlin, like Gee and like Emily Mann in *Still Life,* dramatizes a connection between politically motivated war and domestic battles. *Ourselves Alone* examines the traditionally accepted separation between men and women in wartime and demonstrates both its shortcomings and its falsity. Increasingly, these women are frustrated by their inferior status in this man's army. Frieda, the least political of the lot, announces to her accompanist, "I'm fed up with songs where the women are doormats!" Josie, the activist of the group, confides to Donna that when she makes love with her IRA leader, "I pretend I'm someone else. . . . Sometimes I'm not even a woman. Sometimes I'm a man—his warrior lover, fighting side by side to the death."

But although the women are by no means happy about being taken for granted or forced, like Josie, to accept a subsidiary role in the IRA, they have little room to maneuver. Early in the play, Frieda points to photographs of the dead hunger strikers and angrily tells her father, "We are the dying. Why are we mourning them!" Hard up financially, tied to children, emotionally and sexually tied to men who are either fighting, hiding out, or in jail, these women live narrow, unfulfilling existences. Donna won't even allow herself to be seen talking with another man, for fear that Liam will explode. She later discovers that jealous Liam is having an affair with another woman, at which point she finally breaks off with him, only to take up with another man.

Indeed, a woman's role in this war is largely confined to the sexual realm. When Josie complains about not seeing her IRA lover because he has gone home to his wife, Donna remonstrates, "We're all waiting on men, Josie." Later, after Josie takes up with the Englishman, she believes for a time that they are partners on behalf of the cause. But by the play's end, pregnant with his baby, she realizes that her new lover has both betrayed the IRA and used her. Frieda, broke and rejected by her rigidly patriotic father, moves in with a man who belongs to the anti-IRA Workers' Party, until one day he beats her in a rage and she decides to leave Ireland.

All of these women experience Ireland as a trap woven by war and by men who do nothing but fight. In Shirley Gee's play, love blooms, however briefly, in defiance of political troubles. But in *Ourselves Alone,* men commit to war only, and women are left wanting. Seen through Devlin's realistic gaze, women exist in war primarily to serve men's libidos, a function that ultimately provides the men with only temporary comfort and diminishes the women in both the men's eyes and their own.

That Devlin examines women in war through their sexual relationships with men is no accident. In Western culture, war and sex have entwined at least since the Greeks went to battle over Helen, and the contemporary world has seen the combination horrifically made fact at the rape camps in Bosnia. If war is a rite of passage into manhood, then capturing and raping the enemy's women is apparently one of the actions that stamps a warrior as a true man. More to the point, in defeating the enemy, the rape of the enemy's women seems to have special significance, for it permanently sullies the enemy's most valuable property. At the same time, the conqueror is preserving the sanctity of his own women, safely at home by the fire.

Western myths and literature have continually eroticized war. In their book *Arms and the Woman: War, Gender and Literary Representation* (1989), Helen Cooper, Adrienne Munich, and Susan Squier write:

> The most explicit trope connecting love and war in classical literature occurs when the gods ensnare Mars and Venus in each other's arms. That the two polarized deities make such easy bedfellows illustrates how women's complicity in the aggressivity and violence of war has been allegorized. Love, according to one possible interpretation, is the feminine counterpart to, not the opposite of, war.

In other words, women supposedly find war and warriors sexually titillating.

Aristophanes turned the pairing of love and war comically upside down in *Lysistrata* (411 B.C.), when he tried to show how sex could eradicate war, if women would deny men the pleasure of their bodies. But the example of Shakespeare's *Othello* (1604) is a more frequent approach in Western literature. There, one recalls, Desdemona falls in love with Othello while listening to his stories of "battles, sieges, fortunes" and, in her love and sexual attraction for the Moor, begs the Duke of Venice to let her accompany her husband to war. Othello eventually murders his wife, believing her unfaithful. That his sexual jealousy is somehow connected to his warrior's aggression, Shakespeare may have sensed, but it would take later generations of psychologists and feminist critics to examine.

Among the plays under discussion here, Devlin's *Ourselves Alone* and Mann's *Still Life* determinedly deeroticize war. The sexual relationships in Devlin's play are one-sided: the women are at their men's beck and call, and the men are often physically abusive. In *Still Life,* Mann paints a connection between a soldier's aggression and sexual aggression, without any of the pleasure that sex also brings. In Act 3, when Mark remembers coming home from Vietnam, he recalls, "I wanted to fuck my brains out." He has ended up beating his wife. Earlier in the play, trying to describe his experience in Vietnam, Mark says, "It was power. . . . It's like the best dope you've ever had, the best sex you've ever had." The power to kill has been a turn-on for Mark, and he has brought that desire home, where it translates into waging war on his wife.

Wallace's *In the Heart of America* both deeroticizes war and uses eroticism in an intriguing way. Images of rape occur throughout the script. The description of how children set upon Fairouz when she was a kid, forcing her to take off her shoe and sock and then smashing her foot with a hammer, is essentially a kind of rape. At one point Lue Ming describes how an American soldier took out his knife, cut off her long black braid, and strapped it to the back of his helmet. Lieutenant Boxler, a character who is both a soldier in Iraq and a kind of universal soldier bringing death in wars past and present, describes to Remzi and Craver how he killed an Iraqi, slit his body "all the way down" and "stood inside his body."

But what of Craver's and Remzi's sensuous response to the descriptions of military weapons and the weapons themselves? In a sense, they eventually transfer that eroticism to each other, where, Wallace implies, it belongs. Their relationship is the only nonviolent and lovingly erotic one in the play. After Remzi is beaten to death, Craver describes his body: "Five foot . . . eleven inches. That's how tall you were. I used to run my hand up and down your body like I was reading the bones." And Remzi, appearing as Craver's vision, responds: "I wanted to travel everyplace on your body. Even the places you'd never been." But from where Wallace sits, it is rape, not love, that war nurtures. Craver and Remzi's love cannot survive.

Though these plays are a small portion of women's war writing in the twentieth century, they bring women's experience of war into the theater and broaden ways of viewing war. They temper the notion most often found in literary and other arts that men and women have opposing experiences of battle and that men are always in the heat of it, while women wait docilely at home. Instead, they take the view that war extends from the battlefield to the living room and back again, that violence at the front links itself to violence in the home, a connection that spoils and corrupts the idea of war as a glorious and manly enterprise. Throughout these plays, war is shown as pointless and unrewarding, the destroyer of love and of loving sexual relationships. Women, as well as men, suffer its casualties.

Our Bodies, Ourselves

SHARMAN MACDONALD

SUSAN MILLER

PEARL CLEAGE

૱

Memoir of a Sexual Woman
SHARMAN MACDONALD

Christmas 1969. Louise and me, students on vacation, were pounding the pavements working for the Post Office, delivering Christmas cards. And Ian. Ian was doing it as well. At the end of the first week we stood in line to collect our wages, the three of us. We opened the pay packets. Ian got a pound more than us. We'd worked the same hours, carried the same load. "Why the fuck are you getting paid more than me?" I said. "I'm a man," he said. Like I hadn't noticed. Ian was gorgeous. Still. "You get paid more because you're a man?" I said. That didn't make any sense at all. I was eighteen years old, and it was the first time I had ever come across even a whiff of prejudice. Not that I knew enough to call it prejudice. Embarrassing, that's what it was. Shocking, that's what it was. "For fuck sake," I said, "that's not fair." The following week, me and Louise, we got two pounds more than Ian. Overtime. The postmen liked having a couple of girls in miniskirts around. We didn't have to do any work, just chat and drink hot sweet tea. Caught between a rock and a hard place with a point to prove, we sold our charms, Louise and me.

To get the money to go to Drama School, I go-go-danced on a high shelf, back-lit, in a not very salubrious bar in the Grassmarket in Edinburgh. The costume was thigh-high, platform-soled, red-leather boots and a denim bikini, politely whorish; look, don't touch, but pay me all the same. Selling what I could to get what I wanted.

I've never won the Susan Smith Blackburn Prize. I was runner-up, I think, in 1985 with a play called *When I Was a Girl I Used to Scream and Shout**—"think," because my great friend Christina Reid says she was runner-up with *Tea in a*

At the Bush Theatre in London, Tracy Keating and Sophie Stanton in Jane Coles's Backstroke in a Crowded Pool, *winner of the sixteenth Susan Smith Blackburn Prize in 1994. (Courtesy the Bush Theatre)*

China Cup*. Anyway there we both were at the Garrick Club for the award ceremony—the one and only time I've been inside—it's a Gentleman's Club. Nice irony to have a woman's award presented in a men-only joint. Christina was svelte in a jacket with a brooch on the collar, and I wore dungarees—black dungarees—large, black, parachute-silk dungarees—enormous actually. I was eight months pregnant with my daughter, Keira.

In 1984 my beautiful son, Cal, was five years old, and I gave up acting. Didn't have any idea what I wanted to do instead. Two things I did know: I never wanted to act again and I wanted another child. It's a strange life, the life of a performer. There are great joys in it—huge privilege—but often and often and often—no money. My husband, Will, was an actor then, is an actor now. We absolutely couldn't afford, in any way at all, to have a second child. So. I started to write. Fearfully, anxiously, angrily, joyfully I found a voice. My wonderful husband read what I was writing—challenged it, questioned it, cajoled it and me into rewrite after rewrite. Then he made me a proposition. A bet. If I sold a script, we could have a second child.

I love beaches. Lived across the road from the sea when I was growing up. Important things happen on beaches. So. That was the setting—the edge of all things. It allowed me to put beauty on the stage: sparkling water; glistening rocks; sunshine. My Scottish heritage lent the dialogue rhythm and a languid sharpness—if there is such a thing. I don't claim to be witty, but I was surrounded by wit as I grew up, a mordant wit. I borrowed it. Mischief drove the piece. I wanted to make myself laugh in the hope that if I laughed, others would too. And I was angry. Late seventies feminism had put womankind on a pedestal. I wanted to take the pedestal away. I've never had a head for heights. I wanted woman to be accepted as an equal for what she was: flawed, bright, and beautiful. So. I wrote about sex—the sexual awakening of two girls who grew up by the seaside in Scotland in the sixties.

The Scotland of my childhood was Presbyterian. We had a red-haired, purple-faced minister who preached damnation every Sunday morning, leaning far out of the pulpit to point a warning finger at the congregation. That man was angry. His abiding gift to me was not belief but fear. I don't believe in God, not since praying hard on my knees every night during the Cuban Missile Crisis that there wouldn't be a war; but I do believe the Devil will get me. Hell lives in my nightmares. That's where I'm headed. I can list all the small sins that will take me there. The Devil and the Recording Angel figure in the girls' iconography in *When I Was a Girl . . .* The notion of sin is ever present. There are no heroines.

The play sold for two thousand pounds (approximately three thousand five hundred dollars) to the Bush Theatre. We drank champagne, Will and me, and conceived a child. One thousand pounds bought a car, the other thousand was meant to keep us safe for the rest of our lives.

Back to the award ceremony at the Garrick Club. Shirley Gee won the prize that year. Novelist Beryl Bainbridge made a speech saying that the poet was the highest form of literary being, the novelist came next; the playwright lingered in the murk somewhere far below them. That's not an exact quote, but you get the gist. It rankled. She writes great novels, but hey! Perhaps she meant that plays are lesser works because they're not complete in themselves. They require actors to bring them to life. I love actors. They've been my inspiration all along; to give them the best words I possibly can. Theater requires a glorious team of people working together to make it great; it needs an audience to bring it alive. It is not an activity indulged in alone. That doesn't mean the playwright is a lesser artist—just different.

When I Was a Girl . . . won an Evening Standard Award. The play decided it would look after us. From the Bush Theatre it went up to the Lyceum for the Edinburgh International Festival. Then it transferred to the West End where it ran for a year. It's been performed all over the world, bought our home for us, fed us for years. People wanted *When I Was a Girl* . . . I must have had my finger on a pulse—if I could find that pulse again, I would. It's a great privilege when people want what you have to give. There's been a slow but steady flow of other work from my hand since: some of it has woven a spell; some of it most definitely has not. None of it, so far, has been quite so apposite as *When I Was a Girl* . . . Of course, I've never written for higher stakes.

Keira was born on March 26, 1985. She's nineteen, a sweetheart, and a stunning actor. It's odd writing this piece now. She bought her first flat just this week. She's leaving home. My beloved Cal's already gone. So. That's that bit over. Keira's going marks the end of the *When I Was a Girl* . . . phase of my life. I'm not supporting a family anymore. I don't have to earn as much money and I find I'm not as willing to sell secrets, my own or other people's. I certainly won't be putting my own body center stage ever again, either in a post office or a bar. Age has diminished its charms after all. If only there was a compensatory increase in its store of wisdom. That would be gratifying. The tiny bit of public attention—from press, not audience—*When I Was a Girl* . . . brought me made me feel as if I'd tripped over a paving stone. Anonymity is part of a writer's arsenal—of any artist's arsenal. She has to be an observer. There's a loss of function when the artist becomes the observed.

Today I fancy running a stall in Camden Market—lots of people, hot cups of steaming coffee, mulled wine in winter—selling quilts maybe; I've always liked quilts. Life keeps calling me out of the blue room where I write—husband, children, friends only have to ask. Driving; long smoke-filled lunches; premieres; sunshine; breakfasts in strange corners of the world—pleasure—I can't resist it. It's dialogue that calls me back to the page—its rhythms and flows; the joy of being part of a talented group of people and creating something new; communicating with an audience. And the risk of writing. I like the risk. There is, of course, the occasional overwhelming practical need that forces me to be still and work: outside the blue room door the stair carpet is threadbare; in the kitchen the fridge is empty. Cal and Keira don't need me to provide for them anymore, but I get hungry; and I do love good food and driving and long smoke-filled lunches, breakfast tours of the world, dancing alone in posh hotel rooms, and stair carpets that don't have holes. And I still believe that theater can help change the world, bring peace. And that maybe on a good day, if the wind blows in the right direction, I will write a play that will contribute.

An Excerpt from the Play Sweeping the Nation

SUSAN MILLER

It seems right and fitting that people historically not seen, or seen as outside the main and so not acceptably part of the social fabric—people flawed, beautiful, mundane, accomplished, as exquisitely myriad in human design as everyone and so finally the same—find their way into my next play. And it seems fitting that this play be launched with a celebration of the Susan Smith Blackburn Prize, which recognizes, embraces, and honors the gifts and difficulties that women writers have known over time. And which has supported the life of my plays for over twenty years.

This play takes place as a group of people are creating a television show about lesbians. It is about the creative process and the writers' identities, about the actors' challenges to play their parts within this framework, and about the lesbians they write and portray. It is, I hope, funny and iconoclastic. The representation of gay women here serves to illuminate something beyond itself—the struggle in the writers' room to make an entertainment, to do justice to their subject, to incorporate the larger conversation, to collaborate in bringing their views of things (which are often in conflict) to the public and letting an audience discover what was for so long hidden and unexplored. I'm interested here, as always, in the contradiction in relationship and identity. ("I am a One Breasted, Menopausal, Jewish Bisexual Lesbian Mom": *My Left Breast.*) And I'm interested as well in how these identities allow for characters to step out of their context, to comment, to transform their functions within the play and act, now and then, as guides or narrators. It's been an important challenge to me that the play's structure allow for the irony of taking its own inventions to task. With this in mind, there's a character, who sometimes inhabits the play, named the Playwright. She speaks in this excerpt. And so, my offering.

PLAYWRIGHT/NARRATOR
Flannel shirts.
    (beat)
I mean. Is that all they can think
of? To define ten percent of the
population of the earth. Flannel
shirts? Which to my mind are the
sole property of undergraduates in the
60s and people who live in
Maine who can't all be lesbians. Can they?
Flannel shirts and short hair. Not
any kind of short hair. Bad short hair.

Bad bad short short hair. And the eschewal of
hair products. Which really, oh my
god, if you only knew, is the final
insult. So, I've taken this
opportunity to go undercover and
expose the bathroom shelves of all
the known lesbians in my circle and
adjoining neighborhoods, randomly
detailing their beauty products.

    (A PHOTO OF PRODUCTS is projected)
I count 21 gels, 16 pomades, 12
molding muds, a plethora of shine,
texture gel, manipulating wax,
radical sheen, marine lusterlizer,
paste, configure cream, and gel
fixe. Not to mention spray.

    (beat)
Okay, I have a little test. I'm
going to show you some pictures.
And you decide.

    (Photo of WOMEN'S FACES)
Lesbian or German Tourist?

    (beat)
Lesbian or Straight Soccer Mom from
Iowa?

    (End slides)
Oh. And that we have no sense of humor.
We are not funny! We are humorless
and glum and don't wear makeup and
have tattoos which we hide under our
flannel shirts except when we are
riding on motorcycles flaunting our
breasts in parades. We lack humor
and we're big. Well, like the rest of America, of
course, the unfunny and fat dwell
among us. Like the rest of America,
we're big and small and fat and
thin, and like the rest of America
we obsess about how big and small
and fat and thin we are. I also

think there is something about
shoes, but I'm not sure what it is.
But, just in case, I'm going to
dispel that myth, too. In a little
test I like to call, "Whose feet
are these? Heterosexual or
homosexual?"

     (beat)

I think it all has to do with the
word, Lesbian. I'm sorry. This is a
wrong word. Let's face it, this is
a heavy, glum, scary scary word. It
is the opposite of gay. It reeks of
thick brown orthopedic shoes and
people who never dance. Well, they
can't dance, let's face it, with
those shoes. Lesbian, come on,
equals prison warden. But, gay
women! Women who love other women.
On the mouth. In bed. Wet. Women in
thongs and push up bras. Women in
little tee shirts and sneakers.
Women pulling each other down by
the hair, down to where she wants
it. A woman running her hands along
the inside of another woman's
thighs. Mad, dazed.
Women on the dance floor. Abandoned. Unzipped.
Flirting across the room.
Two women wanting the same thing.
Saying, Oh! Saying, You! Saying,
This. This is so — Two women.
Alive. Beautiful. Full of the taste
of the other. Her
hands. Her breasts. Her ass. Lithe.
Fresh. Supple. Arched.

     (beat)

Gay.

Standing at the Crossroads
PEARL CLEAGE

(with apologies to bluesman Robert Johnson who was here when I arrived and who did not appreciate the interruption, although he probably understood it . . .)

I used to see my task as an African American writer much more clearly. I believed my role was to be part of the vanguard. Part of the word warriors and other cultural workers who would create a new language for a people headed toward freedom, self-determination, and wholeness. I saw my work as deeply rooted in, and reflective of, a community-wide struggle for liberation. I understood the problem. I was involved in the solution, and my work flowed directly out of that Movement energy and optimism.

But things are not the way they used to be. It is wartime in America. Collective optimism has been replaced by unemployment, poverty, rampant substance abuse, the unrelenting scourge of HIV/AIDS, cynicism, and fear. While my own work continues to be an extension of my politics, as well as of my spirit, its direction, like the direction of my community and my country, is currently at a crossroads. Knowing, as I do, the power of that crossroads is second only to the power of the full moon, especially in countless blues songs where a wrong turn is always a turn for the worse, I am trying to pay attention.

My work as a writer has been shaped by the three great movements that energized, illuminated, and defined my generation of Americans: the Civil Rights Movement, and I use the term broadly to include both the nonviolent wing of the African American freedom struggle and the equally diverse group of African Americans who did not subscribe to nonviolence as a philosophy or a tactic and reserved the right to self-defense; the Antiwar Movement, in all its many, often contradictory incarnations, all of which played a vital role in ending the war in Vietnam; and the Women's Movement, imperfect as it was, and is, fighting against the oppression of women, and establishing once and for all that the personal is irrevocably political.

The intersection of these three vibrant social movements during the time when I was learning how to be a playwright created a perfect storm of social consciousness and artistic activity, practically guaranteeing that my work was, from the very beginning, connected to the national and international movement of people toward peace, freedom, and justice. See what I mean? Once a sixties person, always a sixties person, and as the Detroit hipsters used to say when I was growing up in Motown's shadow, "I ain't afraid to cop to it," but that crossroads is still sitting out there in the moonlight, waiting for me to make a move, but first I need to take another look around.

When I teach writing at Spelman College, a historically black institution for women in Atlanta, I give my students an exercise. What if you arrived on the planet earth, I ask them, a sepia-toned, Amazonian space traveler from a distant, all-female galaxy, searching for beings you heard inhabited this place, who looked strikingly like you and your multicolored sisters? Setting your invisible starship soundlessly at the curb, you climb out in almost any urban American black community to see what you can see. It could be Detroit, could be New York, could be L.A., but probably not, since even on your planet, L.A. is regarded as terrain to be explored only by experienced time travelers with nerves of steel and specific questions to study that can be answered best in a post-Apocalyptic dreamscape, frantically playing out its last days under a smog-laden sky that frightens outsiders, until the smiling cab driver confides that the smog is the reason they have such beautiful sunsets. But you could also have landed in Montgomery, New Orleans, even Birmingham or Washington, D.C. You could definitely have pulled over in Atlanta. You are, after all, in search of African American women, and where else would you find us if you don't start in places that call themselves *black meccas,* in spite of all the evidence to the contrary?

So you've come in search of African American women, living their lives at the start of the twenty-first century. And where are we? Everywhere and no place. Thrashing at the center and skulking on the periphery. In my Atlanta neighborhood, you find us on the front page of the daily paper, abused, abandoned, tortured, tormented, raped and slashed and stashed in abandoned cars or vacant lots or empty houses until the neighbors call the police about *that awful smell,* and the newscasters say *she had no identification,* and nobody knows who she is and nobody comes to claim her.

In my neighborhood, you can find us working in strip clubs or running from our ex-lovers, estranged husbands, and possessive boyfriends. You can find us being held hostage by our *baby daddies,* a culturally specific term that evolved to address questions of paternity and commitment in a place where both are frequently challenged or forgotten. You can find us cowering in the corner while the *baby daddy* gone mad with powerlessness, or jealousy, or the rage that has no name, negotiates with the police while he decides whether to kill us or let us go, and the weeping relatives keeping vigil outside wonder who will tell us that he has already slit the baby's throat.

This is not a play. This is a real story. A real young mother and her *baby daddy* gone mad in a way that Ntozake Shange predicted years ago in her classic choreopoem, *for colored girls who have considered suicide/when the rainbow is enuf,* but which isn't any easier to understand just because we were warned that it was coming. Because this is not a play. This is a real dead child, a real weeping woman, and as I look at the color picture in the paper on the morning after the forty-hour hostage standoff, how it could happen is still mysterious to me. Searching for clues, I look closely at the photograph of the murderous young Afro-American father, shirtless and insane, booted and bearded and low slung jeans and smooth, brown, muscled chest, and he looks enough like Tupac Shakur to be his brother.

This scene is not unique. In any urban American community, the images of life we see around us and that must inform the work of the conscious African American woman writer if we are who we say we are, *and who we must be,* are so bereft of hope and wholeness and the possibility, however embattled or imperfect, of some kind, any kind, of future, that the real challenge we face is to continue to be convinced that written language, with all of its beautiful, terrifying, liberating power, is any match for the madness of a twenty-two-year-old father who taped a screaming child's mouth to mute the death cries and then turned him over so, as the killer shouted, "the last thing the little nigger sees on this earth will be my face."

What dramatic moment that I might conjure will ever be able to communicate the horror, the despair, the rage, the sorrow, the absolute fear I feel that this is what we have now become? A community of helpless, damaged women, frightened children, and predatory men. A doomed community, despite *Ebony* magazine's desperate efforts to convince us that the black family is intact, the black economy is thriving, and *all that other stuff* is just the mischief of a few bad apples, and if we could just get them to stop making those nasty rap records and playing their car radios so loud, everything would go back to the way it used to be in that magic, mythical time before we were in the position of cartoonist Walt Kelly's famous Pogo Possum where "we have seen the enemy and he is us."

It is in these moments that I understand the frustration that drove Harlem Renaissance author Countee Cullen to shake his poetic finger in God's face and "marvel at this curious thing: To make a poet black, and bid him sing!" But it is wartime in America, and across the globe, and Cullen may not be a suitable wartime poet. He may not be the one who can make me think writing can still be my weapon of choice against the psychopaths who continue to think it is possible for either side to win at war. Cullen may be too cynical or too refined or simply too conflicted about whether it is worth the effort it takes to do the job we promised to do.

At this terrible moment, perhaps the better guide would be the gentle voice of the poet Mari Evans, who says simply that the black writer's task can be broken down to six small words: Tell the truth to the people. Just that. Always that. Tell the truth to the people. It is her words, not Cullen's, that will help me remember that part of the poet's job (and aren't all playwrights poets?) is always to tell the truth—in all its terribleness—in a way that illuminates our fragile, flawed humanity and manages to love us anyway.

And I do. That love is why I started writing plays in the first place. Because I knew that Che Guevara was right when he said all true revolutionaries begin with feelings of great love, and because I understand the sixties is only a dream decade if we say it is, and I say it ain't. The question now is: what do you say?

Engaging Social Issues, Expressing a Political Outlook

GWYNN MACDONALD

❧

Democracy and theater started in the same place, around the same time. As democracy emerged in fifth-century Athens, theater developed alongside. In its very origins, theater's role was both cultural and political. It was a civic duty for Athenian citizens to attend the theater, and periodically they were officially obligated to judge the plays presented. For them, theater was as much a social and political force in their lives as it was a source of entertainment. Theater gave Athenians an opportunity to gather and reflect as a community on issues of the day, and the dramas themselves helped the citizenry to process the trauma of war and shape their new identity as a powerful, democratic city-state.

Since power and responsibility in Athens were rigidly structured along gender lines, with women confined to the domestic sphere and men exercising power in the city, it is a point of contention for modern scholars whether women were allowed to attend the theater. It is known that women were not eligible for citizenship or any form of political participation, and similarly they had no part in making or presenting theater. This marginalization of women — and other disenfranchised people such as foreigners and slaves — meant that from the outset, theater, like politics, was a public sphere occupied and defined by men.

Thousands of years later, women in the theater, especially playwrights, still struggle against this legacy. The Susan Smith Blackburn Prize was founded in large part to widen the theatrical arena and make clear that both theater and society are impoverished without the input of talented women. Whether prized for their outstanding contributions to theater or not, women playwrights are still perceived mainly as women. The result has been that women playwrights are underproduced or often, when they are produced, thought to possess less value than their male counterparts. When men have written important work,

they have been held as the standard; when women have written plays of consequence, they have been declared—as Robert Brustein wrote in 1992 in the
New Republic—"a significant movement." There is no continuity of history
when one constitutes a movement. So it's not surprising that a little more than
ten years after Brustein's declaration, an article by Jason Zinoman would appear in the December 2003 issue of the *New York Times* and, focusing more on
the phenomenon than the plays, herald yet again "The Season of the Female
Playwright."

In every era, the status of women playwrights and their work has been inextricably linked to the status of women in society. That women dramatists have
written, in the playwright Ellen McLaughlin's words, "from a perspective as figures who live on the margins rather than in the center of political power," has
not only shaped their work but has also made their writing for the stage *inherently* political. It was an event with profound political consequences when
women, previously barred from acting on the English stage, first entered that
public space in 1660 with the restoration of Charles II to the throne. While in
exile, Charles had been exposed to women in the theater during his travels on
the continent, where women were already performing on and writing for the
stage. After reclaiming the English monarchy, he hoped that by opening the
English theater to women, particularly as actors, he would eradicate the practice of sodomy that was thought to be commonplace in the theater and a threat
to the social order.

The critic Laura Rosenthal has pointed out that Charles's maneuver remade
theater into a public space that not only permitted, but *required* women; it was
perhaps the only such public space in Restoration England, and one of the few
venues for female public expression. A number of the actors became England's
first professional female playwrights, and female playwrights were soon successful in writing plays both for the stage and for publication. Working from
the assumption that women were the equals of men, these playwrights infused
the popular culture of their day with a new sensibility, challenging and de-
lighting seventeenth- and eighteenth-century English audiences with complex
female characters and innovative dramatic actions. Their plays presented scores
of female characters who insisted on having it all: their rightful inheritance *and*
a love match. They took on the sociopolitical topics their male counterparts
were writing about: the debate over an authoritarian monarchy, life and fashion in a consumer culture, the politics of marriage and divorce. But they also
tackled new topics, such as life in the American colonies in Aphra Behn's *The
Widow Ranter* (1689) and prison reform in Elizabeth Inchbald's *Such Things
Are* (1787).

These playwrights participated in and stimulated the political discourse of their day. But perhaps in the end, their most political act was in successfully carving out a place for female playwrights in the English-language theater, ending a centuries'-old tradition of male hegemony.

Though the connection between theater and politics continued for women playwrights through the centuries, it was not always recognized, either because political plays by women did not seem to exist or because the content did not on the surface appear especially political. In the first instance, overtly political plays by women, like the majority of plays by women, were just not written into theater history. Not until the 1970s, when feminist literary critics began to uncover long-lost plays by women, were plays with political content rediscovered: plays such as Mercy Otis Warren's *The Group* (1775), which argued the cause of the Patriots during the American Revolutionary War; abolitionist works such as Mariana Starke's *The Sword of Peace* (1788) and Susanna Rowson's *Slaves in Algiers* (1794).

The second reason women were assumed not to have written plays with political content was that, traditionally, a political work was defined as one in which political ideas or a political milieu dominated. This definition, however, has been too narrow to read political content in social issues and domestic dramas—the subjects on which women playwrights most often focused. Re-examining the basis on which a work is considered political has been of special importance to feminist theorists. In *Redefining The Political Novel: American Women Writers, 1797–1901* (1995), Sharon M. Harris advocates, for example, that the family must be considered a legitimate topic for a writer to explore political themes, because "this is where women had most experience and where their knowledge of the need for change most often has been drawn." Harris argues that definitions of political literature need to expand to include literature that acknowledges the dynamic interrelation of the political and the social, as well as the impact of sociopolitical issues on the life of the individual. This expanded definition of political literature has at its core the notion that, not only is there a politicized self (the personal is political), but also that true social change comes from inner and individual change, which eventually spreads out into the community.

Over the course of nearly three decades, the more than three hundred playwrights who became finalists for the Susan Smith Blackburn Prize have engaged contemporary political and social issues in plays that have taken a unique angle on those issues and brought to the fore many others that might have gone unexamined.

The Irish playwright and fiction writer Edna O'Brien and the American author Susan Sontag, employing very different styles, look at society's view of women writers and the relationship between thwarted creativity and female depression, in *Virginia** (1981) and *Alice in Bed** (1993), respectively.

Caryl Churchill and Migdalia Cruz employ verse and heightened language in their scathing critiques of the greed of high finance (Churchill's *Serious Money**, 1987) and corruption in the church (Cruz's *Salt**, 1996). In *Golden Girls** (1985), Louise Page sheds light on the media-driven world of women's sports and the ways in which society perverts female ambition.

Class issues are drawn darkly in Wendy Kesselman's *My Sister in This House** (1988) and are perhaps at the root of two sisters' murder of the upper-class women for whom they work. Social hierarchies are likewise explored in *Mud, River, Stone** (1998), by Lynn Nottage, who examines the stratification of race as experienced by a middle-class African American couple who travel to Africa. And in *Fen** (1982), Caryl Churchill documents the impact of global capitalism, and the persistence of poverty and oppression, among the women who live and toil in an East Anglian fen village.

Looking at the plays that have engaged social issues with a political perspective, it is useful to place them on a spectrum, starting from plays that directly investigate politics as a social phenomenon to — narrowing the view — plays that examine the political dimensions of social issues affecting a community and finally to plays that deal up-close with the extremely personal as political, namely, the female body (and experience) in a male-dominated culture.

In the early years of the Blackburn Prize, from 1978–1979, when it was first awarded, to the mid-1980s, politics in the form of the Women's Movement had a direct impact on women in theater, with theaters dedicated to women's work tripling from the late 1970s to the early 1980s. These playwrights had lived through major social and political movements of the 1960s and 1970s: in the United States, the Civil Rights Movement, the Antiwar Movement spurred by the Vietnam War, the struggle for the Equal Rights Amendment, and *Roe v. Wade;* across the Atlantic, the disintegration of the Labor Party in England and the conflict in Northern Ireland. These movements gave women a sharpened political outlook, and many chose to explore how systems of power affected the lives of women.

In *Cloud Nine** (1978), Churchill tracks a family and its immediate circle at two critical moments in British history, to probe the nature of power relations between the sexes. The central social issue of the play — sexual politics — is framed by an overt political agenda: to explore how personal experience, or sexual interaction, recapitulates social and political experience. "The empire is one big family," a character states in Act 1, and "You can't separate economics and fucking," another declares in Act 2. Churchill writes from a feminist socialist perspective, uniquely formed by coming to adulthood during the feminist movement and maturing as an artist during the rise to power of the conservative Tory Party led by Margaret Thatcher, beginning in 1975.

In a farcical look at Victorian and contemporary sexual and social relations, *Cloud Nine* explodes gender and identity as a social construct by using techniques of cross-gender and cross-racial casting and the doubling of parts. Act 1 presents Clive, a British colonial administrator, his family, and colonial underlings in a Victorian outpost in Africa. Everyone is unhappy with their roles, sexual or social, except for the daughter, Victoria—represented as a doll—and the mother-in-law, Maud. By Act 2, the same family, with a third generation, is living in 1970s London. It is the 1970s, but the characters have aged only twenty-five years. Betty, Clive's wife, has left her husband, has taken a job and her own apartment, and is trying to adjust to the changes that have occurred since the previous century. These changes are manifest in a new and freer range of sexual choices and in less defined social roles for women.

While most of the action in Act 1 ostensibly revolves around the quest to fulfill sexual desires, in Act 2 the action is directed more toward achieving self-hood. Both acts end with a union: Act 1 in the comic resolution of marriage, Act 2 in the symbolic, but more credible, union of Betty with herself. Setting Act 1 in a nineteenth-century imperialist society allows the politics of oppression—here directed toward the natives—to be seen more clearly before being updated as suppression of women in Act 2's twentieth-century, free-market, capitalist society. In the early development of the play, Churchill has said that she and her actors "looked at England's relationship to Ireland and how it is like a male/female relationship." Colonialism, in Africa in Act 1 and in references to the Northern Ireland conflict in Act 2, becomes a metaphor for sexual oppression.

The play was written at a time when Britain was acutely experiencing the worldwide recession and the progressive Labor Party was impotent either to militate this or fend off the Conservative onslaught led by Thatcher, who would become prime minister in 1979, the year *Cloud Nine* reached the stage. This period saw high inflation and diminishing job opportunities for women, with the choice between having a family or having a job becoming extremely curtailed. When half a million women dropped out of the labor force between 1977 and 1980, women's social status lost ground. Deepening this crisis, the culture responded to high general unemployment with a resurgence of traditionalist views of women's domestic function, a trend meant to pressure women into staying at home, thus freeing up more jobs for men. In such an atmosphere, a woman has practically no identity should she refuse the domestic one society assigns.

While *Cloud Nine* is nonrealistic and somewhat ethereal, Nell Dunn's *Steam-*

Six women take to the baths in Theatre Royal Stratford East's production of Steaming *by Nell Dunn, winner of the fourth Susan Smith Blackburn Prize in 1982. (Photograph: Alastair Muir)*

ing* (1981) is a down-to-earth depiction of the women whose lives prompted Churchill's work. In a realistic manner, Dunn writes about women whose identities, life choices, and possibilities for self-development and happiness have been limited by patriarchal power. Like Churchill, Dunn attacks the political order of the day. But she targets her attack very specifically at local government, its corruption and failure to respond to the needs of its constituency, and she does so very directly through the political action in the plot.

The play presents six women of various ages and circumstances coming together in a supportive community during "Ladies' Day" at the steam room of an East End public bath. In this all-female environment, the women can escape their disappointment and anger, as well as gain insight into that anger and channel it toward self-actualization. When the bath is declared "unsafe" by the local council, which prefers to shut it down rather than fund a low-profile service to a marginal community, the women protest. The character Josie is the one who represents their argument to the council, and this act of political engagement transforms her. In the beginning of the play, Josie is sexually exploited and physically abused and feels powerless: "I know you're going to tell me I ought to get myself a job, and stand on my own feet, but what can I do? . . . I want someone to look after me!" By the middle of the play, Josie has a dawning awareness that there should be more to her life: "I want to be somebody, to have done something. At the moment all I'm going to get on my gravestone is: 'She was a good fuck!' " And finally at the end, Josie takes on the council and takes control of her life: "I kept thinking, this can't be me saying all this with all these people listening . . . this can't be Josie, she'd never dare . . . I knew nothing about the world—now I'm going to change all that . . . I'm going somehow or other to get meself . . . Myself an education." For all the women, for Josie in particular, political awakening—an awareness of the political system of power that has shaped their lives—propels personal revelations, which form the dramatic climax of the play.

In *Keeping Tom Nice** (1988) and *Before It Hits Home** (1998), plays from the middle years of the Susan Smith Blackburn Prize, a British playwright and an African American playwright each look at families that struggle as caretakers in the larger context of two very different social issues: care of the disabled and homosexuality and AIDS in the African American community. Writing about the conflicted feelings of parents toward offspring whose "difference" puts them outside the social norm, each author depicts a crisis in the home and reveals its political dimension.

The plays focus not so much on the nature of political power as on its effects. The personal is political when the suppression of people who are not a part of the dominant culture is expressed through interpersonal dysfunction and violence.

Cheryl L. West's *Before It Hits Home* is a two-act play about a bisexual African American musician, Wendal Bailey, who is dying from AIDS and goes back to his family, either to get stronger or to end his days surrounded by loving relatives. West takes the issue of AIDS home on two fronts. In Act 1, she lays the epidemic at the doorstep of a society that was profligate in its response to what was initially a containable health crisis: "All you had to do was tell us," says Wendal to his fourth doctor—"Didn't cost you nothing." And in Act 2, West shows the personal prejudice and denial that made transmission on an epidemic scale possible. "I've lived a lie and I'm gonna have to answer for that," Wendal tells his mother, in a scene where her denial and abdication of responsibility echo his own from the previous act.

That Wendal's mother, aunt, and brother cannot deal with Wendal's homosexuality and illness is a reflection of larger social attitudes linking homophobia in the African American community to racism. Patricia Hill Collins's *Black Sexual Politics: African Americans, Gender, and the New Racism* (2004) describes the African American community as being "noticeably silent about the spread of HIV/AIDS among African Americans largely because they wished to avoid addressing the sexual mechanisms of HIV transmission (prostitution and gay

NINE

Whose Voices Are These?

The Arts of Language in the Plays of
Suzan-Lori Parks, Paula Vogel, and Diana Son

AMY S. GREEN

❧

MAN: So where do all these words come from?

WOMAN: I don't know. When I really get going, it's like a trance
—it's not me writing at all. It's as if I just listen to voices and
I'm taking dictation. . . .

MAN: Doesn't that spook you? I mean, whose voices are these?
Who's in control? . . .

WOMAN: Well, they're the characters speaking, or the script itself. I mean, I know it's me, but I have to get into it. At first
it spooked me a little. But now I know when I hear them, it's
a good sign.

— PAULA VOGEL, *Hot 'n' Throbbing** (1994)

Millennial playwrights draw their dramatic voices from a host of linguistic
models. As postmodern artists, they are unconstrained by the demands of con-
sistency. They do not subscribe to particular "isms." They mix and match, bor-
row and parody the language of everyday discourse and the literary canon. They
play around with text, texts, and modes of speech. Theirs is the language of
the city street and the suburban shopping mall. It grooves to the rhythms of
jazz, doo-wop, hip-hop, and pop. It eschews formal grammar and embraces
profanity. It can be enigmatic and dense with allusion, or deceptively simple.

Suzan-Lori Parks, Paula Vogel, and Diana Son all romp in this linguistic
playground. Lovers of words, sounds, and styles of language, they are facile
chameleons, able to switch voices, dialects, and modes of speech with dazzling
versatility. The result of all this fooling around is language that achieves a kind
of vernacular eloquence, language that is grounded in the many dialects of daily

life in twenty-first-century America, yet able to keep up a running conversation with the past.

Suzan-Lori Parks's language is visceral. It is as much about breath and rhythm, and the feel of the syllable in the mouth or the sound on the ear, as it is about formal definitions of the words. She loves etymology, pores over the dictionary for amusement and inspiration. She believes that "words are spells in our mouths." Her plays are full of puns and double entendres. She writes in prose and in verse, often in the idioms of the African American underclass. Her characters exist outside the parameters of standard American history. They include a pair of contemporary urban brothers named Lincoln and Booth (their father's idea of a joke), who have been abandoned by their parents and the American dream in *Topdog/Underdog** (2001); a single, illiterate mother and her five kids living in a makeshift shelter beneath a bridge landing in *In the Blood* (1998); and embodiments of malicious slave and Reconstruction stereotypes named "Black Man with Watermelon" and "Black Woman with Fried Drumstick" in *The Death of the Last Black Man in the Whole Entire World* (1990). Parks dramatizes their untold stories in a hybrid real-and-imagined language that transcends Standard American English. When she ventures to settings outside the United States, for example, to nineteenth-century London in *Venus** (1996), the characters speak in idioms as different as the Queen's English and a midway barker's vulgar patter. Parks writes about oppression in fabricated dialects of resistance.

Jazz, blues, rap, and hip-hop are essential to her writing. Parks has said that music provides "a surface on which you can build the foundation of the play." She listens to different kinds of music for each piece — jazz for *The Death of the Last Black Man in the Whole Entire World,* opera for *Venus.* She sometimes borrows the structure of a piece of music to shape her nontraditional plots. She goes off on improvisational verbal riffs in which one word or syllable calls up another and then another, to form alliterative strings or permutations of a root. Internal rhymes create syncopated rhythms. Booth is "scheming and dreaming" about his partnership with Link, who describes his own three-card monte technique in rhymes that mimic his patter: "Thuh moves and thuh grooves, thuh talk and thuh walk, thuh patter and thuh pitter pat, thuh flap and thuh rap." Parks dances around while she is writing. It is fun to imagine her as a literary whirling dervish, casting off dried up ideas and ways-of-saying like crusty layers of dead skin to get to the raw, tender flesh where she might find the still-pulsing meat of her story.

Not surprisingly, Parks writes outside the margins of standardized spelling, grammar, and punctuation. She writes a kind of dramatic transliteration akin to a musical score. It includes sounds and silences, tempi and vocal dynamics. Her words look like they sound: "wuhduhnt" for wasn't, "hidedid" for hid, or "SPEC-SHUN" for inspection. Even breath patterns and interjections are marked: "Huh" is a short exhale; "thup" is a slurping sound; "ssnuch," a "reverse snort"; and "gaw" is a "glottal stop," for which may be substituted "a click-clock sound where the tongue tip clicks in front of the mouth." So original is her documentation that Parks put a crib sheet or "guide" in the introduction to her first anthology, *The America Play and Other Works* (1995), to enable her readers to "dive into an examination with great confidence." In winking homage to Strunk and White's famous manual for writers, she calls the guide *Elements of Style*. It includes a glossary of "foreign words & phrases" such as "do in diddly dip didded thuh drop," meaning "unclear." A "(rest)" tells the actor, "Take a little time, a pause, a breather; make a transition," whereas "a spell" indicates "an elongated and heightened (rest)." In *Fucking A* (2000), Parks invents a language she calls TALK. The female characters use it for extreme girl-talk, to speak graphically or obscenely among themselves about sex, hatred, and jealousy.

It's not that Parks enjoys tormenting her audience. In fact, she recommends that productions "present a nonaudible simultaneous English translation" of TALK. If her linguistic quirks and neologisms jar, it is because, like Bertolt Brecht, Parks wants her spectators to listen with all the senses, to think, to grapple with the gnarled and knotty strands of history, culture, and relationships. Tony Kushner has observed that "thinking, piecing together, searching, interpreting, understanding" are gauntlets Parks throws at our feet. There's something of the precocious child about her writing, something playful, impish, testing the limits, daring the grown-ups — those who think they have the answers or should have them — to take that! "Here it is, Mr. or Ms. Critic!" she once told Steven Druckman in a 1995 interview for the *Drama Review*. "You guys go away and think about it and exercise your brains and come up with something thrilling." The plays defy reductive interpretations. There are many ways and no ways to figure them out. They are puzzles, perpetual riddles that seem to lead us toward a solution but wind up where they started, like the optical illusions in the drawings of M. C. Escher. They force us to confront anew the constellation of experiences we think of as race in America and beyond.

Whereas Parks's work emerges from the richness and pain of African American history, Paula Vogel takes the white, suburban, middle class for a joy ride in the fast lane. She, too, writes in a variety of styles and voices. It is almost hard to recognize the same author in works that range from campy, cartoon farce in *The Mineola Twins** (1996) to the delicately observed unraveling of childhood memories in *How I Learned to Drive** (1997), except that both bear her trademark juxtaposition of wisecracks and heartbreaking revelations. Li'l Bit, the apprentice driver of the title, confides to her astonished schoolmates, "Sometimes I feel like these alien life forces, these two mounds of flesh have grafted themselves onto my chest, and they're using me until they can 'propagate' and take over the world." The personification of her ever-expanding breasts is funny, but the humor is muted by Li'l Bit's distress at her budding sexuality.

Vogel writes from a seriously satiric, feminist perspective. Her *Desdemona* (1993) poses and explores a fascinating proposition: what if Shakespeare's virtuous heroine were, in fact, a whore? How/would we reconsider her murder? Would Othello's insane jealousy be somehow justified? Would we apportion her some of the blame? No virtuous lady in Vogel's rendering, "Desi" searches frantically for her missing handkerchief. "Oh, piss and vinegar!!" she grouses. "Where is the crappy little snot rag!" Vogel tackles tough issues, but much to our delight, she seems constitutionally incapable of facing the world's angst with a straight face.

Vogel's work is steeped in American popular culture and its emotional fallout. Sci-fi movies, the Beach Boys, Disneyland, Liberace, and Maidenform girdles are palpable in her plays as background motifs, quotes, references, and, most important, the rhythm track for her language. She supercharges the lingo of the Top Ten hit, the mall, and the movies. Her dialogue croons to Roy Orbison, shimmies to Motown, whines like a bratty adolescent, and crackles with clever puns and punch lines. She peppers lines with verbal bits and pieces of Americana and Western civilization. Great painters and writers make cameo appearances alongside etiquette manuals and topical jokes. The personal is always political and vice versa. In Vogel's dramatic universe, the sober and the comic, the mundane and the intellectual collide and reverberate.

Vogel's plays go no farther back in American history than the span of her own life. Her chronology begins in the 1950s era of prosperity, complacency, and denial. *The Mineola Twins* begins here and skips through the turbulent sixties, seventies, and eighties. The dialogue picks up and amplifies each decade's style and slang. "I want to be pure for you on our Wedding Day," is juxtaposed with "Hey, daddy. . . . I'm trying to 'engage,' dig? I'm dishing politics, man, I'm trying to connect." The lines immediately contrast the teenage twins, one a would-be homemaker who loses it when her Melmac world starts to crack, the other a rebel who wields a countercultural mallet.

So far, *How I Learned to Drive* is Vogel's only play with a rural setting. It flashes back to events that begin in 1962 from the wise hindsight of the 1990s, as Li'l Bit patches together recollections of sexual abuse by a beloved uncle. Her speech is simpler, more eloquent than that of Vogel's more exaggerated characters. When at last she recovers the memory of the first time she was molested, Li'l Bit realizes, "That day was the last day I lived in my body."

*The Baltimore Waltz** (1990) is a kind of autobiographical fantasy. It takes on both the institutionalized homophobia that left gay Americans to waste away from AIDS in the 1980s and the individual struggle to come to terms with the grief left in its wake. The playwright handles both issues with a sense of the absurd. A doctor in Vienna offers an unorthodox experimental treatment. After a preliminary, promising sample, Dr. Todesrochen tells his patient, "We must have many more such specimens from you—for the urinocryoscopy, the urinometer, the urinoglucosometer, the uroacidimeter, uroazotometer, und mein new acquirement in der laboratorium—ein urophosphometer." He comes off as a New Age Frankenstein.

Hot 'n' Throbbing parrots second-wave feminist platitudes about female sexual liberation, but they fail to safeguard the main character from a violent death at the hand of her estranged husband. In each of her plays, Vogel tunes her spirited language to both the historical and the personal moment.

Diana Son is the youngest of the three playwrights being considered here. For her, feminism is a given; the emphasis is on the second part of hyphenated American (her parents are Korean but met, married, and raised her in the United States). Simplicity is the hallmark of her dramatic language. Like Parks and Vogel, Son is a multifaceted artist. Her works include *R.A.W. (Cause I'm a Woman)* (1993), a short, funny, and fiery ensemble rant against the objectification of Asian women in the West. *BOY* (1996) is a comic folktale about a family with three daughters—Labia, Hymen, and Vulva—who are disappointed when their fourth infant turns out to be a girl, so they raise the child as a boy. Magic realism sets the stage for *Fishes* (1998), in which a family that runs a pet shop is surprised when Mom dies suddenly and comes back as an exotic fish. Son's most famous work is *Stop Kiss* (1998), a realistic problem play about female sexual self-discovery, homophobia, and hate crime. The modes of language in Son's plays vary from choral poem to comic-book punch line to intimate pillow talk, yet there is a consistent clarity of expression throughout.

Whereas Parks and Vogel layer a lot of words and images onto page and stage, Son is a minimalist, an aesthetic preference she attributes to her Asian background. Each of her plays is built around a central metaphor. She pares away that which is not essential to telling her story. The semantic simplicity is deceptive, however. Her words are the tip of the dramatic iceberg. Son writes in Everyperson's vocabulary, straying from ordinary, concrete words only for technical specialties like species of fish and gourmet recipes. Single-word lines and single-clause sentences speak volumes. As an audience member, Son says she is not "there to indulge the writer's need to impress [her] with the use of language or with one-liners." In reality, she is not entirely above writing topical jokes. Callie in *Stop Kiss* describes her job as a radio traffic reporter to Sara, a new acquaintance: "I . . . ruin things for everyone else," she says. "You're Rudolph Giuliani?" is Sara's snappy comeback.

Like the other two dramatists, Son loves words, written and spoken. "How the text is arranged on the page, the sounds the words make, the rhythm between them, are as important to me as their meaning," she writes in the introduction to *R.A.W.* for the anthology *Contemporary Plays by Women of Color* (1996), edited by Kathy A. Perkins and Roberta Uno. She says she finds the arrangements of letters "aesthetically beautiful." In *R.A.W.*, she wants the male lines to be projected as slides rather than spoken by an actor, partly for visual effect, partly because she wants the audience to hear them in their own heads, and partly to hedge her bets. "An active audience is not a bored audience," she hopes.

Son, Vogel, and Parks are clearly very different playwrights, yet they share some linguistic and rhetorical strategies that invite more detailed comparison. The musicality of language is important to them. Humor is always waiting in the wings, and much of their work is intertextual: it includes, evokes, or refers to images from other literary texts and artifacts of popular culture. A side-by-side analysis of musicality, humor, and intertextuality in their plays allows a deeper appreciation of their crafts(wo)manship.

Rhythm, rhyme, and repetition are the percussive instruments in the three playwrights' linguistic orchestras. Parks, for instance, relies on what she calls "Rep & Rev"—repetition and revision—an integral element in the oral and musical traditions of Africa and the African Diaspora. Son underscores positive and negative relationships among ideas with sequences of short parallel sentences. Vogel repeats lines at substantial intervals. Each utterance gains resonance from the contrast between its immediate and prior contexts. The three playwrights hear very different internal drums and use the three R's in different ways to get their rhythms to page and stage.

According to her style guide, the *Elements,* Parks uses Rep & Rev to "create a dramatic text that departs from the traditional linear narrative style." She repeats words or phrases in quick succession with small phonic variations. "How many kin kin I hold," wonders Shark-Seer in *Imperceptible Mutabilities in the Third Kingdom* (1989). "Whole hull full," he decides. Soul-Seer continues the phonetic game: "Thuh hullholesfull of bleachin bones." In a later scene, Mrs. Aretha Saxon repeats the first line as she tries to calculate the capacity of her slave ship: "How many kin kin I hold." Parks picks up another pair of homophonic syllables this time: "Whole hold full," she decides. "Depends on thuh size. Thup. Size of the space. Thuup. Depends on the size of thuh kin." This hiccoughing wordplay is followed immediately by the terse and factual language of "Footnote #1: The human cargo capacity of the English slaver, the

Brookes, was about 3,250 square feet. From James A. Rawley, *The Transatlantic Slave Trade,* G. J. McLeod Limited, 1981, page 283." The contrast snaps us out of the fiction into an ugly reality.

The fed-up Raunchy Asian Women of Son's *R.A.W.* chant militant choral poems in which they take turns contributing to a list of stale and offensive male desires:

He wants to be with me.
He wants to know me.
He wants to fuck me.
He wants to see if my clit is sideways.
He wants to make me moan in ancient languages.
He wants me to bark like a Lhasa Apso.
He wants to wow me with the size of his non-Asian dick.

They then set the virtual men straight in the next march-metered passage:

I will not give you a massage.
I will not scrub your back.
I will not cook exotic meals using animal parts that aren't normally eaten.
I will not *not* get on top.
I will not be your Soon Yi.

The rhythm is even, regular, emphatic. The objects of the sentences become more graphic and outrageous with each repetition of the parallel nouns and verbs. The women draw their lines in the sand, marking the boundaries of their territory in economical, coordinated sentences that leave no rhythmic space for modifiers or secondary clauses that could mitigate their resolve.

Vogel uses a creeping, incremental, cumulative type of repetition. Like a musical refrain, the repeated line is amplified and transformed by the new circumstances in which it appears. Within the first five minutes of *The Baltimore Waltz,* Anna, the main character, says three times, "It's the language that terrifies me." The first time, she explains that she has avoided overseas travel ever since she was "traumatized by a junior high school French teacher." "Terrifies" is hyperbole here, a self-deprecating exaggeration that introduces us to Anna's neurotic charm. The next iteration of the line follows a very funny monologue in which Anna's brother recounts his last day on the job as a San Francisco librarian. After he led a symbolic pink-triangle-cutting session with the children who showed up for the final Reading Hour with Uncle Carl, he was promptly forgiven his two weeks' notice and ordered to vacate the premises.

His parting words to his supervisor were, "In a language you might understand: Up-pay ours-yay!" Of course, Anna is not really afraid of pig Latin. "Terrifies" is a verbal roll of the eyes. "My outrageous brother!" she seems to smile. "What will he do next?"

Later in the scene, a doctor's dire diagnosis tells Anna that she is vulnerable now to a host of "various bacteria: streptococci, staphylococci, enterococci, gonococci, gram-negative bacilli," and such awful-sounding symptoms as "eosinophilia, resulting in fibroblastic thickening, persistent tachycardia, hepatomegaly, splenomegaly, serious effusions into the pleural cavity with edema." The sudden bad news and the doctor's rhyming barrage leave Anna and Carl discombobulated. This time the words really do terrify her. They portend her imminent mortality. This third repetition puts the brakes on the earlier levity and is more poignant in light of the first two comic iterations.

All three playwrights write speeches that are essentially torrents of words and images. The cumulative effect may sweep the listener into a state of agitated arousal or near-trance. The passages can build comic momentum, as in *The Mineola Twins*, where Jim leads himself down an illogical path of hyperbolic doom after losing his virginity before marriage:

> So don't you see? The domino-theory? There goes virginity, there goes my promotion, my work ethic, monogamy, mortgages, raising 2.5 children, truth in advertising, belief in a deity, living in the suburbs, caring for my aged parents and saluting the flag.

His partner's deadpan response is the topper: "Wow. Heavy."

The single mom next door in Son's *BOY* is a coiled spring of sexual frustration. When she finally opens the spigot, she spews resentment at her astonished daughter.

> Tell him about the ramshackle house I brought you up in after your father took off at the news of your birth. . . . Tell him about the sour tasting meals I cooked because the only meat I could afford to buy was bad. . . . You think your father was some kind of royal king and I was his favorite concubine? You waiting for some prince to come climbing up your tower and rescue you from your life with me? . . . I'm a woman alone with no skill to sell and your criticizing mouth to feed. You think this house is ugly? You don't like being in the same room as me? Well I got you a handyman, Charlotte, someone who can build you what you need. Who's going to give that to me, Charlotte? Who's going to give me what I need?

In New York, Jeffrey Wright and Don Cheadle in the Public Theater's production of Top-dog/Underdog *by Suzan-Lori Parks, which was a finalist for the twenty-second Susan Smith Blackburn Prize in 2000. (Photograph: Michal Daniel, Billy Rose Theatre Collection, the New York Public Library for the Performing Arts, Astor, Lenox, and Tilden Foundations)*

She doesn't just fly off the handle. She launches herself into outer space and takes the whole door with her.

When Parks's Booth is caught "spunking" into his girlie magazines, he defends himself: "Im hot. I need constant sexual release." He warns that if he didn't relieve his urges, he'd "be out there doing who knows what, shooting people and shit." He turns his feeble defense to a strong offense via a verbal attack on his brother's private parts.

> Not like you, Link. When you dont got a woman you just sit there. Letting yr shit fester. Yr dick, if it aint falled off yet, is hanging there between yr legs, little whiteface shriveled-up blank-shooting grub worm. As goes thuh man so goes thuh mans dick. Thats what I say.

The speech follows an orgasmic trajectory. The insults amplify to a comic climax. Then, spent, the passage leans back and takes a deep breath.

Not all dramatic geysers are funny. *Fucking A* contains the longest list in any of these scripts. The Butcher is the kindest, most reliable, and gentlest man in the play. He and Hester commiserate over their respective incarcerated children. In one such scene, he reels off an exhausting, two-page list of improbable and absurd criminal charges that have been made against his daughter. The offenses range from "prostitution, racketeering, money laundering" to "smiling in the off season," "eating at the table of authority," "playing with herself on the governments nickel," "standing on one leg in a 2-legged zone," and "failing to predict a series of natural disasters." The catalog finally runs out of steam at "having neither gimmick nor schtick," "raising the dead, envisioning the future, remembering the past, speeding—huh." The litany indicts the system in which the Butcher's daughter doesn't stand a chance. Her tragedy is compounded by the fact that her law-abiding father buys into the institutionally promoted idea that she is "rotten to the core."

Other waterfalls of language can be hypnotic. Lincoln's sing-song, three-card monte patter is incantatory. "Lean in close and watch me now," he beckons. The lull of what follows is irresistible:

> Who see thuh black card who see thuh black card? You pick thuh red card you pick a loser you pick that red card you pick a loser you pick thuh black card thuh deuce of spades you pick a winner who sees thuh deuce of spades thuh one who sees it never fades watch me now as I throw thuh cards. Red losers black winner follow thuh deuce of spades chase thuh black deuce. Dark deuce will get you thuh win. 10 will get you 20, 20 will get you 40. One good pickll get you in 2 good picks and you gone win.

Booth envies his brother's extraordinary talent and wishes some of it would rub off on him. When he tries to match his brother's flair, his amateur attempt falls flat, marred by forced rhymes, jagged rhythms, and extraneous embellishments. Parks annotates his awkwardness with hyphens: Theres-thuh-loser, yeah, theres-thuh-black-card, theres-thuh-other-loser-and-theres-thuh-red-card, thuh-winner." Booth tips his hand by letting the effort show. The spell is broken. We don't fall for his con.

Humor leavens darker impulses in the work of all three playwrights. It relies on incongruity, puns, double entendres, comic exaggeration, and verbal surprise endings. In *Topdog/Underdog*, Booth boasts that he "stole and stole generously." Vogel's Desdemona fondles a long, pointy metal object: "If I could find a man with just such a hoof-pick—," she muses, "he could pluck out my stone— eh, Emilia?" Son interprets the realities behind the promises in personal ads:

> East Asian scholar.
> Geek.

Vietnam vet.
Psycho.
Ivy leaguer.
Jock.
New Age philosopher.
Pot head.
Long-haired musician.
Slob.

In *Fishes,* Junebug tells her mom about a dream: "I still looked like me but my body was bigger and I liked kissing boys and I ate green salads and I won a vacuuming contest!" Mom's bittersweet punch line, "That's called a nightmare, Junebug," settles, sadly resigned, into the last four syllables.

Vogel's humor has many parents. Although she might cringe at the comparison, her one-liners rival those of Neil Simon. They sucker-punch the audience by starting a speech in all seriousness and then zinging us with an unexpected fillip. "We almost blew up together, just like any other happy nuclear family" (*The Mineola Twins*), for example, and "It's not normal for a baby to smile all the time. It's either gas or mental retardation" (*And Baby Makes Seven*). Vogel might prefer comparing her sarcastic adages with those of Oscar Wilde: "Virginity is a state of mind" (*The Mineola Twins*); "When the Master Piddles the Servant holds the Pot" (*Desdemona*); and "Leave it to a cuckold to be jealous of a eunuch" (*Desdemona*). Her sense of the ridiculous and the Ridiculous call to mind the camp Charleses, Ludlam and Busch. Camp hyperbole and winks at sex and sexual orientation abound in *The Mineola Twins,* a pastiche of prefeminist stereotypes and sci-fi creepiness. When Myrna, the good Mineola Twin, learns that her otherwise-identical-but-flat-chested twin robbed a bank in a padded bra, she is indignant: "My sister used my knockers as terrorist camouflage!" She also blows a gasket when her teenage son, Kenny, identifies a fabric color. "I don't like hearing the word 'mauve' in your mouth," she scolds. "Only boys who grow up to be interior decorators use words like 'mauve.'"

Parks calls humor the seventh sense (the sixth, according to her style guide, "helps you feel another's pulse at great distances"). Humor is what happens when the playwright "get[s] out of the way," she told Druckman during their interview. A "great way of getting to the deep shit." Her comic touches belong to the category Pirandello called *humorismo,* the kind of laugh that chokes up when we recognize the pain underneath. Booth is caught up in a fervid effort to get a commitment from his waffling girlfriend. He tells his brother:

> I got her this ring today. Diamond. Well, diamond-esque, but it looks just as good as the real thing. Asked her what size she wore. She say 7 so I go boost a size 6 and a half, right? Show it to her and she loves it and I shove it on her finger and its a tight fit right, so she can't just take it off on a whim, like she did the last one I gave her. Smooth, right?

It's a typically sly maneuver, recounted in energetic verbs like "boost" and "shove" and crowned with the euphemistic "diamond-esque." There's a wrenching gap, however, between the enthusiasm with which Booth tells the story and the pitiful desperation it reveals. The dynamic is reciprocal: the humor lightens the emotional turmoil, just as the turmoil tempers the laugh.

Another lens—or prism—through which to compare and contrast the three playwrights' use of language is intertextuality. Many of the plays quote, allude to, or model themselves on other writing. These borrowed or echoed elements affirm the postmodern idea that there is nothing new, that every work of art ultimately responds to or recycles something that came before. Parks and Vogel especially embrace that interdependence and interconnectedness and pick up their secondhand materials from the Bible, Shakespeare, modern literature, official documents, pop songs, current events, and cultural artifacts as varied as the minstrel show and a driver's ed manual. The intertextual references situate the plays in a virtual cosmic echo chamber, where voices usually separated by time, place, and culture can talk to one another.

A mock minstrel show adds dimension to Parks's portrait of abandonment and immobility in *Topdog/Underdog.* Lincoln and Booth's parents left them to fend for themselves. Their relationship is a strained symbiosis of dependence and resentment, reminiscent of Cain and Abel. They are also figurative orphans of a broad, multigenerational decline of family and social bonds in the African American community, a regrettable consequence of life in a society that has little use for young black men. Parks puts them in a telling historical light when they celebrate payday by play-acting a Negro vaudeville routine:

> BOOTH: Lordamighty, Pa, I smells money!
> LINCOLN: Sho nuff, Ma. Pappas brung home thuh bacon.
> BOOTH: Bringitherebringitherebringithere.
>   *With a series of very elaborate moves*
>   *Lincoln brings the money over to Booth.*
> BOOTH: Put it in my hands, Pa!
> LINCOLN: I want ya tuh smells it first, Ma!
> BOOTH: Put it neath my nose then, Pa!

LINCOLN: Take yrself a good long whiff of them greenbacks.
BOOTH: Oh lordamighty Ima faint, Pa! Get me muh med-sin!
    Lincoln quickly pours two large glasses of whiskey.
LINCOLN: Dont die on me, Ma!
BOOTH: I'm fading fast, Pa!
LINCOLN: Thinka thuh children, Ma! Thinka thuh farm!

Instead of staging a contrived debate about the impact of negative images on the fortunes of contemporary African Americans, Parks invokes this loaded cultural icon that carries the twin specters of good-hearted self-deprecation and humiliating subjugation. The brothers may think they are light-years beyond the minstrel show, but they live in its lingering shadow. Like the old-world, homespun rubes they love to imitate, Link and Booth are stuck on the outskirts of the American dream, living hand-to-mouth with no real prospects. Our delight in their game is offset by the recognition of how small a leap of imagination it actually requires.

A driver-safety manual provides a structural and thematic framework for Vogel's *How I Learned to Drive.* Voiceover excerpts from that overconfident and emphatic document create a counterpoint to the seduction and incestuous abuse that are the play's central focus. The play opens with the manual's title, *Safety First—You and Driver Education;* chapter headings and longer excerpts sprinkled throughout the play comment on the action and steer us through the nonlinear plot. Most are ominous warnings, or tips for preventing or coping with dangerous situations: "By thinking ahead, the defensive driver can adjust to weather, road conditions and road kill. Good defensive driving involves mental and physical preparation. Are you prepared?" The irony, of course, is that Li'l Bit is not safe in the car. Behind the wheel will prove to be her most vulnerable position, the place where Uncle Peck first lays hands on her. Despite its promises, the manual does not cover all eventualities. Its omniscience is a pose. What use are the rules, Vogel implies, if they don't hold up in the real world? If Li'l Bit can't protect herself from a smiling predator?

Vogel, the inveterate conjuror of pop-cult references, is also the author of the most highbrow example of intertextuality. An excerpt from James Joyce's novel *Ulysses* (1922) at the end of *Hot 'n' Throbbing,* which Vogel revised for the 2005 New York production at Signature Theatre Company, creates a harrowing ironic tension between itself and the onstage action. Onstage, Clyde, the husband, strangles his wife, Charlene, with his belt; the male Voice reads from Charlene's "pending coroner's report," while the female Voice Over speaks aloud Charlene's desperate interior conversation with herself.

Get to the door can you keep calm—no—you can get out of this—no—
keep fighting try to get—ask him with your eyes—no theres no air left—
no for the kids stay calm stars put your arms round him keep your eyes
open ask no to say no my god no no air I can't no

With its free association, lack of punctuation, and repetition of key words,
the speech echoes Joyce's remarkable stream-of-consciousness monologue at
the end of *Ulysses*. In that famous passage, Molly Bloom celebrates her sexual
awakening. Her cadence is one of ever-deepening breaths, of gulping the fresh
air, of increasing arousal. Vogel inverts Joyce's technique. Charlene is running
out of breath, gasping for air, losing consciousness.

When Clyde "redoubles his grip" on Charlene's throat, Vogel interpolates a
tape recording of the male Voice reading from Molly Bloom's interior monologue. At Signature, the recording was hushed and gentle, almost a lullaby for
Charlene's slip into death.

I asked him with my eyes to ask again yes and then he asked me would
I yes to say yes my mountain flower and first I put my arms around
him yes . . .

To underscore her contrapuntal intent, Vogel twists the irony once more. The
stage direction requires that "the tape recording slow down, warped, breaking
down," as we hear the end of Molly's speech.

. . . and drew him down to me so he could feel my breasts all perfume yes
and his heart was going like mad and yes I said yes I will Yes.

The broken recording warps Molly's exuberance into Charlene's death throe.
By the end of Molly's passage, Charlene's body is limp. Vogel's poignant quot-
ing and manipulation of Joyce intensifies the brutality and senselessness of
Charlene's suffocation.

Getting back to the questions in the quotation that begins this essay, where
do all these words come from? Whose voices are they? They come from across
the spectrum of American demographics, from our African, Asian, and European pasts, and from the fertile imaginations and skilled pens of three thinking playwrights. All three have emerged in recent years from the coterie of the
experimental/avant-garde theater to a wider commercial audience. *Stop Kiss*
won the Obie for Best Play, the *New York Times* Best of 1999, and the GLAAD
Media Award for Outstanding Production. *Topdog/Underdog* played Broadway

in 2002 and won that year's Pulitzer Prize in drama. (The Blackburn Prize was ahead of the pack when its judges named the play a finalist in 1999–2000, two years before it premiered at the Public Theater in New York.) Signature Theatre Company in New York devoted its 2004–2005 season to the plays of Paula Vogel.

What explains their theatrical ascendance? Have they just been around long enough to garner wider recognition? Is the theater attracting a younger, more adventurous audience, one that is ready to listen as intently as they watch their movies and television shows? Or are the playwrights making compromises with accessibility? *How I Learned to Drive* (1998 Pulitzer, Obie, Drama Desk, and New York Drama Critics Circle awards) and *Stop Kiss* derive some acclaim from their advocating of good causes through familiar characters, language, and settings, but that does not mean they pander to a lowbrow audience. *Drive*, especially, is a fearless journey through previously uncharted dramatic territory.

Some critics complain that Parks's later work abandons her early experiments in favor of scripts with beginnings, middles, and ends, recognizable characters, and accessible language. The charge is unfair. *In the Blood, Topdog/Underdog,* and *Fucking A* reflect a maturing of Parks's craft. She no longer has to start from scratch every time to dazzle us with her dramaturgical virtuosity. The wild oats she sowed in her developmental plays built the surefootedness with which she now returns to more traditional forms. As her early work redefined the theatrical event that is a play, the recent work transfigures the traditional play. That said, we can rest assured that she will reinvent her work again, to surprise and provoke us with new styles and forms.

A hunger for substance and freewheeling imagination in the theater has made the zeitgeist right for the plays of Suzan-Lori Parks, Paula Vogel, and Diana Son. We can look forward to hearing more from them, in voices old and new, near and far, as familiar as this morning's coffee and as remarkable as an out-of-body experience. Let's keep listening.

First-Person Singular

Female Writers Embrace the One-Person Play

MANDY GREENFIELD

᳅

One person stands alone onstage, and her words, spoken aloud, become powerful tools to command an audience's attention.

From *The Search for Signs of Intelligent Life in the Universe* (1985) — Jane Wagner's commercially successful play starring Lily Tomlin — to the alternative creations of artists such as Holly Hughes, Deb Margolin, and Rhodessa Jones; from Whoopi Goldberg's lacerating comic turns to the dramatic political statements of Sarah Jones, Eve Ensler, and Heather Raffo, the sheer volume of one-woman shows — too many to list here — begs consideration of the form as a unique vehicle for theatrical expression. In particular, the form allows these women the flexibility to experiment with the nature and uses of storytelling.

In the preface to her book, *Extreme Exposure: An Anthology of Solo Performance Texts from the Twentieth Century* (2000), the director Jo Bonney affirms that "despite their limitless backgrounds and performance styles, all solo performers are storytellers." But Bonney is primarily interested in the phenomenon of "solo performance," that brand of one-person show which is neither purely text based nor entirely performance art but seems a hybrid of the two. She, like many of us, is dazzled by the form, and she comments that by "presenting their personal observations, convictions and fears, [solo performers] share an intimacy with their audience, built purely from their live presence and their words." She is, in effect, describing idiosyncratic artists such as Laurie Anderson and Karen Finley, whose texts only truly live when they themselves perform the work.

Bonney's description doesn't embrace a play for one actor that is stable enough to stand apart from its creator, for any actor to perform. We begin to see an important distinction between a solo performance and the one-person play. The one-person play lives and breathes outside of — or perhaps before —

its performance or its performer. Whether text invented by an author (or authors), or drawn from other sources and arranged by an author, or codified by an author as the result of improvisation, the one-person play exists on the page and does not rely on any specific actor to give it life. The dramatic impact of the words is as palpable and powerful (or humorous and entertaining) on the page as on the stage.

An examination of a few female-authored one-person plays makes it clear that the form also serves a particularly utilitarian function. One-person plays, especially by female writers, can become instruments for affecting social change, for pointedly criticizing the status quo, for healing, or for creating roles for female performers where they otherwise might not have existed.

In terms of the contemporary one-woman play in the United States, there is no better place to start than with the work of Anna Deavere Smith. An artist who is deeply concerned with social issues, since 1982 Smith has created and performed one-woman pieces composed of interviews she conducts in distinct communities of Americans as a means of deconstructing those communities.

Part of a project she dubbed "On the Road: A Search for American Character," her work began with an interest in the relationship of language to character. Initially, Smith developed a language-based technique for teaching acting, during which she used media interviews with celebrities and public figures (who, in her technique, were the "characters") to reveal the psychological truth of a particular character. Smith was convinced that the words a person/character spoke — indeed, the act of speaking those words — was the mark of individuality and, therefore, the key to that person/character's psychological reality. By contrast, many other acting techniques ask the actor to match his or her emotional reality to the words a character speaks, to give a truthful performance. Ultimately, Smith applied this "selfless" technique to her own performances; she began interviewing people on her own and developed her signature style.

Influenced as much by artists such as the soloist Spalding Gray and the author Studs Terkel, by Shakespeare and the playwright Adrienne Kennedy, as she was by the feminist theater movement of the 1970s and early 1980s, Smith resists the notion that there is anything particular to the one-woman show that makes it distinct from the one-man show. However, she cites the overall better level of theatrical training and education, a spirit of adventure, and the greater sense of authority among women since the Women's Movement to explain the proliferation of one-woman plays in the contemporary American theater. Identity politics, she notes, has also spurred the growth of the form.

Among Smith's most notable plays, *Fires in the Mirror** (1992) and *Twilight: Los Angeles, 1992** (1993), consist entirely of verbatim excerpts of interviews with real people. The words of these plays are not Smith's words. But it is in

At the Public Theater in New York, Anna Deavere Smith performs her one-person play Fires in the Mirror, *a finalist for the fifteenth Susan Smith Blackburn Prize in 1994. (Photograph: Martha Swope)*

the composition of these plays—the order of the interviews, the recipe of ideas, the conflation of personalities, the cacophony of points of view, the startling poetry Smith extracts from her interviewees' spoken words—that the brilliance of Smith's work reveals itself.

Fires in the Mirror, for example, is a compilation of the thoughts, feelings, hopes, and regrets of individuals from the Hasidic and African American communities in Crown Heights, Brooklyn, in 1991, following an incident that polarized these two groups: an eight-year-old African American boy named Gavin Cato was hit by a car in a rabbi's motorcade and died. Rumors that a Hasidic-run ambulance service had helped the members of the motorcade rather than the child incited African Americans to respond with rioting and violence, culminating with the murder of a Hasidic student named Yankel Rosenbaum.

In the piece, Smith juxtaposes people of different colors, races, ages, and cultural strands into a tapestry recognizable as one complicated America. While not every monologue in the piece directly relates to the incident itself, each reveals a deeply personal, highly individual, and culturally relevant beam in the hologram of this disparate community, bound only by proximity. Smith's text can jump from the Reverend Al Sharpton's arrestingly percussive words about his hair to the vowel-laden, tentative language of Rivkah Siegal, a Lubavitcher woman discussing her relationship to the wig she is obligated to wear. From there, the text can move to the deliberate, erudite opinions of Professor Angela Davis and culminate in the powerfully lyrical, rhythmic, image-driven pronouncements of Carmel Cato, the deceased boy's father. In that way, Smith recreates the Crown Heights of 1991 — its contradictions and its complications — for us.

To read Smith's work is to recognize both the sheer, raw power of human speech and the ingenuity of an artist committed to connecting with her audience, harnessing the power of theatrical convention, to create, as she says, "a more democratic theater where the stage is a reflection of the diverse world around us." In *Fires in the Mirror,* there is no exposition — from word one, we leap headlong into the world of people who observe, speak out, riot, cower in their homes, agree, disagree, and sympathize — all in relation to the events that polarized their community.

Much ink has been spent — especially in academic circles — on the performative aspects of Smith's work. Academics question how an audience "reads" Smith's performance, given that she is a highly educated, African American woman shifting among figures of various races, genders, socioeconomic backgrounds, and education levels. While we can leave the theoretical questions aside, it is worth noting that the cumulative impact of reading these monologues forces us to recognize where our own sympathies lie, where our own preconceptions about African Americans and Jews reside, how our own complicity in cultural stereotyping prevents us from a deeper understanding of the world around us. Once we acknowledge to ourselves where we stand, *Fires in the Mirror* asks us, like the woman performing the play, to embody "the other" — to step into the shoes of someone else — for just a few minutes.

Audience response to *Fires in the Mirror* and *Twilight: Los Angeles, 1992* was so overwhelming, Smith asked, "If an audience is willing to stand on their feet and give an ovation, what would it take to get them to come backstage and say, 'What can I do about the social problems being addressed in the play?'" To answer her own question, in 1997 Smith created the Harvard-based Institute on Arts and Civic Dialogue, "to convene the public around serious social issues and [to] make relationships with organizers and others who do progressive work." There was, as she mentions, a "civic impact" of these plays on audiences. Of course there was a civic impact! How can we not be moved by the words of Carmel Cato, the father of the deceased boy, when, at the end of the play, he recognizes the tensions and pain inside himself and acknowledges that something is deeply wrong in his community?

> The whole week
> before Gavin died
> my body was changing,
> I was having different feelings.
> I stop eating,
> I didn't et
> nothin',
> only drink water,
> for two weeks;
> and I was very touchy—
> any least thing that drop
> or any song I hear
> it would effect me.
> Every time I try to do something
> I would have to stop.
> I was
> lingering, lingering, lingering,
> all the time.
> But I can do things,
> I can see things,
> I know that for a fact.
> I was telling myself,
> "Something is wrong somewhere,"
> but I didn't want to see,
> I didn't want to accept,
> And it was inside of me, . . .

Carmel Cato, the man, and Carmel Cato, the character in *Fires in the Mirror,* reveals his pain and anguish through his words: the repetition of the "I + verb" construction thrusts us into his world—into the actions he took, couldn't take, wanted to take—in the face of unspeakable pain over this incident. In the aching refrain of "lingering, lingering, lingering," we experience his sense of helplessness, of impotence in the face of mounting tensions within his community. And even though his voice is particularly rich and innately sympathetic (he is, after all, the deceased boy's father), his monologue is just the final punctuation to a slew of equally exposing words from many of the people affected by this event, each of whom Smith treats with equal time, space, and dignity. We must decide who—if anyone or anything—is the protagonist, who the antagonist, in this multifaceted play of words.

Whereas Smith set out to write a play dedicated to exploring character and found that it evolved into meaningful political discourse, Anna Reynolds and Moira Buffini began with a political instinct to critique the British prison system but also wound up with a searing character portrait in *Jordan** (1992). Their one-woman play was inspired by the case of Shirley Jones, a single parent who, in 1986, smothered her baby boy and attempted suicide, after escaping an abusive husband and turning to prostitution as a means of survival.

Anna Reynolds met Shirley Jones when both were incarcerated in an English prison. Moira Buffini, who taught drama in the prison system, met and co-wrote *Jordan* with Reynolds. Buffini, as she remarked in a recent interview, very organically took "the poetry and prose that Anna had written, this clay," and turned it into a play. Primarily trained as an actor, Buffini went on to write several plays following *Jordan,* including *Gabriel* (1997), *Silence** (1999), and *Dinner* (2002). In addition to co-winning the 1992 Writers' Guild Award for Best Fringe Play for *Jordan,* Buffini received the Time Out Award for her performance as Shirley.

The play is affecting and at times profoundly difficult even to read, given the sheer frankness with which the character of Shirley recounts the events leading to her incarceration, trial, and eventual release from prison. Surprisingly, it is this very frankness in tone that lends the play its payoff, for the facts—unadorned, unembellished, unsentimental—of this woman's story are harrowing. Shirley delivers the words of the play both to Jordan, her deceased baby, and to us, the audience, but never does she justify or rationalize, cajole or manipulate. We listen as she is cheated on while pregnant, beaten up shortly after giving birth, and left for dead by the baby's father who, in an awful irony, takes legal action to remove Jordan from Shirley's custody, because he claims she is an unfit mother. It is at this moment—when the possibility arises that her child will be removed from her care and placed in the custody of the man who abused her—that Shirley is moved to kill the baby and also herself:

> I know where I am going. I buy a bottle of vodka and four packets of aspirin and that's it: the end of the money. On the way back, we go down to the sea. I take you out of your pram and we watch the waves, black and silver in the darkness . . . I leave the pram sitting on the shore; a gift

for the waves. We won't be needing it anymore. We'll be up there, in that space, gliding on the water to the moon . . .

I drink the vodka, gagging on the strength of the aspirins! Then, I can't remember . . .

I take up a pillow and without looking I place it over you, so so gently and I press down on it for a long time, without looking. I can't look . . . in case . . . I see you kick.

Shirley's first attempt to kill herself fails. Her second does not. When we learn in the final moment of the play, through a slide projection, that, upon her acquittal and release from prison, Shirley succeeds in committing suicide, we are deeply saddened, even deflated, but not surprised.

Shirley doesn't explain her choice to kill her baby and herself. The explanation comes by way of a revision to the well-known fairy tale about Rumpelstiltskin, which she tells in pieces, interspersed throughout Reynolds' and Buffini's text. In the popular Grimm's fairy tale, a miller's daughter makes a deal with a little man to give him her firstborn, if he will help her spin straw into gold and become queen. But ultimately, when she becomes queen, she does *not* give up her first child. The little man takes pity on her when he sees how heartsick she is over the possibility of losing her baby, and he tells her that if she can guess his name, he will not demand the baby. Of course, in Grimm's version, she is able to guess the little man's name—with help from a trusted messenger who has overheard it—and she, the child, and the kingdom, presumably, live happily ever after. In *Jordan,* by contrast, the Queen cannot guess the little man's name; she has no trusted messenger; she has no resources; she cannot come out on the winning side of the deal she's made with any man. Instead, Shirley says:

As dawn was breaking, she made her decision. She took up her child and fled into the fading darkness . . .

Freedom. The Queen and her child rode by horse for many days, over mountains, through rivers and dark forests, until at last they came to a magical land where food was plenteous and the dazzling sun always shone, a land where they played in the trees and grass and danced together on the path toward the moon. And of course, they lived happily ever after.

In both excerpts, Shirley is focused on "darkness" and a place near "the moon." Fleeing into the darkness and toward the moon becomes a refrain in which darkness represents death and the moon a place of great freedom. Lacking the human or financial resources to fight the "little man" who fathered her child and unable to survive in the kingdom, which is London, Shirley chooses death as a means of finding freedom for her child and finally herself.

The revised telling of Rumpelstiltskin is significant in and of itself. Through it, we understand in theatrical terms the psychological space that Shirley, the character, occupies. At the same time, the inclusion of a fairy tale — of a "once upon a time . . ." construction juxtaposed to Shirley's first-person, present-tense narrative — illuminates the power of the one-person form. Unlike a fairy tale set in a remote time and place, Shirley's story is immediate, it is happening now, before us, and we don't need exposition to understand or experience the events. If we trust our storyteller, she will take us right where we need to go, even if we don't know when the curtain rises exactly where we are or with whom.

Because the storyteller is also the only character onstage, the audience's relationship to the storyteller informs — in fact, dictates — the audience's relationship to the character, Shirley. Whatever we may think of infanticidal mothers — whatever we may think about *this* infanticidal mother, who, we may assume, had her share of media exposure in 1986 — the revelation of character happens with such immediacy and simultaneity during the storytelling process that the gap between the facts of Shirley and our experience of Shirley is closed. Not until the end of the play do we, readers or audience, formulate some interpretive closure of her character and story. We close the pages of the play or we leave the theater, and only then do we form our judgment of Shirley. No judgment is made for us.

In contrast to *Fires in the Mirror* and *Jordan,* there is a brand of one-person play that is distinctly and purposefully autobiographical. Here the author-storyteller recounts her own tale. Susan Miller, whose body of work runs the gamut from full-length plays to screenplays and television shows, found herself using the one-person form to dramatize a deeply personal story. In *My Left Breast** (1994), Susan, the character, tells us directly — with incredible humor, pain, and pathos — the story of being a "One Breasted, Menopausal, Jewish Bisexual Lesbian Mom" surviving breast cancer.

Miller wrote *My Left Breast* as a one-person play because, as she describes it, she needed in a certain raw way to tell this story — her story. She didn't want an intermediary in the process. In fact, for the play's premiere at the Humana Festival of the Actors Theatre of Louisville, Miller, a writer with no formal acting training, performed *My Left Breast* and continues to do so, periodically, in regional theaters all over the country. The courage it must have taken Miller to write this highly personal, irreverent, and profoundly moving play is amplified when we consider the courage it must have taken to speak the following words to an audience:

> I miss it but it's not a hand.
> I miss it but it's not my mind.
> I miss it but it's not the roof over my head.
> I miss it but it's not a word I need.
> It's not a sentence I can't live without.
> I miss it, but it's not a conversation with my son.
> It's not my courage or my lack of faith.
> (Beat.)
> I miss it — but it's not HER.

Clearly, as with both Shirley and Carmel Cato, the repetition of the "I + verb" construction establishes the emotional immediacy and primacy of the storyteller. But here, by contrast, the specificity of the construction, "I miss it but . . . ," establishes another character as well: "It," the third-person singular, a thing, unspecified. Because Miller tells us in the opening lines of the play that one of her breasts is not "real," we have a referent for "it": "I" establishes Miller as the storyteller/protagonist, and "it" establishes her left breast as the antagonist, the thing that opposes her, stands in her way, and must be overcome for there to be resolution to her drama.

Interestingly, the repetition of the construction, "I miss it but it's not ____," also affords Miller the opportunity to establish some of the supporting characters of her play: a hand (a traditional symbol of the individual's agency or will); her mind (the faculties); "a word" and "a sentence" (language). Her will, her faculties, and language will figure prominently in the battle between her and her left breast. And what is a one-woman play if not a conflation of an artist's will, faculties, and language? This one-woman play is the site where the drama of Miller's ordeal plays out: she must tell this tale to beat the antagonist, to overcome the obstacle of cancer in her left breast, to arrive, victorious, at the denouement. Courage and faith will also play roles in this tale, as will her son and a mysterious "her." A protagonist, an antagonist, a supporting cast, and a conflict — all the ingredients of great drama unfold before us, with just one woman onstage.

In an April 2004 article for *American Theatre* magazine, Miller focused on the phenomenon of others playing the role of Susan and remarked that "the issue in [the] collision or merging of autobiography and fiction is whether a character has life beyond its creator and whether its creator will give over that life." She has, in fact, given over that life many, many times to actors nationally and internationally, and that the play has gone on to have a robust life through other performers is a tribute to the strength of the text. Miller's impulse to write this autobiographical story as a one-woman play is a tribute to the form as a vehicle for self-expression.

By many accounts a semiautobiographical work, Dael Orlandersmith's *The Gimmick** (1998) is a riveting, poetic, and tender monologue, delivered by Alexis, a teenage African American girl who lives in Harlem in 1968. Orlandersmith's admission in the foreword to the published version of the script is noteworthy:

> I began to write again because of the lack of roles offered to me as an actor—especially as a black female actor. Many before me had to and, I hope, fewer after me will have to deal with lack of work and stereotyping. As a large, black female I am offered roles as welfare mothers, prostitutes, religious fanatics, the jolly, wise-cracking, fat girlfriend (sidekick to the pretty woman who gets the man), or the strong, big, black woman who is a thinly disguised "mammie." I'm also offered roles playing much older women. . . . [B]lack females and other women of color deal with the triple whammy of sexism, racism and ageism. In my case it is sexism, racism, ageism and sizeism.

Orlandersmith's text pulsates with the need to fill the void she has identified, to create a character so rich and rare that only a woman of a great and particular talent, size, age, and color can play it. How many actors—and not for lack of talent—could credibly speak the following section of Alexis's words, as she struggles to find something to wear to her friend Jimmy's art opening?

> We go to the women's section/size 6, 10, 12/I'm still having a hard time finding things in a size sixteen/the dresses are still old lady dresses/ polyester and sickly yellow/I'm getting depressed/more depressed/I'm feeling fat/ugly/fatter/uglier . . . Jimmy says "don't worry, Alexis/Mr. K's daughter/Genevieve . . . maybe she can help/let's go" . . .

> "Hi I'm Genevieve/Jimmy says you need something to wear/how about a long shirt with a vest/we can do that/there are no dresses in your size/but there's some nice shirts that are long/they cover the hips" . . .

> . . . the clothes are fine/she/Genevieve knows the world likes skinny girls/ skinny/thin/white Modigliani girls/the world does not like big/black/ girls at all/not at all

Alexis is not one of the clichés of African American womanhood that we find all too often in our culture. She is neither a welfare mother, a prostitute, a religious fanatic; a jolly, wise-cracking, fat girlfriend (sidekick of the pretty woman who gets the man); nor a strong, big, dark woman who is a thinly disguised "mammy." Alexis is a thinking, feeling, hurting young woman, who wants to look good at her friend Jimmy's art opening but who feels defeated at some level by the world. We are invested in her, we care about her, and we pull for her in a complete way. She is not a stereotype. In setting out to create a role for herself, Orlandersmith expanded the repertoire for any African American actor of a certain age and physical stature who shares her frustration with the dearth of good roles available.

I have focused closely on a handful of British and American one-woman plays, but it is worth noting that the form is widely embraced and exploding internationally. Women such as Brazil's Denise Stoklos, Mexico's Jesusa Rodriguez, Northern Ireland's Geraldine Hughes, England's Fiona Shaw (who's actually Irish-born), and Australia's Caroline O'Connor, among many others, have made major contributions to the growing scene.

And the scene is, in fact, growing. But why women choose this form for their stories and why audiences are so content to listen to them are matters of varied opinion. The New York–based writer and performer Lisa Kron, whose comic and intense one-woman plays include *101 Humiliating Stories* (1993) and *2.5 Minute Ride* (1999), feels there is something uniquely American about the form and attributes the current proliferation and popularity of the one-person play to what she calls "the culture of confession" in the United States. Critics often attribute the boom of one-person plays to Americans' obsession with personal stories, brought about by the talk-show revolution. We might even consider the degree to which so-called reality television whets the appetite for telling and hearing "real" stories on the stage, personal experience being the source for many one-person shows.

But something else—not particularly culturally specific—seems to be at work as we canvas the vast landscape of contemporary one-woman plays, both in the United States and abroad. Kron, alongside many other theater artists and producers, views economics as a huge impetus for the number of such solo turns on contemporary stages. Simply put, a play requiring one actor costs a lot less to produce than a play that requires ten. For traditionally underrepresented or marginalized voices—those of women, people of color, gays and lesbians—the one-person play becomes the most viable way to be heard, to push alternative stories into the mainstream. Anna Deavere Smith posits, "A theater may not want to commit to a whole play about an Asian family for example. They may wonder if they have the audience for it, or if they could develop the audience for it. On the other hand, they might be willing to host the charismatic storyteller who is willing to get up in front of strangers and tell the story all alone!"

But American cultural zeitgeists and economic realities aside, the vitality of this form, at this moment in time, feels far more active than reactive. Women embrace this form to tell their stories for a host of reasons, to a number of ends and by a number of means. Whether overtly political, deeply personal, or some combination thereof, the writer who engages with the one-woman play can mold the form to suit her needs and, with great economy, create an entire theatrical universe onstage. A complete drama for one actor.

ELEVEN

Women's Imaginations

Experimenting with Theatrical Form

CAROLE WODDIS

Some years ago, in Mary Remnant's introduction to volume 6 of Methuen's *Plays by Women* (1987), the estimable British theater critic Michael Billington was quoted as saying that "in art you cannot ignore an audience's age-old hunger for structure and shape."

Nearly two decades on, Billington's comment has lost little of its force. The form that Ibsen made famous in the second half of the nineteenth century — the realistic drama of psychological conflict, with its recognizable language and its linear action that unfolds logically to a climactic moment — still holds a good deal of sway, despite challenges from other quarters. And when women in particular veer from that course, then they must be prepared for vitriolic repercussions, be it those dished out to the lesbian playwright Sarah Daniels in the 1980s or, more recently, to Charlotte Jones. Previously lauded for *Humble Boy** (2001), a play that made its heady and ideas-packed exploration of bees, galaxies, and the English way of life accessible through a clever use of characters and "shadow" equivalents from *Hamlet,* Jones was then lambasted for attempting the infinitely more daring *The Dark* (2004), an exploration of urban fear and disconnection played out through a split-action, real-time structure.

This essay looks at how three women dramatists have defied this conundrum in their plays, for it is the case that when women deviate from the norm, they run the risk of incurring personalized criticism (which is not to say that male playwrights who experiment with form haven't also incurred abuse and insult). But women dramatists who put their concepts out in the world in a form not adhering to that reassuringly familiar, realistic model run added risks. It takes a thick skin and a big heart to run the public gauntlet, to stay true to creative juices in the face of convention.

What makes them do it? Sheer cussedness? A rebellious streak? Or is there

Simon Russell Beale in London's Royal National Theatre production of Humble Boy *by Charlotte Jones, winner of the twenty-third Susan Smith Blackburn Prize in 2001. (Photograph: Catherine Ashmore)*

something inherently "other" in the synapses of the female mind? Has the lateral, multitasking way of life that many women lead engendered a creative process that naturally expresses itself with a less linear, more fragmented mode of writing?

Twenty years ago, this was thought to be so. But even the proponents of this theory now think that both sexes' experience of our fragmented life has so merged as to neutralize that particular argument. So what is it that still pushes women into formal experimentation?

Over twenty-five years of active theater reviewing, I have gathered the genuine impression that women dramatists have often been prepared to take unfashionably daring, formalistic risks in order to uncover uncomfortable truths hitherto untold. Not, of course, that this necessarily implies any degree of uniformity in the way women approach their responses. As Elaine Aston has written in *Feminist Views on the English Stage: Women Playwrights, 1990–2000* (2003):

> "Writing women" can take many different forms and there is no one style to characterise the work of women playwrights in the 1990s. Stylistically, they defy categorisation. What they do share, however, is, as [Christopher] Innes observed of post-1970s women's playwriting, a refusal of "standard dramatic forms," whether this is a revisioning of (white) realism by black and Asian women writers, [Sarah] Kane's more explosive treatment of realism in *Blasted*, [Phyllis] Nagy's jazz-style compositions, [Caryl] Churchill's experiments with words and bodies, or [Judy] Upton's techniques of mimetic distortion.

Indeed, Sarah Kane abhorred realism, the dominant strain in British new writing of the 1990s. In Heidi Stephenson and Natasha Langridge's *Rage and Reason: Women Playwrights on Playwriting* (1997), Kane comments perceptively on the critical furor that followed *Blasted*, her first play, in 1995:

> But much more important than the content of the play is the form. All good art is subversive, either in form or content. And the best art is subversive in form *and* content. And often, the element that most outrages those who seek to impose censorship is form. Beckett, Barker, Pinter, Bond — they have all been criticised not so much for the content of their work, but because they use non-naturalistic forms that elude simplistic interpretation. I suspect that if *Blasted* had been a piece of social realism it wouldn't have been so harshly received.

"Sometimes," Kane also told Stephenson and Langridge, "we have to descend into hell imaginatively in order to avoid going there in reality." Interestingly, Kane detested the whole notion of the category "female playwright."

The three writers discussed in this essay — Bryony Lavery, Rona Munro, and Liz Lochhead — have also been bold mold-breakers. I've chosen Lavery and Lochhead because they are true adventurers — buccaneers with a mischievous, subversive wit who take exhilarating formalistic risks. I've included Rona Munro because, like Lochhead, she is part of a Scottish renaissance that should be acknowledged (there is a strange predisposition in the United Kingdom that favors Irish work over its Caledonian counterpart, a subject worthy, at some date, of further scrutiny). But just as importantly, Munro also manifests her own steely sense of uncompromising, formalistic inquiry.

Lavery is prolific. Over twenty-five years, she has poured out a volume of work that amounts to thirty-five to forty pieces (even she has lost count), ranging through stage plays, radio adaptations of fiction such as *Wuthering Heights* (1995), plays for children, feminist cabaret—most, until comparatively recently, relegated to the margins. She has been a performer (an unforgettably naughty Good Fairy in one of her reworked pantos), a teacher, and, for a short time, codirector of Britain's leading gay company, Gay Sweatshop. Her work has run the gamut of styles, with satire, pastiche, and parody her forte. "I am a playwright," she has said. "I like to play . . . with words, with structure . . . to build the right construction for the embodiment of the idea. Naturalism, I don't think I've EVER written naturalism."

Ironically, one of her early plays, *Origin of the Species* (1984), deals precisely with the legacies of the Great Naturalist himself, Charles Darwin. Showing the daring that is her hallmark, she revisited Darwinism by addressing herself to humankind's evolutionary history from the (as yet) untold female side. A play of richly imagined assumptions and guesses, it takes us back to the very beginning of the world through Molly, an older woman and archaeologist, who uncovers a four-million-year-old female, slowly brings her back to life, and introduces her to the ways of "civilization." Molly and Victoria, her discovery, are the only characters in the play.

This "civilizing" of Victoria allows Lavery to weave a latticework of issues and critiques regarding social conditioning, the role of women, mothering, and nurturing. And all of this is a symbiotic process, since Molly also comes to learn things from Victoria, things that make her question the male-centered account of evolution as she has understood it.

In the process, Lavery has enormous fun inventing sounds, making puns, and playing on the idea of language itself, largely through Victoria's growing understanding of it. There is a wonderful exchange at one point where Lavery, always keen to get in a cinematic, popular cue if she can, brings the 1942 film *Casablanca* into the proceedings. Victoria by this time has learned a modicum of speech, and she and Molly are singing an old English song, "On Ilkley Moor bah T'At." Victoria says, "Plaie id again Molly! Plaie id again!" Molly, picking up on Victoria's innocent duplication of Humphrey Bogart's famous lines, responds by saying, "Of all the piano bars in all the towns in all the world . . . and she walks into my piano bar!" Victoria, of course, does not recognize this reference, so Molly explains it, as Victoria asserts, "Id's nodd a piano. Id's a hah-moan-i-yum."

Notwithstanding the playfulness, there's also a serious didactic intent. The relationship between Molly and Victoria turns to love, and the lesbian aesthetic at work here becomes both reference point and subtext. Lavery uses it to question traditional cultural attitudes, challenge taboos, and suggest a different (better) society.

Many years after *Origin of the Species*, Lavery again used these twin strategies of playfulness and subversion in *A Wedding Story* (2000), a moving, twin-tracked love story played out against the fog of (once again) the film *Casablanca*. Here, the cinematic reference point becomes a metaphor mainly for memory loss and bewilderment, as a mother descends into the mental oblivion of Alzheimer's, and her young, cynical, lesbian daughter, who previously had never wanted to be fettered by anything or anybody, surrenders to the demands of her female lover for long-term commitment.

Playfulness abounds. Words take on double meanings. Quick-fire scenes with titles such as "The Engagement" (actually a very naughty scene in the ladies' loo at a wedding) follow in rapid succession. Time present is mixed with times past, and there is a constant juxtaposing of opposing but parallel lives. Scenes of the unspeakable — the mother, Evelyn, in the full throes of Alzheimer's confusion and verbal violence — are juxtaposed to scenes depicting Evelyn as she once was, a distinguished pathopsychologist in her healthy mind. Scenes of the daughter Sally courting her new love are juxtaposed to Evelyn's own courtship and marriage. *Wedding Story* finally is a brilliant structural, thematic, and emotional juggling act — a celebration of love explored in cinematic, jump-cut style, spiced with cultural references (Lavery has an unerring eye for what's modish), deceptive flippancy, and a text in which characters' truncated lines and the spaces between them are written, says Lavery in an Author's Note,

Because   often
They are in   torment.

It is a case of style absolutely mirroring content.

Frozen* (1998) is undoubtedly Lavery's greatest commercial success to date. In advance of a countrywide furor about pedophilia and a flood of plays referring to child abuse, Lavery wrote a play that dared to feature a pedophile as a protagonist, to get inside his head and present him with, if not sympathy, an attempt to understand the reasons for his behavior. Staged by Birmingham Repertory's artistic director Bill Alexander, *Frozen* premiered at the Rep, and in June 2002 the play opened in London at the National Theatre. Two months later came the United Kingdom's worst pedophile crime in years: the murder of two schoolgirls, Holly Wells and Jessica Chapman.

Aside from the eerie confluence of play and event, *Frozen's* success was due to the form Lavery adopted, a form that apparently went against straight narrative but in fact contained an internal logic. She continued the device of parallel lives explored in *Wedding Story* but in triplicate, using monologues.

Lavery has in the past often used the monologue as the most direct route to an audience's feelings. Sometimes this technique can be counterproductive, but in *Frozen,* parallel monologues reflect the interior feelings and journeys to resolution of the victim's mother, the perpetrator, and an American female psychiatrist. Both formally and metaphorically, the monologues reflect individuals locked in frozen emotional states. Then, as the characters unthaw and change, they shift into dialogue. There are no screeching confrontations or noisy resolutions, just the steady drip, drip, drip of events being recalled, information being conveyed, and recrimination tiptoeing up on the pedophile.

The structure shows lives being lived in parallel, but their intersection, when it happens, becomes a force for change. For example, after Nancy, the mother of the victim, visits Ralph, the pedophile, in prison, he begins to feel something small, glittering, and hard — a realization akin to remorse — swelling in his chest. Finally, a dialogue between Nancy and the psychiatrist at Ralph's graveside brings the play to its close, although, unconventionally and uncomfortably, Lavery doesn't round off the proceedings with closure. Leaving questions concerning the nature of forgiveness and the ability to go on hanging in the air, Lavery places responsibility with each audience member.

In a note to this writer, in response to a question about the play's antecedents, Lavery wrote:

> I keep giving different answers to this . . . I wanted to write about the stupidity of evil, the uncreativeness of it . . . the effect of a terrible tragedy on a family. And Forgiveness . . . Revenge . . . and their relative effects and strengths and weaknesses. I don't know where Ralph came from . . . except that he came very easily! But like Evelyn in *Wedding Story* he's a creation that is very interesting to work on because the leap to him is a huge one from him to me, I think, and that is always very rewarding! He's got a closed mind, Evelyn's got a mind that is disappearing . . . and finding the arrangement of words for that is . . . great writing FUN!

When *Frozen* transferred to Broadway in 2004, Lavery noted that, in the intervening years, "there were several places where what had seemed hard to get to . . . suddenly seemed very clear!" She cut some scenes and speeches, added others: "Clearly I overwrote more back then. So it was rather a joy and an adventure to find faster dramatic ways of telling the story."

Lavery's descriptions hint at the seductiveness of the playwriting process itself, at once an Everest and a playpen. Unfortunately, playwriting can also be a precarious business. In September 2004, Lavery found herself at the center of an accusation of plagiarism in regard to *Frozen,* a situation that, as of this writing, remains unresolved. Still, from *Origin* to *Frozen,* Lavery has continued her imaginative exploration of form.

Rona Munro was twenty-two when she wrote *Fugue* (1983), "nearly passing out with excitement all through rehearsals," as she stated in the introduction to the published play. A four-hander working on many levels, its central character is Kay One, a young woman apparently suffering from a nervous breakdown, an event represented by Kay One's memory, Kay Two. There are also a ghost and a psychiatrist, who bear the same name as the central character. Alter egos and split personalities have perhaps now become stylistic clichés, but in 1983, when still a fledgling dramatist, Munro took courage in both hands and used the device with precocity to dramatize confusion and collapse. Kay Two serves the function of that running commentary, the interior voice we all carry around with us that can be critic or support.

Playing Kay One's story of herself against Kay Two's commentary, with interjections from the Ghost and the Psychiatrist, Munro creates a contrapuntal effect that also heightens tension, destabilizing the emotional equilibrium of the audience. The atmosphere the play engenders is of a noose being tightened, which in a sense it is. As in an interrogation, Kay One, both victim and defendant, is trying to answer questions within and outside herself about what has prompted her behavior. Why has she been found wandering in the Scottish highlands in her night clothes? And what is the source of her overwhelming fear? As Kay One speaks, or tries to recall or explain events, Kay Two interrupts, contradicts, and in later stages exhorts—the inner voice made concrete.

Through these various voices—and various answers, justifications, descriptions, hopes for the future, and subsequent disillusionments—Munro builds an account that shimmers with truth, terrifies, and poses disturbing questions. "Fugue" describes the play's structure. As in a piece of music, a theme is started, taken up by another voice, interwoven, and then developed. "Fugue" is also a fascinatingly layered depiction of a clinically recognized psychological state, involving loss of identity and flight from the home environment, in this case Kay One's holiday cottage in the Scottish highlands.

At once a ghost story and a haunting, *Fugue* is, in many senses, the play of a young, overexcited mind. It is overwritten, but it also throbs with ideas about fate and chance, and it is one of the most successful evocations of free-floating, existential female terror I have ever encountered in a play script.

How much of this came from Munro's own experience is not recorded. But she has written of the potency for her of nature and of her Scottish cultural inheritance. *Piper's Cave* (1985), a didactic but fascinating neorealistic account of the forging of a new female identity (again, with doppelgänger effects), is set in an actual physical spot in Scotland and was partly inspired by experiences from Munro's youth. "It came," Munro wrote in an introduction to the play, "out of a childhood spent mainly on my own crawling around woods and cliffs, and out of a desire to try and write about the weird relationship people have with landscape even now we're nearly all living in towns." Again, adventurously, she broke with contemporary dramatic convention, attempting to give metaphorical and emotional qualities to nature by depicting it through a speaking character, Helen, who, it is suggested, might also be the female protagonist's lover.

Piper's Cave explores stereotypes about earth mother identity and male violence. Much later, in *The Maiden Stone* (1994), Munro makes a dense, voluble, bravely ambitious exploration into another aspect of female identity: the question of whether to choose childbearing or a career. Set in nineteenth-century Scotland, *Maiden Stone* finds Munro using Scottish myth, mixing fantasy and symbolism, and employing a distinctive and, to southern British ears, almost incomprehensible Aberdonian dialect. Needless to say, staged at London's Hampstead Theatre, the play might as well have come from another planet, so reviled was it for the intensity of its female preoccupations (to do with fertility, both physiological and artistic), its rejection of straight narrative, and its dense metaphorical language.

Beside these experiments in style and language, *Bold Girls** (1990) and *Iron* (2002) stand out as plays in which Munro appears to adhere to more accessible structures and language. But even *Bold Girls,* a play about working-class Belfast women who are frustrated by the conflict between the English and the Northern Irish, has its non-naturalistic elements. And in *Iron,* Munro plays with memory and time to write about the relationship between a daughter and her mother, who is incarcerated in prison for life.

Iron appears at first to follow the constraints of a docudrama in its verisimilitude; it is set in a prison, where the mother has been sent for killing her husband. But formal experimentation exists in the texture of the conversations between mother and daughter, a texture that reactivates the past in the moment of telling. Through these conversations, Munro weaves the past into the present: the unlocking of the past for the daughter by the only person who can give her the memories she has blocked out since a child and by the only witness to the murder of her father. *Iron* becomes an exercise in multilayering, a play of recall and response in which a daughter finds her identity and frees herself and a mother learns to let go.

For the Scottish playwright Liz Lochhead, cultural inheritance also serves as a fertile launchpad, although one less connected to Scotland's physical landscape than to its linguistic and historical associations.

Since she first broke onto the theater scene with *Blood and Ice* — a difficult birth that extended from 1981 to 1986 — Lochhead has become the acknowledged doyenne of Scottish drama, confronting political issues with verve, caustic wit, and a feminist guile disguised by humor and invention. In certain plays, her language is a mixture of the prosaic and the poetic. *Blood and Ice,* her exploration of Mary Shelley, the author of *Frankenstein, or the Modern Prometheus* (1818), falls into this category. At other times, for example, in *Mary Queen of Scots Got Her Head Chopped Off* (1987), Lochhead's contemporary Scottish vernacular and critical, ironic voice amount to a reassertion of Scottishness over English cultural domination.

A wonderfully fertile reimagining of the historic rivalry between Mary, Queen of Scots, and Elizabeth I of England, Lochhead's play largely dispenses with straight narrative. Created in collaboration with the Scottish Communicado Theatre Company, which specializes in a highly physical form of theater, and first performed at the Lyceum Studio Theatre in Edinburgh, the play emphasizes quick visual transformations: at the crack of a whip, a proud Elizabeth becomes the humble Bessie, loyal serving woman to Mary, Queen of Scots; at the sound of a drumbeat, Mary transforms into modest Marian, gentlewoman to Elizabeth. Lochhead pushes the action along with scenes that are mirror images of each other: first Mary talks, then Elizabeth talks. Circus tricks abound, and a gleeful irreverence that takes its cue from Scotland's strong music hall tradition, which favors direct, broad comedy, often to the point of bad taste.

Politically, Mary and Elizabeth were indeed mirror images of each other: one a Catholic, the other a Protestant; both female rulers in a world dominated by male power; both subject to dynastic determinants that affected the way they conducted their private lives. But their outcomes were different. One lost her head, and the other ruled over a golden age for forty-five years. Lochhead uses the concept of mirror image as a theatrical metaphor to run like indelible ink throughout the play's construction, through the play's songs, rhymes, children's games, and visual and linguistic puns, as well as its political illustrations. Indeed, at the play's end, Lochhead performs a thrilling coup de théâtre by summing up the historical-religious clash between Mary's Catholic supporters and Elizabeth's Protestants in a harsh, ten-minute lampoon. On a contemporary children's playground, the Scottish queen's martyrdom and the English queen's ascendancy are figuratively reflected when a Catholic girl named Marie suffers persecution at the hands of a group of Protestant youngsters. Yesterday's history as today's sectarianism.

Similarly, in *Blood and Ice,* Lochhead does not fix on a linear, cause-and-effect narrative to explain why Mary Shelley came to write *Frankenstein,* although that is certainly there. Instead, like the theatrical painter she also is, she tries to grapple with the very act of creativity itself by evoking atmosphere, creating a canvas of impressionistic images, and again using mirror images to explore female biological determinism and the sacrifices a woman makes to be an artist.

During the play's painful gestation, Lochhead honed and pruned. She used characters in Mary Shelley's life—the poet Byron; her husband, the poet Percy Bysshe Shelley; and her half sister, Claire—to exemplify aspects of Shelley's consciousness and imagination. Eventually she added a servant to the story line and put the monster onstage from the very beginning.

Through the servant Elise, Lochhead tries to show the contradictions within Mary Shelley. Daughter of Mary Wollstonecraft, the author of *The Vindication of the Rights of Women* (1792), Mary is unable to live up to her intellectual inheritance. She may talk idealism and liberation with her friends, but in reality she is still imprisoned by class and social prejudice. When Elise becomes pregnant, Mary reverts to traditional norms: she sacks Elise and insists that she marry the putative father, a response that points to Mary's hypocrisy as well as, in the case of Elise, to the restrictions that nineteenth-century society still foisted onto ordinary working women.

As for the monster itself, its presence is felt as a permanent, if shadowy, stage figure, as though always on the edge of our—and Mary's—consciousness. The monster is a being whose significance ranges from the obvious one of being "other" to Lochhead's far more interesting and original invention: the terror of creativity itself.

Comparisons are frequently invidious, but the contrast between the playwright Howard Brenton's treatment of the same characters and events in *Bloody Poetry* (1984) and Lochhead's *Blood and Ice* is instructive. Brenton takes a linear, male-centered approach to writing his play. He brings to the fore Byron and Percy Bysshe Shelley as the all-important creative protagonists and pushes the women to the background.

Lochhead's protagonist is clearly Mary Shelley, who attempts to combine motherhood, domestic life, and literary creativity. In Lochhead's approach,

Mary Shelley's attempt is articulated through metaphor, mirror imagery, and the physical manifestation of the monster. His words close the play: "Come, pursue This, chase This, till This shall catch you . . . ," an indication of Lochhead's fresh, allusive handling of a familiar subject: the difficult, often compromised, gestation and pursuit of female creativity.

TWELVE

Joking Aside

A Conversation about Comedy with Christopher Durang, Gina Gionfriddo, Sarah Ruhl, and Wendy Wasserstein

❦

The following conversation took place with the playwrights Christopher Durang, who was a judge for the Susan Smith Blackburn Prize in 2002–2003; Gina Gion-friddo, who was a co-winner of the prize in 2002–2003 for her comedy U.S. Drag; *Sarah Ruhl, whose play* The Clean House *received the prize in 2003–2004; and Wendy Wasserstein, who was a finalist with* Uncommon Women and Others *during the prize's first year, 1978–1979, and again in 1981–1982 for* Isn't It Romantic. *Wasserstein won the Blackburn Prize in 1988–1989 for* The Heidi Chronicles. *During the conversation, the editor was on hand to serve as moderator, although after the first question—"What do you laugh at?"—a moderator was unnecessary.*

WENDY WASSERSTEIN: One thing I've often noticed is that the playwrights I know have some of the best laughs. And I can recognize them in the theater in the dark. I can hear Christopher's laugh. I used to be able to hear [playwright] Albert Innaurato's laugh. I have a very high-pitched and childish laugh. I've often noticed that at plays—certainly at their own plays—if you hear this lone howl in the wilderness, it's the playwright. Do you think that's true?

CHRISTOPHER DURANG: Well, I do have a distinctive laugh. Do you mean, do lots of people who work in comedy have distinctive and noticeable laughs? I had a conversation with my aunt yesterday. She's been having some health issues, and I've discovered that if I send her tapes of *I Love Lucy*, bought through Amazon, it cheers her up. So I just sent her a new five-episode tape, and she was telling me that she was enjoying it and laughing, and a friend of hers came in who also liked it but didn't make a sound with her laughter. Would open her mouth and move her body, but wouldn't make any sound.

And my aunt said, "Are you laughing?" I wonder whether you have to laugh out loud to be connected to it. Do you both laugh out loud, or not?

SARAH RUHL: I do, but I have a quiet laugh. I'll kind of snicker quietly. Maybe it's because my mom has a very loud laugh, which is nice, you know, to hear your mother's laugh. But maybe I purposely don't have a loud one.

GINA GIONFRIDDO: I don't think I laugh out loud. I know I never laugh at purely slapstick, purely physical, comedy. I went to see the screening of a Buster Keaton movie in Providence, Rhode Island, and everyone was laughing. And I enjoyed it, but it didn't get a laugh out of me. The Three Stooges have never gotten a laugh out of me. The falling-down-on-the-banana-peel stuff, I never have really risen to in terms of laughing out loud. I don't think I have a distinctive laugh, but I now know the stuff that I laugh at — I seek out political lampooning. And then I don't laugh, but I sit in my apartment in front of the television and go, "Oh, no, you didn't just do that. Oh, no, you didn't just do that." I talk back more than laugh.

WW: Because I have a four-year-old daughter, I notice what makes her laugh. She will laugh at the slapstick, she will laugh at the chocolate falling on the floor, or someone getting covered in chocolate. She will laugh, and it's such a genuine laugh, that I'll start laughing, too. But if I wasn't with her, I, like you, would never laugh at Buster Keaton or anything like that.

SR: Often, even infants have a sense of humor, and you can look at them and know that they can tell when their parents are joking. How is it they can tell? It's not language based.

WW: It's not a sense of irony. I know that my daughter's sense of humor has been developed over time. But the initial things she found funny tended to be slapstick, and that still makes her laugh.

CD: I also am not a big fan of silent film comedies, because of the slapstick. But I have to admit, I'm such a corny person, I've grown fond of watching reruns of *Candid Camera*. In one of the live situations, they were set up on a moving train to serve food, and they had a trick tray, so that they would go toward the person, and all the dishes would almost fall, and the people's jerking-back response actually did make me laugh. And I have no idea why.

WW: My daughter's name is Lucy Jane, and I partially named her for Lucille Ball. Once, on a terrible night in Rochester, New York, I was stuck at an Omni Hotel — a really bad night — and at three o'clock in the morning, on came Lucille Ball. And I thought, "This woman has just saved my life." There she was, and watching her, I thought, "This is so funny, and her craft is so great."

SR: I think women are taught to be beautiful and to laugh at men's jokes. So it's rare to find a woman who is outside of that paradigm.

CD: With a couple of friends, particularly when I was in my twenties, I've had what a therapist would call inappropriate laughter, because we were telling stories that at their core were upsetting. Something that did happen in my life, which I put in my play *The Marriage of Bette and Boo* (1985), was that my father, who had a drinking problem, knocked gravy on the rug, and my mother got real angry. He was a little drunk, and so she told him to clean it up, and he came out with the vacuum and started vacuuming. And she kept screaming, "You don't vacuum gravy." And "You don't vacuum gravy" is actually funny on some level when, fifteen years later, with distance and perspective, you tell it to somebody.

I think of that famous *Mary Tyler Moore* episode where Mary laughs at the funeral of Chuckles the Clown. It's an episode about inappropriate laughter, and it's very funny. Also, the setup was that the whole first half of the episode, Mary is angry at everybody who's laughing that Chuckles the Clown died because he was stepped on by an elephant. Then she ends up laughing uncontrollably at the funeral. Delayed inappropriate laughter.

GG: There definitely is a class of humor that is aggressive, and I would put in there that *Candid Camera* routine. There's something funny about victimizing the innocent and laughing at people who don't know the joke is on them. It's an aggressive impulse in some way. In fact, *Candid Camera* was just sued for humiliating a man. It was an airline security joke, which was inappropriate to begin with, but they told a guy he had to lie down in order to go through the metal detector. And he did and he was injured. He had some terrible bruise (I watched this on *Court TV,* which is my other addiction): *Comedy Central, Court TV.* Until somebody really gets hurt, a joke is funny.

SR: I remember hearing the critic John Lahr speak about humor and aggression, and I thought his ideas were so sexist, because he kept saying that humor was masculine and aggressive, that comic metaphors were masculine. You know, you "stick it to him." He was talking about all these sexualized metaphors for why comedians make people laugh, and that it was an act of masculine sexual aggression. But I think comedy can be quite the opposite. You're taking something in and accepting it as true, and that can be funny. Life is funny, because it's both tragic and bizarre. Laughter is a kind of acceptance.

CD: I don't think that there is one theory of why we laugh. Sometimes in comedy, anger makes me laugh. There's a British actress, Penelope Keith, who plays this really angry person in the television version of *The Norman Conquests* (1978). She just wants to set the table. And when somebody switches things so that the table isn't set right, she goes into a fury. Not just irritation; fury. And her fury is funny.

I remembered something this morning on the bus, and it was, "Getting the first laugh is so important in a play." It's one of Mike Nichols's paradigms about direction, that the director and actors have to communicate permission to laugh.

WW: Gerald Gutierrez, who was a very good director of comedy, would talk about not only getting your first laugh but also what kind of laugh it was. Because if you're putting on the musical *The Producers* (2001) or Aristophanes' *The Clouds* (423 B.C.), you're establishing a different kind of comedy than if you're doing a play of wit. I find also, that when a reviewer has said a play is funny, suddenly the audience is laughing at things like, "I washed my socks today." And if you listen to the language, you think, "Well, that's not really funny."

SR: In *The Clean House* (2004), a Brazilian maid tells a long joke in Portuguese to the audience and then she exits. And when I wrote that, I didn't intend it to be funny particularly. I was just interested in the question of translation, and would you know if someone was telling a joke in another language, would that be formally communicated. Recently we did a reading where we actually had the maid tell a joke. I'd been trying to collect the perfect joke in Portuguese, and we got a Spanish professor to help us, and he's not that funny, but he has this whole file of jokes. And he was telling them to me, and I thought, "Oh, damn, they don't translate. It's not funny to hear them in another language." Because he was reading them as though they were on a language tape, very formally. But then the actress took the joke he had given her, and she was very funny, because gesturally she was funny and rhythmically she was funny. So I don't know why this continues to fascinate me, whether or not jokes are really translatable. Some of the jokes I've collected in Portuguese are absolutely not. They have a lot of parrot jokes.

CD: When I read the play, I assumed that the main humor of it was that an English-speaking audience was listening to someone tell something in Portuguese that was a joke, that there was no way they could understand it, and that was actually what you expected the audience to find funny. Is that right?

SR: I suppose so. I guess I never expect audiences to find something funny or not funny. I was just interested in the problem of translation. Maybe it secretly amused me, and I wasn't aware of it.

CD: What about the conversations between the maid who doesn't want to clean, which is to me a funny setup, and the woman she's working for, who is angry about it and keeps confronting her? I think those situations are funny. Do you think they're funny?

SR: Yes, I think they're funny. But sometimes you don't know something is funny until you write. The impulse for the play was a true story that I had heard about a maid from Brazil who was depressed and wouldn't clean the house. And her employer, a doctor, took her to the hospital and had her medicated, and she still wouldn't clean. I found that tragic. Also absurd. And when I started writing, there was anger at the doctor who had medicated her and then was up in arms that her maid still wouldn't clean.

ww: What's really funny in the play is that it comes from the character, that the maid won't clean. It plays as funny because you've captured the character there. I find that when the character work is good, then things become funny. For myself, I find it harder to say, "Oh, I'm going to be funny, and this will be my vessel," than to show what particular characters do.

I was struck, Sarah, by what you said about comedy being considered masculine. I don't agree with that either. My writing comes from that school of women writers—Clare Boothe Luce, Anita Loos, Edna Ferber—who wrote witty women. I know a lot about this, because Christopher used to take me to see their movies when I was young. That tradition has sort of fallen down; a lot of it gets filtered into television now. But basically the women whom I write are witty people, and they're witty and funny for a reason, whether they're deflecting, whether they're trying to puncture male pretentiousness, whether this is how they get by in society. These people happen to be funny or witty or ironic for a reason. Line for line, it scales as funny, but it actually has to do with character.

sr: It's interesting to me that not only is it difficult to be funny as a writer, but even characters, if they try to be funny, would be unfunny. There are two levels of distancing. There has to be a rhetorical situation where the characters are not trying to be funny but they're funny anyway, and as a writer you have to be writing about something else in order for humor to emerge. Chris, can you try to be funny and then be funny?

cd: Uh, no. Particularly not in person. When I have a meeting with movie people, I usually say up front: I'm not funny in person. They think I'm going to be Robin Williams, and Robin Williams is Robin Williams. No, I'm mostly drawn to comedy that comes out of character, which I think probably works best in most theater comedy. Even in farce, where the character might be stuck in certain traits.

gg: I watch a lot of sketch comedy; I love sketch comedy. Yet I don't think that's a skill I have. I would be terrified to have to go into a room and write David Letterman's monologues: "Here are the events of the day, give me your best one-liners." I couldn't do it. I do think I can write comically, but it has to come out of story and character and situation. I can't really do jokes.

ww: I can't either. If someone told me, "Write jokes," I couldn't do it. Monologues, maybe. I can't give a toast. Someone will say, "Oh, you're so funny, give a toast." I can't do it. It's just not funny, because it needs that character in a situation.

CD: The rhythm of a line is important, too, in comedy, and not just because a key word will be funny, although sometimes a crisp sound will be funny. I'm thinking of a line from *Isn't It Romantic* (1981). The girl is shy, and she's sitting with her arms crossed, clutching her purse . . .

WW: Someone says, "You're clutching your purse." And the girl says, "I have valuables."

CD: Right, right. "I have valuables." There is something to the brevity of the line that's comic. It would never be funny if she said, "I could never put this purse down of course, you see, because, you know, I have valuables." There's something about it being at the ready that's funny.

When I wrote plays in high school, I was startled when I got laughs. Even when I was writing *Sister Mary Ignatius Explains It All for You* (1979). The impetus for writing the play was serious: my mother was dying of cancer. I no longer believed in the Catholic faith I'd been brought up in and I was wishing I did, because it's very hard to deal with someone who's dying and not be able to say, "Don't worry, you're going to Heaven," and all this stuff. So I found myself (a) wishing that I had the belief a little and (b) thinking back on the rules, which were intricate. So my impulse in writing the play was not to be funny but to have a representative of the church come out and explain absolutely everything in the world. And as I was writing, I would say, "Oh, non-Catholics won't know that," so I expanded it so that Sister Mary was talking to non-Catholics, too.

I had not a clue how funny that play really was, especially the first half. But by just presenting it straight, it frankly struck many people's ears, as it soon struck mine, as funny. The presenting of debatable thoughts as fact ended up sounding funny. The first time I heard the play aloud, which was a reading with Jane Hoffman, I knew it was funny. But just writing it, I didn't. The juxtapositions of things, or the way they were said, would sometimes make them funny.

Though one part of the play is not meant to be funny at all. One of the characters who shows up is an ex-student who's both been raped and had two abortions, and her mother died of cancer. She gets very mad at Sister and tells her off and talks about losing her own faith. And when I wrote it, I thought, "Oh, my God, what am I writing? This isn't funny at all, this is just serious." And that is true. It's still uncomfortable for me to sit through that speech, because I can't tell if the audience is interested, bored—I just can't tell. I'm so used to judging things by humor, which of course you don't do with a noncomic play—or with a noncomic section of a comedy. Not to mention you're changing tone.

GG: There's a line in that play that's always stuck with me, and I'm going to get it wrong, but it's an example of dark comedy. Somebody says, "Well, God doesn't answer," and the Sister says, "Well, He always answers, it's just sometimes He says 'No.'"

CD: And by the way that is one of the biggest laughs in the play, and it's simply what we were told. I wasn't literally quoting, but you know, "God never closes a door without opening a window." That was a really big laugh.

SR: Catholicism is just sort of inherently funny. [Laughter]

CD: I do think that knowing what's funny is an instinct. I seem to know it in my gut. It's not like a science. I don't think you can teach comic writing.

WW: Do you remember the Famous Artists School? They used to have pictures: "If you can draw this, you can be an artist." If you can draw this comic writer, you too . . .

CD: I think writers can be mentored. People can read your script and say, "I have this reaction." It's not that the mentor necessarily knows the truth, but you're getting feedback. When I teach at Juilliard, I have some writers who are innately comic and then others who are very good writers but aren't comic—just as there are good actors who aren't comic. And then there are some writers who are in the middle. But I've found to my surprise that one of the things I have to tell my students about is exposition. You know how some people cannot tell a joke, and usually the people who can't tell a joke, they leave out the important parts of the setup? They've forgotten to tell you that they're sitting behind a bookcase or something? Especially with a comedy, everything has to be very well defined for the joke to work. It's a boring word, "exposition," but it's one of the few things I think can be discussed in teaching. Although, practice makes perfect. Sometimes just working on plays is where you learn, as opposed to a classroom.

WW: Definitely. After you've been writing plays for a while and working with directors. Gerry Gutierrez asking, "What kind of first laugh are you getting?" I didn't know about that. I learned from standing with Gerry watching *Isn't It Romantic* and waiting for the first laugh. Trying to set up what kind of comedy it was, that it was a boulevard comedy, that there was permission to laugh.

CD: Audience expectations.

WW: Yes, audience expectations.

SR: I'm still interested in what you said about a director asking you to cut a joke because there were too many jokes.

WW: I get this all the time. I got it from Dan Sullivan at the first preview of *The*

Sisters Rosensweig (1993). It's a well-made boulevard comedy, but it starred two comic geniuses, Madeline Kahn and Robert Klein. So we go to the first preview of this play, and Madeline is so funny that when she goes off stage, you lose the through-line of the play, which is about Jewish identity, American identity. A woman lights the Sabbath candle, her sister blows it out, somebody's had a hysterectomy. All sorts of stuff going on there. From the audience you'd hear cough, cough, cough. So afterward, Dan took me out and said, "We're going to have to look at the story you're trying to tell, and you're going to have to cut some of Dr. Gorgeous, because when it's too funny, you've got a problem. You've got almost hysteria, and then the play just drops." It was almost as if the rustics had run off with the play.

I've noticed that with my plays, because the comic characters, which I write best — sometimes I think this is true of Chris's plays, too — are the more vivid supporting roles. They're larger, they're funnier. And the through-line character — the Heidi, the observer, Sara Goode in *The Sisters Rosensweig* — they're a beige color. So what happens is, the brighter comedy, the people in red with the bright red hair, the people that make me laugh, too — can change the shape of the show.

CD: Did you end up cutting a lot?

WW: I did end up cutting a lot. Sometimes I look at that material and think it would have been nice just to do an evening of Madeline Kahn and Dr. Gorgeous. It was bliss. It was true bliss.

CD: I think the balance in the finished product is quite good.

WW: That's half an hour less of that play, after the first preview. And it's very hard to cut, if you're a comic writer and people are laughing at it. You want to go, "No, no."

CD: Jerry Zaks would tell an actor, if he had a speech that maybe had four laughs in it, "Don't stop for the first three, push through, because if you don't take a breath, you'll get a big laugh at the end. Otherwise you'll get four small ones." That was a smart and interesting hint. [Pause]

SR: Comedy can be subversive. Laughing at a nun, laughing at a dictator. It's a democratic thing.

CD: Yeah, it can be subversive. I don't watch David Letterman or Jay Leno too much, but sometimes, if they're poking fun at the president, and there's some sting to it, that really can have a big effect. If you have straight political discourse, it's very unlikely that you will be able to change anyone's point of view. A year after *Sister Mary Ignatius* opened in New York, it was protested by what I would call conservative groups, and they tried to shut the play down in St. Louis and then in Boston. There was a *Phil Donahue Show* about it, which actually made the box office go up in both New York and Los Angeles. I gave permission for the Donahue people to use footage from the L.A. production, and even the audience that was objecting to the play stood up and said, "Well, I have to admit it's funny."

I didn't expect people to be angry with the play. I thought everyone would just agree with me. I thought I was just saying sensible things. But some people literally believed everything that Sister taught, and the idea of a roomful of people laughing at her was just infuriating to them. And some people didn't believe in Limbo anymore, but nonetheless they had strict reverence for what they had been taught and still partially believed in. It was like a family who doesn't allow criticism of the family. Those people I angered a great deal.

SR: You take someone's power away, even for a moment, if you can laugh at them.

GG: Political comedy is being done very well on television. In theater, the problem is that the time between writing and production takes so long, you risk having the comedy become dated by the time the play goes on.

SR: I think comedy is a tool for anyone who has a bit of distance from the thing itself, who is outside looking in.

GG: These political satirists on television, I feel as though I need them at the end of the day. I need my cleansing bit of lampooning. I definitely feel purged and healed in some way, which is one of the major ways that comedy functions for me. You talked about sending *I Love Lucy* tapes to your aunt, Chris, and I know that the times in my life when I was going through illness, I really needed comedy, and I needed a certain kind of comedy. I'm not sure what that phenomenon is, but I think there is a way in which comedy heals us.

WW: My daughter was a premature baby, and I found that the way to get through hospital stays was to have been a comic writer and have a comic eye on the whole situation. On whatever level, I found it all sort of funny. Also, because I had worked in the theater, I had that ability to collaborate, so I actually didn't think all these doctors were maniacs; the lights are low, let's just do this. But if I had gone through that without a sense of humor, it would have been devastating. Just devastating.

CD: When I've had some depressed periods, I've chosen to watch *Fawlty Towers* or *Monty Python,* and they actually have succeeded in helping. I mostly can't write when I'm depressed or in the midst of whatever's upsetting me. When I do write, I'm usually either in a good mood or a neutral mood.

SR: In relation to that, I wonder about what you mentioned earlier, Chris—the story of your father spilling the gravy. You have a horrible experience, you stage it, and then all these people laugh at this horrible experience.

CD: I felt the topic was tamed for me psychologically. It was put in a little construct. Plus, it was many years later, there was now distance from the event. In a really nutty play of mine called *Titanic* (1983), there's a really sicko family on the *Titanic,* and the *Titanic* keeps not sinking, and they want it to sink and they drill holes in the bottom. I thought it was just a surreal fantasy that popped into my head. Years after writing it, I realized, "Oh, strong-willed people hitting heads and doing terrible things to each other—I recognize this theme from my past." These surreal, over-the-top characters came from feelings I had about my extended family, but I didn't know that when I was writing the play. But I did feel a kind of relief, putting this mishmash of characters butting heads on the stage, putting it out there.

SR: Did you know that there is a disease where you laugh all the time? It's called excessive mirth.

PART FOUR

The Expanding World of Women's Plays

The Expanding World of Women's Plays

Women have traveled a long way in the theater that owes its traditions to ancient Greece. Once excluded from the production of theater completely, then looked upon mainly as actors, women are now producers, directors, designers, and, of course, playwrights. Since the 1970s, when the second wave of feminism brought an influx of female dramatists, women have remained steadfast adherents of the playwright's art. In a mere three decades, they have forged a history to which new playwrights can turn for inspiration, education, and mentoring.

This is not to say that women have attained parity with their male colleagues in terms of the numbers of plays produced. Quite the contrary. In the United Kingdom, a 1994 survey of theaters funded by the Arts Council of Great Britain revealed that productions "written, devised or adapted by women or from books by women" accounted for merely 20 percent of all the work performed in 1994. In 1985–1986, the figure had actually been higher: 22 percent.

In the United States, the situation is similar. According to the 2002 report released by the Theatre Program of the New York State Council on the Arts — prepared by Suzanne Bennett and Susan Jonas and titled *Report on the Status of Women in Theatre: A Limited Engagement?* — during the 1994–1995 season, plays authored by women represented 17 percent of the productions at Off-Broadway and regional theaters that are members of Theatre Communications Group (TCG), the national service organization for nonprofit theaters. Using a later database — the 1,900 productions staged in 2000–2001 by TCG theaters — Bennett and Jonas discovered that 20 percent of the plays had a woman "on the writing team." The following season, however — 2001–2002 — the proportion of female playwrights represented at TCG theaters had dropped back to 17 percent. So far, this study is the only one of its kind in the United States.

And there are larger difficulties facing women who write plays, as there are facing men. In the past three decades, the challenges to freedom of expression continue to arise, from individuals and communities who live under, or represent, all forms of government. In 1989, after the Anglo-Indian writer Salman Rushdie published his novel *The Satanic Verses,* the Ayatollah Ruhollah Khomeini, then the spiritual leader of Iran, called on Muslims to assassinate Rushdie for what Khomeini considered a blasphemous book that insulted Islam (the novel was banned in India and South Africa and burned on the streets in Bradford, England). Rushdie went into hiding.

In the United States in 1990, the chairman of the National Endowment for the Arts, John Frohnmayer, vetoed grants that had been awarded to four solo performers, Karen Finley, Tim Miller, John Fleck, and Holly Hughes; he cited the works' sexual content (courts eventually ruled that Frohnmayer's directive had been unconstitutional). In December 2004, when England's Birmingham Repertory Theatre produced Gurpreet Kaur Bhatti's play *Behzti* (*Dishonour*)*, members of Birmingham's Sikh community protested. After one protest turned violent and Bhatti, a British-born Sikh, received death threats, the theater shuttered the production. Bhatti went into hiding for many weeks.

The events surrounding *Behzti,* which won the Susan Smith Blackburn Prize in 2005, raise issues of concern to playwrights and audiences alike. Most of the Sikhs who protested the play had neither seen it nor read it; they had only heard about its content. They objected in particular to Bhatti's putting a rape of a woman, and the subsequent murder of the rapist, in a Sikh temple, a religious place where, they asserted, such acts could never occur. Sikh community leaders in Birmingham had asked the Repertory Theatre and Bhatti to change the play's setting; the theater's administration and the playwright had refused, proclaiming an artist's right to freedom of expression.

Protests were generally peaceful, but one night a few Sikh men broke into the theater during a performance, destroying property and frightening the theater's staff. The Birmingham police and the Sikh leaders indicated that if the production continued they could not guarantee that the violence would stop.

There is much to think about in this situation, including the purpose of art and the role of an arts institution in a community. Most playwrights would agree that theater, at its best, challenges and confronts an audience — that theater does not exist to encourage unanimity or emotional and intellectual safety but to ask questions, some of which may be unpleasant to hear.

But what responsibility does a theater have to its potential audience? In a world where tensions between differing cultures run so high, how and where does a theater set limits on its own responsiveness? Perhaps even more important, how does an arts organization teach a community not to be afraid of art?

The status of Rushdie's *fatwa* is uncertain, although he no longer lives in hiding. In 2005, he wrote an article for the April 17 issue of the *New York Times Book Review* on the occasion of PEN World Voices: The New York Festival on International Literature. He wrote, "In many parts of the world . . . the free imagination is still considered dangerous," and it is essential to defend writers who come under attack "by powerful interests who fear and threaten them." But he also wrote that it is important to engage in a "global dialogue" and see "what bridges can be built."

Drawing on her own experience, Gurpreet Kaur Bhatti also addresses a human being's right to imagination, in a brief essay, "The Freedom to Create." Ongoing creativity, she notes, is an artist's strongest affirmation.

The residue from artistic censorship affects all playwrights, even if they have not had to confront it directly. But on a day-to-day basis, most dramatists wrestle with issues of survival: how to find the time and the quiet to write; how to get their plays produced; whether to write for film and television and risk abandoning theater; how to maintain psychological health in the face of rejection; how to establish personal relationships.

The two major waves of feminism that swept across part of the world, at the end of the nineteenth century and again in the second half of the twentieth, liberated women from hundreds of years of restriction. As a result, women in many countries can work in the theater and be largely free from society's criticism, can travel where they want to pursue their careers — can have careers in the first place. The only thing that holds them back is the theater itself. As women's freedoms have expanded, the theater in some respects has contracted. Though there are numerous theaters, tight budgets limit the number of new plays artistic directors can produce. Theaters suffering from tight budgets take fewer artistic risks, for fear of alienating the audiences and the funding sources they need so badly.

Despite the difficulties they encounter, women continue to write plays for the English-speaking stage. As the essays from dramatists in Canada, South Africa, Australia, and New Zealand indicate, the world of women's plays is always growing. And unquestionably, newly dedicated women are moved to write for the theater. Like Sarah Ruhl in the United States and Moira Buffini and Rukhsana Ahmad in the United Kingdom, they find that plays provide a unique means of expression for their imaginations and ideas.

But different generations of women see their places in theater differently. Judith Thompson of Canada, whose drama *Habitat* was a finalist for the Susan Smith Blackburn Prize in 2002–2003, and Jean Betts of New Zealand, whose *The Collective** was a finalist in 2003–2004, both came to playwriting when the Women's Movement steamed at full throttle, and they staunchly maintain their identities as women playwrights and advocate greater strength and visibility for women in the theater. Rukhsana Ahmad, although she has come to theater relatively late in her literary career, also drew inspiration from the Women's Movement and declares herself a feminist.

The youngest generation of playwrights is not so sure. They do not want to be categorized as "women playwrights" — like Moira Buffini, they want to talk about politics, they want to talk about their art; they leave that other discussion behind, as if it were a dress they had finally outgrown. The exuberant communities of theater women that emerged in the 1970s and early 1980s have largely disappeared, replaced by women seeking their individual fortunes. But an independent racer does not necessarily find the track easier to run. As Sarah Ruhl notes in her interview, women are often aware that they have to work harder than men to be noticed in the theater. The advantage, says Ruhl, is that women's art is better for the struggle.

And playwriting is a struggle, Timberlake Wertenbaker writes frankly and humorously in her letter to the fictitious Emily. Marsha Norman, in her introduction to this book, points accusingly to what she considers the scourge of play development in the United States, notably, readings that often do not lead to productions. Norman warns, also, against the danger to inspiration lurking in the temptingly high-paying worlds of film and television. Yes, she acknowledges, looking back on her own career, there are certainly more women writing plays than when she burst on the scene in the 1970s. The newest generation of female playwrights is equipped with extraordinary artistry. But how long will talented women remain in a field that often still disregards their art and usually underpays them?

Looking back at Norman's introduction, it is as much a warning to the theater as a heart-to-heart with playwrights. Unless the attitudes within contemporary theater change, she suggests, it may lose the voices for whom the past three decades of women writing plays have paved the way.

THIRTEEN

The Freedom to Create

GURPREET KAUR BHATTI

❦

I like to play. The word itself excites me. As an adult, I claim it in the theatrical arena: I am a writer of plays. But it is the child in whom play encompasses absolute freedom of the spirit. In the school yard, where the conflicts of life are enacted, children rejoice in the seemingly effortless arc of invention.

Whereas the games of adults are ordered and controlled, the fearlessness of youth demands that play examine all areas of the soul—the unpalatable and the dark alongside the joyful and the light.

When we connect with this boundless liberty, we create. This connection can be uncomfortable and painful, and it requires bravery and endurance. In the process of theater, I believe it is the duty of the writer to undertake this journey, to inhabit the core of the imagination and celebrate the power of the word.

This freedom to play, to dream and pretend, is a human right. Without such freedom there could be no art, and without art we would be inhuman beings, unable to properly exist and fulfill our potential. Our creativity sustains us in the same way as breathing, eating, and sleeping.

If each human life is a miracle, then we all possess the miraculous gift of imagination. This ought to be cherished and encouraged, because it is the core of our humanity and, aside from physical appearance, is the very thing that sets us apart from each other. Without imagination, we would be devoid of the extraordinary possibility of our own thinking.

God is often referred to as the Creator. Creativity is godly, if born of honest and passionate truth. And as long as this is the case, I consider that no individual has the right to censor another's art.

Artists have always had to fight for the right of self-expression. Challenging ideas, and a propensity to provoke, often sit uneasily with social mores, governments, and the agendas of organized institutions. That's fine, as long as the work is allowed to happen. When the law ceases to protect the artist, then society is left with a set of sorry questions: Why is it that some people so fear the power of another's imagination? And why can they not bear the threat of lawful offense?

In such situations, artists are forced to fight harder than ever. And I think the best way to fight is to continue to create. But please note that this is a triumphant battle, because we are simply doing what sustains us and keeps us alive.

It is none of my business what anyone says or thinks about me; while people disappoint and fail and err (and thank God they do, they are simply human beings), the truth has yet to let me down. I only know that I have learned great lessons of tolerance and courage and that as an artist, nothing can restore me more than the flourishing of my imagination. So it is up to me to be brave and to approach my work with the exquisite freedom found in an animated school yard.

FOURTEEN

Beyond the U.S.A., Beyond the U.K.

FATIMA DIKE, PETA TAIT, JEAN BETTS,
AND JUDITH THOMPSON

❦

A View from South Africa
FATIMA DIKE

Writing came to me in the early 1970s, not as an artistic outlet, but as a way of expressing the pain within, the pain of not understanding the oppression of black people in South Africa. The 1970s were significant in South Africa, because it was at this time that the very first black poets of the struggle emerged. Oswald Mtshali, Sipho Sepamla. Wally Serote's poetry was like a coiled spring ready to uncoil. His description of Johannesburg, the City of Gold, used metaphors that made you understand the writer's understanding of oppression.

I came into writing at a time of hope and at a time of despair. America was experiencing the Black Power Movement, which was sweeping the world, bringing hope to oppressed peoples everywhere. South Africa was going through one of its most oppressive periods: the Treason Trials plus the Rivonia Trials sent our leadership into prison for life. Our political parties were banned, and the cream of black South Africa left their homeland to go into exile, leaving a deadly silence behind.

We sustained our struggle by listening to black music, we watched black films born out of the sixties struggle in the United States. We knew the stories of the Black Panthers, Malcolm X, Martin Luther King Jr., Angela Davis, Stokely Carmichael, Nikki Giovanni, to name just a few. Then, in the early seventies, Steve Biko made waves in South Africa with his Black Consciousness Movement, and we quickly latched onto it.

Protest theater came into its own at the same time. It was Black and Proud and very dignified. It made us feel the same way, too, but most of all it left us thinking very deeply about who we were at the time and how we had accepted oppression. This theater was outspoken and unafraid. In fact, it challenged the very system that was oppressing us. This theater was about the castration of black men by a white system, performed by black men. They played the roles of blacks and whites, giving the audience their understanding of white people. These companies were made up of men mostly, but you could find a few sisters here and there. But the roles they played were written by men, and therefore I always felt that the characters were interpretations of women through male eyes. Most of the plays were patronizing, although some of them tried to portray us in a somewhat dignified manner. But the bottom line was that we had not come into our own in the theater. Most of these ladies came from the school of Gibson Kente, the father of Township Theater, and they were cast in these plays because they could sing, because some could act, and others could dance. They were brought into these male-led companies because of these talents, and they would end up learning stagecraft hands-on, since there were no drama schools for black people.

This was the state of theater in South Africa when I started to write.

I was born in Cape Town in the township of Langa; my parents came from Somerset East in the Eastern Cape Province. My father passed on when I was seven years old, and my mother carried the burden of bringing us up single-handedly, along with my brother's children, who were born out of wedlock. Although my mother came from the country, she did not look rural; she looked royal. Even though she worked as a domestic for most of her life, there was a regalness about her. In the way she put on her makeup, the way she dressed, and the way in which she brought us up. Both my elder sisters had bicycles, something that was rare in the townships in the 1950s. They both went to boarding school for their high school education, and so did I. I ended up in a Catholic boarding school in the Transvaal, where I was taught by Irish nuns whose headquarters were in Birmingham, England.

I began to read voraciously at this time, because in each of our classrooms there were bookshelves with books in English, Afrikaans, and Setswana. The English books caught my eye, and I read like I had never read in my life. By the time I had finished my secondary school education at St. Anne's, I had read over a hundred books, most of which were English classics: Charles Dickens, Robert Louis Stevenson, Emily Brontë. Through these books, I traveled in my mind to places far away. English became my favorite subject at school, but, since it was a second language, the art of essay and letter writing proved to be a challenge, a challenge that prevented me from getting 300 out of 300 in the English exam. I tried very hard to improve my letter writing and my essays, but alas, I never got all the marks in any English exam. After English, history was my favorite subject.

Around 1968 and 1969, I met white friends through my best friend, Cussien Mngqolo, whom I grew up with. They were mostly University of Cape Town (UCT) students who were studying architecture, but they were also interested in the arts. This is how I met my friend Sue Clark. She is a poet, a lover of the arts, and she loves artists. She threw parties at her house, and you could meet a cross section of people at any given time at her parties. There were students from UCT, of course, as well as lecturers, poets, and professors. She got me interested in the poetry of Sylvia Plath. But Sylvia didn't speak to me about my problems. Then, when the black poets emerged, Sue found their books and bought them for me to read. Immediately, I was captured by their understanding of my problems as a black woman growing up in South Africa. She took me to summer school at the university, so that I could hear them reading their poetry. A whole new world opened up for me, and another era of reading came to me. Very slowly, my two worlds came together: I was given books to read by my white friends in town, and my black friends in the township were also discovering books. I was introduced to Credo Mutwa's *Indaba, My Children* (1966), on whose heels soon followed his most dynamic book, *Africa Is My Witness* (1966), which was banned immediately after it was published.

Credo Mutwa is a divine/healer, who has been researching the history of Africa and Africans. *Africa Is My Witness* was banned because it revealed the wisdom of Africa and Africans, but also brought the evils of colonialism and racism to light. The first half of the book gave a history of the continent of Africa, the wealth, the art, spirituality, and so on. The second half spoke about the oppression of black people by white people, especially the Afrikaners who were in power then.

I and my friends frequented the United States Information Services library in the middle of town, where we could read banned books as long as we did so inside the building. When we sat down to discuss the plight of the African and the African American, and how the African American was dealing with his oppression, poetry came out of me. We formed a group called the Black Mambas in 1970–1971 and went around the townships reading our poetry and spreading the gospel of Black Consciousness until about 1973–1974, when some of our group members went missing because the Special Branch, South Africa's version of the CIA, was looking for them. The group broke up after that because some went to jail and others skipped the country.

In 1972, the Space Theatre in Cape Town opened its doors to the public. Sue Clark had taken me to the theater when it was still a warehouse and was being renovated. We became volunteers and used to do odd jobs around the place, until the day when they ran out of money and decided to hold a fund-raiser. I was asked to come and read the works of the black poets. I was very honored. This is where I met Barney Simon, with whom I was to work until his death in 1995. Barney Simon had a real love for theater, and he had a real love for black theater, because he loved the stories black people told about their lives. After working with him on that fund-raising concert, I worked with him on my first play, *The Sacrifice of Kreli* (1976), about the king of the Gcalekas, who chose exile rather than enslavement by the British colonizers. I wrote it in both English and Xhosa. Rob Amato, whom I had met in 1975 at the Space Theatre, produced the play; in fact, he gave me the research he had discovered on the king of the Gcalekas, because he felt the play needed to be written by a Xhosa person.

This period was the most beautiful and at the same time the most scary for me. I was entering the world of show biz and I had not planned for it. It fell into my lap. Rob Amato gave us everything we needed for that production, but we also paid for it emotionally, because there were days when he himself was not sure whether he was using his money for the right thing, for the right reasons. What was different about me coming into theater was that, usually, if you were black, you held down a job and continued to be an actor, because in our tradition acting was not a career.

In South Africa, it was unthought of for a woman to be an actor and make it a career, let alone be a writer. Being a writer in the middle of a repertory company was an even bigger challenge. It was as if I was the queen, and anybody else was a worker bee, because I could call the shots. The men in the group did not take kindly to this. They had to find ways of leveling the playing field, either by making me aware of our age difference or by trying to jump into bed with me. The other thing was experience. Since I had no experience whatsoever, I was getting advice on a daily basis: they told me what to do and what not to do. I kept my peace, listening and nodding at every suggestion, knowing that finally I would make the decisions that suited me best, based on what they told me. The lessons I learned from this time have carried me through my writing career.

In the 1980s, the scenario changed, because women playwrights emerged in full force. The women in male-led companies broke away, found their voices, and began to express themselves. I had seen Gcina Hlophe in a production of *Black Dog* (1984), by John Ledwaba, at the Baxter Theatre under the direction of Barney Simon; she was an actor then, but she also wrote poetry and prose. A few years later she wrote *Have You Seen Zandile?* (1988). Phyllis Klotz, a white director and producer who worked with black groups, staged *You Strike the*

Woman, You Strike the Rock (1985), workshopped from a script by Itumeleng Wa-Lehulere. The play was conceived by Itumeleng, and Phyllis came to help him develop the script in the same way that Barney Simon worked with John Ledwaba on *Black Dog,* although Phyllis did not recognize Itumeleng's authorship, and so he took her to court. This play was dynamic, and its four actors—four unknown women—moved into the spotlight internationally.

Women writers in South Africa are marginalized: they work under extremely difficult circumstances. To be a writer you need to be courageous, believe in yourself, be strong, challenging, because a lot of work out there is by men for men. Another difficulty is that we do not meet. There is one person who is trying to make us meet, and that is Tembeka Mbobo. She cofounded the Women in Writing Community Project, which holds a conference every year in Johannesburg and invites women from all over—as far as Zimbabwe, Namibia, Zambia, and Kenya. I have been able to survive because I am always working with a group, mostly youth, and I am focusing on women as subjects in my plays. I also have made it my aim and objective to nurture the youth of our country through theater. We are the walking libraries of our immediate past, the history of the struggle for the freedom of our people. It is good that our children should know our stories and not hear them from other races, that they should be told orally, as it has always been done.

Theater in South Africa is growing, and I know that more and more black women playwrights will emerge. Now we have the freedom to choose, and our parents have seen how we, the pathfinders, have succeeded in bringing recognition to our efforts in the struggle, through our writing.

A View from Australia
PETA TAIT

The performing arts have two distinct heritages in Australia: one from indigenous arts that have a central function within traditional communities and one from transplanted European models. While a distinctive Australian style became apparent in the mid-twentieth century, theater culture was not self-sustaining until the 1960s, in line with other areas in the arts. The emergence of a group of male playwrights, and their realistic domestic dramas about Australian society, established the foundation of what became a flourishing professional industry. However, geographic distance and socioeconomic differences mean that this recent theater history and practice varies among the eight states and territories and their capital cities; Melbourne and Sydney continue to be the largest centers for theater.

In 1974, I was a young, impressionable audience member at the group-devised shows produced by the formative Melbourne Women's Theatre Group, the first of its kind in Australia. At the time, I thought there had been few women playwrights. Thirty years on, scholars have overturned this misconception by uncovering the history of women dramatists: as supporters of suffrage at the turn of the twentieth century; as writers for commercial theater and for public radio in that century's first fifty years; and as champions of left-wing and political issues over decades. Women have been writing drama in Australia for over a hundred years, but it was the social changes that came with the second-wave Women's Movement of the 1970s that increased the numbers and elevated the profile of Australian women writers nationally and internationally.

What distinguishes women's theater work is its long-standing questioning of conventional gender, racial, sexual, and migrant identities, a questioning that continues to challenge the dominant values, even within comparatively more conservative main-stage productions. Although this phenomenon is not unique to Australia, it is worth noting that drama and performance by women remain the art forms that most overtly explore the promise of social change.

One noticeable feature of post-1970s women's drama is the proliferation of depictions of female artists, as fictional or historical characters. As a camou-flaged manifestation of a playwright's perception of artistic struggle, this may not, again, be particularly Australian. But it does provide a fascinating insight into artistic responsiveness to subtle shifts in social moods. Playwrights and other artists present ideas, but they also work with less tangible qualities such as emotions, and these remain central to theater. I contend that in creating a female character who is an artist, a playwright can frame emotions that reach beyond stereotypical female expressions.

In considering how women's drama has changed theatrical practice, it becomes evident that the expanded range of emotions presented by female characters is significant. In the Eurocentric tradition, theater has been a sphere in which female actors participated in both the policing and the public expression of emotions. Drama with moral themes that condemned women's unconventional love and behavior also informed society about the acceptable limits of that behavior and expression. In opposition to masculine rationality, emotionality was associated with a femininity that needed to be managed and controlled. In the nineteenth century, this was most evident in the treatment of hysteria as a female disease.

But ironically, theater is also a domain for embodying and performing social languages of emotions and their breaches. Thus, in the late twentieth century, theater sanctioned a large-scale public expression of women's indignation about restrictions on their social experience, and female playwrights explored strongly felt emotions of love, anger, and revenge.

Australia's most esteemed woman playwright, Dorothy Hewett, set an influential precedent with her depictions of heightened female emotions. Her pioneering protofeminist play from the early 1970s, *The Chapel Perilous* (1972), is an Australian classic, depicting a woman writer's life and struggles within the historical and political events of twentieth-century Australia.

Since her school days, the play's central figure, Sally Banner, has rebelled against social propriety and conventional values in her love affairs, particularly her lesbian love for her friend Judith. The play chronicles how Sally passionately adopts left-wing causes that bring her into conflict with the state and how she rejects her marriage and motherhood at a time when this is scandalous. A stylistic mix of poetic refrains, songs, realistic dialogue, and vivid images conveys a wide range of emotional moods. Indeed, female characters and their rejection of orthodox social behavior are central to Hewett's plays. She writes with humor across realistic and nonrealistic styles, to depict the personal, social, and political struggles of women and other marginalized people. Always controversial, Hewett's dramas encapsulate not only how social relations have an impact on personal lives but also how these lives are shaped by extreme passion.

Another major writer exploring the emotions of women artists is Alma De Groen, a New Zealander who has lived and worked in Australia for three decades and writes intellectually sophisticated drama, both serious and comic. While most of De Groen's plays use established dramatic forms, her important *The Rivers of China* (1987), which won the 1988 State Premiers Literary Award for Drama in New South Wales and Victoria, was considered experimental in form and content at that time.

In this radical play's view of the future, women control society in a gender reversal that makes men dependent, and this vision is interspersed with the world of the 1920s, where the tubercular Australian short-story writer Katherine Mansfield travels to meet the Russian Armenian spiritual leader Gurdjieff. In De Groen's imagined future, a female doctor, Rahel, adopts the strategy of hypnotizing a depressed character called Man, to save his life. In contrast, De Groen's *The Woman in the Window* (1998) depicts the courageous endurance and personal despair of the Russian Anna Akhmatova, whose poetry was banned in her country from 1925 until 1940. In this play, the future is a technological world where women have lost their rights.

Hewett and De Groen are part of an artistic movement evident in Australia since the early 1980s, in which women's theater writing embraced experimentation with form, often in collaboration with visual artists. The Melbourne writer and director Jenny Kemp, for instance, also designs her own highly visual productions, creating work that centers on female characters' subjective experience. Over twenty-five years, in addition to directing more conventional plays, Kemp has developed seven original and four collaborative works. Her impressionistic *Call of the Wild* (1989) has the male character delivering extracts from novels in French and Spanish and refers to specific paintings of women. A woman is isolated in a tower that doubles as a suburban home, while two bare-breasted women in long gloves and full dresses attend a garden party. A later play, *Still Angela* (2002), uses the device of having one central persona played by three female performers, in a text that moves backward and forward in time to show Angela at different stages of her life. The characters—the three Angelas; her family; her partner, Jack, and other men in her life—interact in fragmented episodes that explore the experience of living through the intrusion of memory. This journey takes us from domestic worlds to a train trip into the Simpson Desert, at the symbolic heart of Australia, and the text's apparent simplicity belies the complex ideas captured in poetic juxtaposition.

By the 1990s, realist female playwrights such as Hannie Rayson and Joanna Murray-Smith were receiving main-stage productions and attracting international attention, although Australia remained better known around the world for its film actors and directors. Rayson's dramas from this period present large-scale, character-based plots that progress to emotional revelations at the climax. These include *Hotel Sorrento* (1990), which is about three sisters who return home for a reunion, one of them a successful novelist grappling with Australian identity and the dismissive accusation that women writers only write autobiography. In *Life after George* (2000), three women who have been married to an aging university lecturer reflect generational and intellectual change across three decades; and in *Inheritance* (2003), the lives of two elderly sisters expose the problems of a farming community and the dilemmas of indigenous land rights. By contrast, Joanna Murray-Smith writes tightly crafted, clipped dialogue in the style of the 1990s, and her plays pivot on the numerous emotional shifts in intimate relationships: in *Love Child* (1994), an adopted daughter meets her birth mother; in *Honour* (1995), a younger woman intrudes on a well-established marriage; and in *Rapture* (2002), a couple move into a hotel for a year without telling their friends.

In addition to realist plays, Australian theater in the 1990s responded to changing attitudes in social identity, with plays that ranged from the ironic queer parody of the imaginative writer-performer Moira Finucane to the very Australian dynamism of indigenous writer-performers like Eva Johnson, Ningali Lawford, Deborah Mailman, and Leah Purcell, who evolved a distinctive solo form about indigenous experience.

Overall, Australia sustains a vibrant range of theatrical work by women, reflected, for instance, in productions by the Adelaide-based Vitalstatistix National Women's Theatre. Playwrights such as Sandra Shotlander, Alison Lyssa, and Sarah Hardy have written some of Australia's first lesbian characters. Tes Lyssiotis wrote the first plays on female migrant identity, and Peta Murray and Beatrix Christian revisit mythic and socially assigned female domains. The theater has attracted women who have garnered reputations in other literary forms, including the fiction writer Tobsha Learner and the novelist Noelle Janaczewska (a finalist for the Susan Smith Blackburn Prize in 1997–1998 for *Cold Harvest*) and Jill Shearer, who has written poetry and short stories. Hilary Bell, who was a finalist for the Blackburn Prize in 1998–1999 for *Shot While Dancing*, is fairly well known in the United States.

The constraints for women writers remain those imposed by the available opportunities within the arts-funded theater industry, although community-based theaters and fringe companies continue to give emerging writers opportunities, and young writers can now study creative writing in university courses.

As a writer for live performance in Australia, my own history reflects some of the shifts in theater and society over time. I wrote short polemical sketches in the 1970s, drama for a women's theater group in the early 1980s, and I was the writer on contemporary performance productions funded by the Arts Council during the 1990s.

Indeed, in the 1990s, I worked collaboratively with the Sydney-based physical theater group, the Party Line, and I also cowrote two plays with Matra Robertson. She and I are interested in an intellectual theater (culture) of ideas that are not specifically Australian. Our plays include *Mesmerized* (1991), about Dr. Jean-Martin Charcot's patient, the hysteric Augustine, who performed in his lectures; and *Breath by Breath* (2003), in which Chekhov's world of the Moscow Art Theatre and his love affair with the company's leading female actor, Olga Knipper, are poised against the persecution of the Jews in the Crimea. A massacre of Jewish people in that region marks the beginning of what became the mass displacement of refugees worldwide over the next century.

These plays critique theater history as well as cultural history, and although the characters are historical figures and the plays depict some circumstances in their lives, the plays are not intended to be biographical. Instead, *Mesmerized* considers the relationship between the performer and the emotionality of the hysteric body, and *Breath by Breath* ironically positions a male playwright against a background of catastrophic occurrences in order to explore artistic responsibility.

Matra and I started to write *Breath by Breath* because we were both profoundly disturbed by ethnic cleansing, and while we were writing the play, asylum-seeking became a hugely contentious issue in Australian national politics. We chose to adopt a Brechtian approach and frame the present in relation to the past, but we focused on Chekhov, because he wrote plays of subtle, complex emotions—plays that influenced the development of twentieth-century theater. I wanted to frame the persecution of a minority as emotionally compelling—requiring compassion, not only reasoned, intellectual arguments. Perhaps my experience as a female dramatist has made me aware of how theater can contribute to a wider understanding, and application, of social languages of emotion as a force for change.

A View from New Zealand
JEAN BETTS

In the early 1970s, when for a while my father was secretary of the New Zealand Theatre Federation (an organization of amateur theaters), he was astonished to learn that New Zealand had the highest number of theaters per capita in the Western world. I suspect this was largely due to the very popular national one-act play competitions that flourished from the 1930s to the 1960s, for they were an excellent training ground for actors and directors. In addition, they provided opportunities for New Zealand's first women playwrights, who wrote many one-acts for this annual event.

This activity declined somewhat when the first of our five major theater companies was formed in the late 1960s, but by the 1970s, a handful of women playwrights began to gain acceptance in the professional arena. Arriving at a time of great turmoil nationally, when our own energetic Women's Liberation Movement was under way, these playwrights felt a deep responsibility to address women's lives. However, they were fighting to be heard among the glorious, overbearing, political, male mob who dominated our theaters so confidently then. In addition to adoring its own male playwrights, New Zealand was in thrall to Stoppard, Hare, Shepard, Barker, Brenton, and company: motorbikes roared across our main stages, and as an actor and director, I have to say I enjoyed every minute of it. Perhaps women playwrights didn't arrive in numbers until the 1980s, partly because we were anxious that we might court ridicule by entering a domain that was so clearly the preserve of beautiful, angry, leatherjacketed young men. Worrying perhaps that if women weren't there, maybe they weren't supposed to be? Or that we might be mocked for writing about things that theater is not supposed to address, that people don't want to see or hear? Wondering if Caryl Churchill was as much as they could handle. This was about the time when I couldn't find plays I wanted to direct or act in anymore, and I began to think about writing my own.

In London in the early 1980s, on my O.E. (Overseas Experience, a rite of passage for us isolated kiwis), I was part of a very successful trip to Scotland's Edinburgh Festival (also a New Zealand rite of passage) with an all-N.Z. theater group. Led by and mostly made up of women and performing predominantly N.Z. women's plays, we won several important awards — and we were inspired and motivated by this achievement. My own confidence was also boosted by an experience with a U.K. political theater group, which was devising street theater to protest the latest bill threatening to restrict women's right to abortion. The script was appalling: the audience was encouraged to hurl abuse at the central character, Big Cath, played as a gross Irish Catholic woman, with dozens of cloth-puppet children dangling from all parts of her voluminous costume, and squealing offensive appeals to the pope and the Virgin in a very bad Irish accent. The last straw for me came at a meeting where the group hotly debated whether mothers with baby boys should be allowed to join. I left, confident that New Zealand political theater had nothing to be ashamed of.

Back in New Zealand in 1990, several of the women involved in the Edinburgh experience met, to see if we could set up a publishing cooperative as our contribution to the upcoming celebration of New Zealand's centenary of women's suffrage in 1993. (In 1893, New Zealand had been the first country in the world to grant women the vote, a campaign which grew out of the Temperance Movement rather than feminist protest. Women were the keepers of civilized society, these women argued — moral guardians with a God-given responsibility to fulfill the traditional woman's role as He intended and ensure that their wayward men did not stray from the straight and narrow. Without women's enlightened vote, they argued, the country would be in danger of going into moral decline!) Our group of dramatists calculated that, up to this point, several dozen male playwrights but only three female playwrights had been published in New Zealand. During our meetings, we became aware that each of us had a new play on the way, and so we decided to stage a small festival. Two local theaters supported us, and in September 1993, with funding from various arts organizations, we staged a season of five new plays that subsequently became the first publications from our new venture, the Women's Play Press.

I wasn't very fussed about publication and couldn't really see the point of it at the time. I had long happily accepted that the ephemeral nature of theater is part of its charm; however, when the boxes of books arrived, and we began sending copies out to schools and libraries, began seeing them enter university curricula, be discussed in classes, performed both at homegrown functions and overseas—the penny dropped. When we reprinted plays over the years to meet a rising demand, when film rights were bought and radio versions commissioned, the pennies not only dropped but began to add up. I rolled over my earnings from my play—a rewritten *Hamlet* called *Ophelia Thinks Harder* (1993)—into other plays and recently into a new venture, the Play Press, which publishes (carefully selected) men as well.

So 1993 was a watershed year for women playwrights, and we have come to realize that publishing is vital for us. New Zealand's small population—a mere four million—keeps theater seasons short and returns small. There are several touring possibilities within New Zealand, and some productions travel offshore, usually to Australia or the Edinburgh Festival, or the Pacific Islands in the case of our P.I. writers. But the most usual way for New Zealand plays to journey overseas is via the published script—anything else can be prohibitively expensive. Most women's plays are on the "risk list" of the established theaters (even though three major theaters are run by women), and we don't generally expect many return seasons. This makes publication that much more important, as it keeps our work alive and helps to generate new productions.

In 2000, I was involved in another festival of new women's plays. Called Shebang, it included work from younger, up-and-coming women, including Maori and Pacific Island women, who have emerged as major players. They write provocatively about the violence and misogyny of their respective cultures. New Zealand seems finally to be ridding itself of the notion that rough treatment of Maori and Pacific women is culturally acceptable and feminist ideas of domestic abuse a Western ploy to deplete their cultures further. Thankfully, this penny has also dropped globally. Such a lot has changed.

David O'Donnell, in his introduction to *Fold & Shudder* (2001)—two plays by the young writers Jo Randerson and Pip Hall respectively—writes that there is now "a second wave of women's playwriting, sharing some of the concerns of the previous generation, but with an assured sense that many of the previous gender taboos have already been broken. . . . While the first generation of women playwrights had a huge confidence in their political views, born of outrage and the urgent desire to address the historical oppression of women, the new generation has a global perspective and less focus on gender divisions."

Recent years have seen the emergence of much more varied and confident voices and, conversely, men who are writing about relationships and babies. The atmosphere feels good.

Recently a pedophile priest pled guilty to a series of abuses against boys at a New Zealand school during the late 1970s and 1980s. Some of the boys in question, now angry adults lamenting blighted lives, have been appearing on the television news. It seems the school hired a priest even though he had a previous known conviction for sexual assault, and during his time at the school there were numerous complaints, which were ignored. One excuse from the Catholic hierarchy was that little was known then about the extent of the devastation this sort of abuse caused. They claimed that had they known, they would have dealt with the abuse quite differently.

I can remember back then that women were still having trouble persuading men — quite decent men! — that rape jokes weren't actually funny; that we ought to have a law against marital rape; that rape crisis centers should be supported, not ridiculed. However, now that the long-lasting damage done to boys and men by sexual abuse is at last taken seriously, perhaps they finally do understand and will be aware that the justice and healing these damaged men receive will be largely due to the work of those maligned feminist pioneers. On the other hand, last week a young murderer received an extremely lenient sentence, because the jury accepted that he was provoked by "unwanted sexual advances" from his male victim. Hmmm. If women could be confident of receiving the same justice, the streets would be littered with dead men. Perhaps we have some way to go.

The obstacles to writing are much the same for all New Zealand dramatists now. In spite of the Internet (heavily used here) and cheaper travel, we are very aware of our distance from the places deemed the Center. We have to fight apathy rather than overstimulation. We have to find ways to celebrate our isolation and enjoy our loneliness, and turn all the difficulties of working for a small population to our advantage. We have privacy and fewer distractions than a more populous country, and we are far more nurtured by visitors. We are far more likely to diversify and build up an exciting range of talents in order to make the most of our small population. (It helps, too, that New Zealand is a Pacific paradise.)

Ironically, while the success of New Zealand films has recently given writers new confidence, it has also switched so much attention from theater to movies that only one of the students at the local university's scriptwriting course is writing for the stage. The rest are penning screenplays! I give them two years before they lose patience with that interminable, thankless process and adapt their screenplays for the theater.

But even though all New Zealand playwrights face the same difficult road, have the same fight to get people to listen and to earn a crust, women should be wary of our male colleagues who tend to be pushier, more confident, more demanding, more ruthlessly competitive. Women should still take care to give special support to our shyer, more diffident female playwrights. In a recent review of one of my plays, one (old, male) reviewer could still suggest that it might have been better if I'd had a man to help me. Another (old, male) critic was outraged that I could suggest that the earliest versions of the Cinderella story had wicked step*fathers* (true). Another was astounded that a playwright as "separatist" as I (I have *never* been a separatist) could possibly be attracted to an all-male play like Gregory Burke's *Gagarin Way* (2001), which I had recently directed. And I've just received some advertising guff about the upcoming annual comedy festival, which, as usual, is 95 percent men.

So we must be careful not to become complacent. We must stay sensitive to the peculiar injustices meted out to our sex both at home and around the world, and be ready to leap up and rant, sit down and write, and do whatever else is necessary. We must complain loudly when productions of those magnificent classics mindlessly reinforce outdated and dangerous views of women and relationships, and we must dare to rewrite those classics shamelessly. We must support men like John Fuegi, whose book *Brecht and Company* (1994) alerts us to the huge female input in that great cheat's work, returning those amazing forgotten women to their rightful place in history. We must recognize those moments when our voice can provide the important alternate angle, the valuable insight that will make a difference in the world, and speak up with courage and confidence.

A View from Canada
JUDITH THOMPSON

If you asked a random person on the streets of Toronto or Halifax, Moosejaw or Whitehorse, to name one female Canadian playwright, I guarantee you they would be stumped.

If they were committed theatergoers, they might be able to name Djanet Sears, Joanna Glass, and Judith Thompson; Linda Griffiths, Carole Fréchette, and Florence Gibson; Ann-Marie MacDonald and Sally Clark, Maureen Hunter and very few others.

The theatergoer with a burning passion for Canadian drama would certainly name Sharon Pollock and Carol Bolt, Erika Ritter and Betty Lambert, Betty Jane Wylie, Anne Chislet, and even Mavis Gallant. They might actually know of the younger, red-hot playwrights, like Claudia Dey and Kristen Thomson, M. J. Kang, Celia MacBride, and d'bi young.

More politically aware theatergoers would know of First Nation (Native Canadian) playwrights Monique Mojica and Marie Clements, Yvette Nolan and Shirley Cheechoo.

But nobody who is not a serious theater scholar would be able to name more than seven or eight all together. Yet there are hundreds of women in Canada whose stunning plays are being produced in small, out-of-the-way venues all over the world, or once and never again in commercial venues. I know, because I recently edited a book of monologues for women, *She Speaks* (2004). There are over eighty time-stopping monologues in this book, with at least seventy by Canadian women.

I am a professor in the theater program at the University of Guelph, and one day I asked a colleague what he knew about women playwrights before 1970. He said that there were "dozens" of books on the subject, and he would loan me a couple he had lying around the office. I followed him, red-faced with shame at my own ignorance, and gratefully received the two books he pulled out for me.

A quick glance at *Women Pioneers: Canada's Lost Plays* (1979), and I learned about Eliza Lanesford Curshing, who wrote *The Fatal Ring* (1840); Sarah Ann Curzon, who wrote *Laura Secord; or, the Heroine of 1812* (1887) and *The Sweet Girl Graduate* (1882). Another book borrowed from a colleague, Kym Bird's *Redressing the Past: The Politics of Early English-Canadian Women's Drama, 1880–1920* (2004), included plays by the feminist firebrand Kate Simpson Hayes: *A Domestic Disturbance* (1892) and *T'Other from Which* (1894).

I am overwhelmed by the courage of these women, in such a thoroughly sexist era, to insist on their voices being heard and to enter into such a male-dominated arena. After all, a play brashly penetrates the consciousness of the audience. I am in awe of these women's energy, considering that they undoubtedly had many dependents and few conveniences and that at the time everything was written in ink—there were no little monks at the ready to make copies, no carbon copies—so multiple copies had to be written out painstakingly by hand.

And then, of course, there was stern societal disapproval to contend with. I would bet that many of these women didn't give an owl's hoot about approval. They were goddesses. Early feminists, these pioneers were absolutely certain of the righteousness of their struggle. They believed that their voices needed to be heard and knew that there were women who needed desperately to hear what they had to say.

There is something extraordinarily bold about writing a play and actually allowing it to be produced—having the gall to think that the words we put in characters' mouths should be heard, especially the words we put in the mouths of male characters. To have male actors giving their souls to words written by a woman is a marvel, even today in this supposedly postfeminist, don't-they-have-everything-they-want-now? era.

I was born in Montreal in 1954. We lived in Kingston, Ontario, for two years and then moved to Middletown, Connecticut, for the next ten, while my father taught at Wesleyan University. My family returned to Canada in 1967, when Canada was celebrating her one hundredth birthday. I was twelve, so I adapted immediately to my surroundings, developing the Scots-Irish-inflected southern Ontario accent, mastering the local dialect and attitude within weeks.

I had played Helen Keller for my mother in *The Miracle Worker* at the Wesleyan University Faculty Players, and I knew that I was an actor, that nothing would ever deter me from my destiny. I also loved to read, having read every *Nancy Drew* mystery by the age of nine, and by the summer of 1967 I had started seriously on Charles Dickens. But I had no notion that I would write, despite editing a classmate's first notebook-novel during recess. I do remember being exasperated by her choices and clichés and enjoying directing her revisions.

I soon began a career at the local amateur theater, playing Betty Parris in Arthur Miller's *The Crucible* (1953). There, at fourteen, I also first encountered a female playwright: Edna St. Vincent Millay. I adored her dreamlike play *Aria da Capo* (1919) — the absurdity, the existential horror, and the profoundly female version of the truth. When I was sixteen, I was cast in *The Prime of Miss Jean Brodie* (1966), Jay Presson Allen's stage adaptation of Muriel Spark's novel, and I became Sandy — the observer, the spy, the future writer.

Clearly, this role planted seeds deep inside me. But at the time, the thought of actually being the aloof observer was anathema. I was an actor, and I found playing the role, with its emotional hills and valleys and intellectual challenges, gratifying. I loved escaping my own life and walking onto the stage, into the frightening and complex world of Miss Brodie and her acolyte-turned-enemy, Sandy. It was, in a way, a metaphor for my own emergence as a feminist and writer: I was in the slow process of throwing off the mantles of the Catholic church and the misogynist society in which I had been living. I was coming to understand that being a girl was largely a performance in a play written for us by men.

My first encounter with a play written by a *Canadian* woman began as a long, crazy poem called *Dr. Umlaut's Earthly Kingdom* (1974), by the Toronto writer Phyllis Gotlieb. When I was seventeen and in the twelfth grade, a drama educator and true mentor, Nancy Helwig, introduced me to Gotlieb's wild-and-wooly rhyming poem about a mad autocrat, and adapted it for the stage into a stimulating, nontraditional piece of theater.

It was very exciting to be working on the voice of a Canadian woman. All the plays performed in my local high school had been written by men, none of them Canadian. At that time, in the sixties and early seventies, much of Canadian culture was still borrowed; the great tidal wave of nationalism was beginning politically but was still at a distance culturally. But it never occurred to me that my *own* stories would be worth listening to.

My family spent 1972, my father's sabbatical year, in Brisbane, Australia, where I immediately joined a theater company and began performing the same mix of classics and commercial hits I was accustomed to.

But here was a much hipper group of young people, and they were doing new Australian work, which I couldn't even audition for because of my accent. The plays were electrifying and caused an earthquake inside my growing consciousness. Yes, I thought, we can tell our own stories. We are not appendages of Britain or cultural appendages of the United States. We are not appendages of men. Our voices have been strangled for thousands of years, but it is possible to remove the hand of imperialism and sexism from our throats and sing out.

I returned to Canada and did a degree in drama at Queen's University in Kingston, where the only Canadian plays I encountered were Herschel Hardin's tragedy of Inuit life, *Esker Mike & His Wife, Agiluk* (1971); a drama by Robertson Davies; and a play by a fellow student.

Then Keith Johnstone, the improvisation guru from Britain, came to teach, and he turned all my ideas about theater upside down. He taught that the canon, or what we had been taught was great, might be garbage and that what the world considered garbage could be great. The least successful person in his class was the most successful. The stars became the outsiders. I didn't know it then, but Johnstone's political approach would have a profound effect on my work. But despite my Australian epiphany, at that time I was still in a firmly colonial mind-set. I believed that "real" theater was in New York or London. "Real" literature was written by people we didn't know living in "real" cultural centers.

After graduation, I auditioned for the acting program at the National Theatre School and was admitted. I was fulfilling my destiny: I was an actor. But except for Martha Henry, who came in briefly, all our acting teachers were men — most of them patriarchal, self-serving, lecherous, antiartistic men.

Only one teacher was more pure artist than man: Pierre Lefevre, who taught us to work with masks. He brought his box of simple masks into the studio and changed my life. As soon as I put on a mask, a character would not just start forming, but foaming at the mouth. Another's personal history would move into my body, and my own identity would disappear. Yet I had never felt more present and alive; my unconscious life poured into the mask.

Lefevre asked each of us to find a monologue that suited our mask, and I began with a thin monologue by the American dramatist Jules Feiffer (at this point I still would not have thought about finding a Canadian monologue). The piece was amorphous, but the character was well defined: an overprivileged gossip with a distinct and overbearing persona. Soon, however, I began improvising my own monologues, and my performances of these elicited a response that was both shocking and exhilarating: I had found my path in the world.

I still didn't know I was a playwright. In fact, the school's director, an American expatriate named Joel Miller, told me in my annual critique that, although I had had some success with these monologues, I must not *ever* think of myself as a playwright. I quickly concurred: "Oh, no, Mr. Miller. Me? Write? What would I have to say?"

I am glad this happened, as it is a perfect example of the silencing of women, in this case by a man who was an avowed feminist. Years later I had the opportunity, at the opening of my play *The Crackwalker* (1980), to remind Joel Miller of what he had said. The blood drained from his face, and he turned away, for once at a loss for words.

Men have not always been my silencers. The actor and director Michael Mawson supported me fully and suggested that I find the work of the great American monologist Ruth Draper. Day after day, I went to the library and listened to recordings of her extraordinary art, to her channeling of people from all walks of life, especially the silenced, the disadvantaged, and the oppressed. She shaped their stories into unforgettable monologues that were chronicles of real people, oral histories of distinct and disappearing cultures.

The first time I actually sat down and wrote was one very lonely weekend in Montreal. My roommate was out of town, I had neglected to make any plans, and everyone was busy. I felt a loneliness more intense than I have ever felt before or since. Family and close friends were three hours away in Kingston. With crushing and pathetic self-pity, I reflected that nobody cared whether I got up in the morning or stayed in bed, ate or starved.

I now realize that the reason I felt so empty was because, until then, I had only existed in the gazes of the people around me. If they were looking at me, talking to me, criticizing me, I was alive, I existed. Now that there was no one at all with me, I felt as though I did not exist. It was as if the act of writing kept me from disappearing off the page entirely. I existed so long as I was writing.

My roommate's typewriter was sitting there, beckoning, ready for me on the kitchen table. I wandered over, and I began writing Theresa, one of my mask characters. I thought it would be fun for her to have a friend, and in walked Sandy. I had no plan whatsoever. I then thought there should be a couple of men in the picture, and I created Alan and Joe. The horror is that the play emerged without warning. The play literally fell out of me, with past experience finding its place, and the silenced finding their voices through me. *The Crackwalker,* for that was the play that flowed out of me, is still produced constantly around the world, in many languages. I marvel at the simplicity of the creation of this first play. Creation has never again been so simple.

I gave the play to Michael Mawson, who gave it in turn to Clarke Rogers of Théâtre Passe Muraille, which agreed to produce it. I will never forget the first reading in 1979, with professional actors: it was Christmas morning times ten. I was honored and floored and yet not floored enough to be cowed. I had plenty of notes for the poor actors.

The play was produced in a fifty-seat theater and then in a large theater in Montreal. Because of its frank and explicit revelations about four extremely disadvantaged people in small-town Ontario, there were a few hate-filled reviews. But there were also full-out raves in esteemed magazines and newspapers. Some thought the play an evil walk through the sewers; some called it a masterpiece. The audience responded very strongly, and the buzz grew louder and louder, and the play became part of Canadian theater history.

After that first play was produced, I became eligible for Canada Council grants. In those days, I could easily live for a year on the twelve thousand dollars a grant awarded, and I wrote my next play, *White Biting Dog* (1984), which was produced by Urjo Kareda at the Tarragon Theatre in Toronto. So began a twenty-year artistic collaboration that would include *I Am Yours* (1987), *Lion in the Streets* (1990), *Sled* (1997), and *Perfect Pie* (2000). Urjo supported me through challenging work, and I owe much of my success to him.

I do venture out of the theater. I have written countless radio plays, a few television movies of the week, including *Life with Billy* (1994). I have written two feature films: *Lost and Delirious* (2001), which sold to twenty-three countries and has a cult following; and *Perfect Pie* (2002), which was beset by conflict but in the end is quite a good film. I enjoy writing for film, but the theater is my passion, and I will never stop writing for it.

Currently I am creating a new piece by improvising with masks; the working title is *The Secret Creed.* I am going to force myself to perform it, because now that I am turning fifty, I need to do what really scares me.

A while ago, a German graduate student who was doing her thesis on Canadian theater interviewed me in a local Italian coffeehouse. As I ate spoonfuls of foamed milk, she told me that other Canadian theater practitioners had told her I had "paved the way" for women playwrights. I regret that I became a little icy at that moment, for I found this offensive. I imagined it on my tombstone: "She Paved the Way." It makes me sound so workaday, dependable—and it just ain't true. The way is not paved for women. The way is thorny, steep, and treacherous.

A casual look at the upcoming theater seasons across Canada reveals that at least 80 percent of the plays being presented are by men, and in theaters that seat eight hundred or more, 80 percent are by American or British playwrights. A glance at the Toronto Theatre Awards, the Dora's, and you see that nominees for best play have always been overwhelmingly plays by men. The juries might respond that their choices were governed by the reality that most of the plays presented were by men. And so we must look to the artistic directors, who are also overwhelmingly men.

There is one answer: Youth. Young women of all backgrounds must be sought out and encouraged to write for the theater. We "veterans" must give our time and energy to support them, and the theater audiences and critics must make a commitment to their work.

Nightwood Theatre, the first visible feminist theater in Toronto, was founded in 1979 by Kim Renders, Mary Vingoe, Cynthia Grant, and Maureen White, and it developed Ann-Marie MacDonald's megahit, *Good Night Desdemona (Good Morning Juliet)* (1990), as well as Djanet Sears's *Harlem Duet* (1997) and *The Adventures of a Black Girl in Search of God* (2002). The theater runs a development program for women playwrights who are starting out. Called Write from the Hip, the group meets once a week, and playwrights, directors, and producers are brought in to talk with the women and listen to their work. I met with the group recently in the beautiful, historic Distillery District. There was a thunderstorm during our meeting, and after the readings, when the storm was over, the sunset glowing through the clouds left us all breathless and bonded, glad that we were playwrights, and with an unspoken agreement that we will never stop writing, that we will not be silent.

FIFTEEN

New Voices

Moira Buffini, Sarah Ruhl, and Rukhsana Ahmad

ALEXIS GREENE

❦

Julia Cho, a finalist for the 2001–2002 Susan Smith Blackburn Prize for her play 99 Histories, *New York, 2004:*

I'm a playwright in the age of readings. In other words, people of my generation can be playwrights without actually being produced. The majority of people my age—I'm twenty-nine—become playwrights knowing our first production would be years away. I think that's kind of wrongheaded; you should become a playwright because you're getting a production.

I don't mind readings and development, but there are different types of readings, some of which help the playwright and some of which do not. One that does not is a reading that is really an audition; that is, you are auditioning your play for a theater. It's as if the theater were saying, "We like your play, but we don't know how much, so let's do a reading of it." This is a horrible situation, because of the pressure this puts on you and your play. And inevitably, the four perfect actors for your four parts are all out of town, so you go to the B and C lists, and you end up with a reading of the play that may not even convey what the play really is.

The ideal is when a theater knows it wants to produce your play and is doing a reading just to hear it. That's great, because then you go into the reading knowing the theater is behind you, and that the reading is to make your play better.

I'm only now realizing that I can pick and choose.

Younger playwrights tend to say "yes" to every opportunity. Because *99 Histories* was my first play, I agreed to countless readings and went into every one thinking, "Now I'll make it better. Now I'll make it better."

Shelley Calene-Black and Alex Kilgore in Houston's Stages Repertory Theatre production of Refuge *by Jessica Goldberg, winner of the twenty-first Susan Smith Blackburn Prize in 1999. (Photograph: George Craig)*

And the play eventually suffered for it. The road was paved with good intentions; nobody was trying to get me to change my play. But I'd think, "Well, I have this reading. I guess I'm expected to work on the play some more." And of course, that's not the way plays are. They don't need endless work. At a certain point, in fact, working on a play will make it worse, not better.

An Interview with Moira Buffini

Moira Buffini's plays include the one-woman drama Jordan* *(1992), written with Anna Reynolds;* Blavatsky's Tower *(1996);* Gabriel *(1997);* Silence *(1999), which won the Susan Smith Blackburn Prize in 1997–1998;* Loveplay *(2001); and* Dinner *(2002). This interview took place in London in June 2004.*

ALEXIS GREENE: Where were you born?

MOIRA BUFFINI: I was born in Middlewich, which is a small town in Cheshire in the north of England. It's between Manchester and Liverpool. My parents are both Irish, so I'm of Irish descent, despite my Italian surname. The Buffinis turned up in Ireland well over a hundred years ago, from Tuscany we think. My Irish relatives consider me to be very English, but I have never quite felt as if I belong here. Perhaps that's no bad thing. I have always had a critical eye on the character of this country.

AG: You grew up in England then?

MB: Yes, I grew up here. Small-town girl.

AG: And you have a sister who is a theater director?

MB: Yes. Her name is Fiona Buffini. We've collaborated several times, and she's great at her job.

AG: When did you first start to write?

A glowing Moira Buffini accepts the twentieth Susan Smith Blackburn Prize for Silence. *Two first prizes were awarded in honor of SSBP's twentieth anniversary, one to Buffini and the other to Paula Vogel for* How I Learned to Drive. *The Alley Theatre, Houston, February 23, 1998. The Century Association, New York, February 24, 1993. (Courtesy Susan Smith Blackburn Prize)*

MB: In my teens. Fiona and I went to the local school, and once a year they did something called the Arts Festival. Someone had to write a play, and one year the person doing it dropped out. I took it over and loved it. So I wrote my first play when I was about fourteen. But I didn't want to be a writer. I couldn't bear the idea of spending that much time in a room, alone. The thought of the loneliness and isolation that a writer must endure made me push it away.

So I trained to be an actor. After taking a degree, I went to drama school. I was an actor for about five years—but writing never really went away. It slowly began to take over, and in the end I found I was turning down acting work so that I could concentrate on it. I'm glad I trained as an actor; I think it is the best training that a playwright could have. I've got a gut feeling for stagecraft that is invaluable. And I think that I approach creating a character in the way I used to approach taking on a role—instinctively. As an actor, I always thought that a part began and ended with what a character said and did onstage, and that if you were vividly, openly present in each moment of speaking, action, and reaction, then you were probably doing the job. To me, character is the most mysterious ingredient in the writing of a play. You can't study it, like structure, and you can't really plan it. I find that my characters are constantly confounding my expectations. They often refuse to fit into preimagined plots, and even when I think I've got them nailed, I find them manipulating me at every turn. I only think about archetypes before I start writing character. Then I let go. I just see what falls onto the paper. If you allow enough uncensored space, something will come.

AG: In *Dinner,* the character of Paige, the hostess, is simply present. I've no idea where or what she comes from. That adds to the mystery of the play.

MB: *Dinner* is entirely character and language driven. When I was most inspired, the writing felt effortless, as if all I was doing was taking dictation. I was simply listening in on what the characters were saying. At the start of writing any play, I improvise endlessly—another thing I used to love doing as an actor.

AG: Would you talk about *Jordan*? It was based on the actual story of a woman who murdered her child after being brutalized by her husband. She was released from prison and subsequently committed suicide. It was one of your earliest plays.

MB: I think for all of its faults, it's one of the things I'm most proud of, still. The main writing plaudit goes to Anna Reynolds. I'm proud of *Jordan* because I performed it, produced it, and turned it from poetry/prose into a vividly characterized play. And I made the tea. The production was garlanded with glowing reviews—it won awards—and I spent a year afterward temping to pay off the debts it incurred. Big lesson about theater, that one. I'd been working in a women's prison, teaching drama, and I had met Anna through the prison network. We felt similarly about so many issues that the prison experience highlights: injustice, poverty and its relationship to crime. Mostly, we shared an enormous compassion for people who were eaten up with remorse. It's a truly terrible thing, an agony that never goes. The play is a monologue in which a young mother addresses the beloved thirteen-month-old son that she killed. A searing piece. Its effect on audiences was profound.

Jordan succeeded on a number of levels. It was an immensely humane and compassionate play, and it was also everything we wanted to say about the prison system. I haven't directly written about prison since, because I think *Jordan* says it all. You see, I think I'm a political writer. No one else seems to, but I think I am. I never write overtly politically about anything, because that doesn't work for me. But I think *Jordan* was a political play. It changed people's opinions about single mothers, about women in prison. Through that human being's journey, you got a clear-eyed view of the system she was in. And because people had been so powerfully, emotionally affected, it made them able to empathize with a character they might otherwise have dismissed.

In this country there's a definite idea of what a political writer is, and it's very overt. Okay, I'll say it. In my view, it's very male. We have the "state-of-the-nation" play, which I don't think you have in America. Very fortunate not to. There's a big argument in England that the theater is a forum for political debate. Of course it is. But it should *inspire* debate, not labor tediously to elucidate all the pros and cons. The theater has to be first and foremost a place of wild imaginings and outrageous actions. It's capable of reaching an emotional and metaphysical level that political debate alone doesn't get near. I think there could be a different kind of political play, a play where the words "earnest" and "worthy" are banished, a play that doesn't confine itself to the here and now or to facts. A truly shocking, challenging play about war that I recently saw was Katie Mitchell's inspiring production of *Iphigenia in Aulis*. Euripides created a haunting play-world where gods, men, and mothers battle it out for the body and soul of a girl, and through doing so, illuminate the injustices of a whole society. He was writing about the politics of his own Athens, and he made them timeless by his mythical setting.

I think we are living in bewildering times. And I find myself more and more suspicious of people who are certain about things. Where do they get this certainty? What is it covering? My position is one of uncertainty. I have become disillusioned with two big creeds in my life: Catholicism and Capitalism. So I'm spiritually searching. I'm politically suspicious. Our society seems to function on the brink of chaos. I'm confused — and let's face it, most of us, apart from the fundamentalists these days, are. I find that all I can do is ask questions. So I don't know whether that's what a political writer is, by definition.

AG: I find that in several of your plays, you show women struggling against unfair odds, often trapped or abused. If somebody asked me whether Moira Buffini was a political playwright, I would say yes.

MB: It's so funny. In reviews, I've been called both a radical feminist (male critic) and a misogynist (female critic), which I think is quite a result. I suppose that must mean that the questions I'm asking are uncomfortable. I always try to be fair to men in my plays, but at the end of the day, especially when you're setting something in the historical past, as with *Loveplay* and *Silence,* it's difficult not to think, "Thank Christ I wasn't born then." Power was so unevenly distributed between men and women, and if you're to write honestly about the past, what else can you say?

I've come to realize the value of subverting archetypes — I love subversiveness, I have scant respect for authority. *Silence* is a play full of mythic archetypes. You've got the hero, the priest, the damsel in distress, her servant, the warrior knight, the king. They exist within their archetypes, but within those limits you can do anything. The hero turns out to be a girl. The damsel turns out to be a warrior. It's the same with *Dinner.* You've got archetypes: the drunken hostess, the successful writer, the liberal artist, the scientist, the beautiful young woman, the uninvited guest. In *Dinner,* I just wanted to take one of those nice polite plays and have blood on the carpet at the end.

When I started, I didn't know whose blood it was going to be. Didn't know for a long time. It's so funny how a play comes together; it takes so long. I wrote the wrong ending, the first time *Dinner* was on. The ending for the first draft is the same ending the play has now: Paige arranges her very own public murder. But after the first draft, I lost my courage. I thought, "You can't kill your heroine. Our whole dramatic tradition is scattered with difficult women that playwrights kill at the end of the play. Don't do it." The Uninvited Guest died instead. But it just didn't work. My instincts were right. The heroine had to go. Because what the play's actually about is excess. The richest class in our society eating itself.

AG: Is the play humorous in performance?

MB: Oh, it's hilarious. And unsettlingly dark. When *Dinner* was on in the West End, I was exhausted. I'd just had two kids, and my youngest, my son, was born six weeks before the first production of *Dinner* went on. So I was in rehearsals with a six-week-old baby and I was just shattered. I think I did the whole first year of Joe's life on adrenaline. Then it just suddenly hit me, and I almost dropped dead with exhaustion. I used to sit in the back of the auditorium and hear the audience laughing uproariously at this play, but I would think it was the darkest, most terrifyingly nihilistic vision, and wonder where did that come from? I think you can go into the darkness when you're making people laugh. Paige is one of the liveliest, wittiest women you can imagine. And yet this is a woman who is suicidal from the minute the play starts. Nothing that happens in the play shakes her from her intent, and that is very, very dark. I think the only reason I could write it is that I was so happy in my personal life. I could leave this horrible dark place every day and go back to my beautiful children. I think *Dinner* is about all my own worst fears. Comedy is fertile for exploring despair. It seems to come naturally to me as well.

AG: To change the subject slightly, what is the status of women in the British theater these days? And is there a sisterhood of playwrights?

MB: I think unofficially there is. I think female playwrights are incredibly supportive to one another. I certainly have found it so. The liberating thing about being a writer—having been an actor, where the odds are stacked against you if you are female—is that you are judged solely on the quality of your work. I find myself patronized by reviewers because of my sex, and I find people have preconceptions about my work because of my sex. But I've been lucky—my work has always been done. I think in every woman's life there are periods when she feels hard done by, or in conflict with the opposite sex. To be in conflict with men is to find conflict everywhere, in everything. It's a bad place to be. And I'm not sure that conflict is the way forward. I think that the way forward is the Big Question.

It's strange. I wouldn't consider myself a powerful woman, yet I am the daughter of one, and they people my plays. The experience of women will always be at the heart of my work. And our position in the world is so rapidly changing. These are extraordinary times for a woman to live in. No wonder we can't keep up. Women need to ask questions of each other, as well as of men. It is so difficult to articulate where you find yourself in the power struggle of things. So I'll keep working away at it. And as for feminism . . . I can only go on asking questions.

I taught a group of six writers at the National Theatre Studio last year, in a regional writers' workshop. These were six writers from the regions who had all been judged on the quality of their work. Now to my delight, the six writers happened to be female. We got on like a house on fire. We had a great week. We discussed form, we discussed structure, we discussed language, we discussed politics, we had a laugh, we went to the pub. And never at any time did we do a big thing about women. Never at any time was that under discussion. We were seven writers at the National Theatre Studio, seven female playwrights. Enough said.

AG: Are you working on a new play?

MB: I haven't written a full-length play in two years. I've been writing film, and my heart is aching to write another play. Since my children were born, the space, the emptiness that you need to create a play, has not been forthcoming. I've found myself stuck in the financial trap of having to earn enough money to pay for the child care in order to earn the money. That is so common to women. But I've been saving my money up. *Dinner* transferring to the West End and going on tour means that I can buy myself enough time to write a play.

It delights me, the journey of a play once it leaves the nest. You have no idea, the slow burn of being a writer. My heart broke over *Silence,* because it was on in the provinces for six weeks and that was it. It didn't get a London production. And I thought that was the end of it. Because every time you finish a play, you think, "That's my best play. I'll never write another one again." But *Silence* has gone all over the world: Australia, Russia, Canada, San Francisco, Poland, Chicago, New York. You cannot gauge the life of a play at the end of its first production. The rewards of being a writer are very slow in coming but very rich when they come. The idea that students in whatever country are doing *Silence* just thrills me to the core. That's the reward of being a playwright. It's much more about that than about financial rewards. I don't think people write plays for money. You'd be a fool to try.

❦

British playwright Lucy Prebble, a finalist for the 2003–2004 Susan Smith Blackburn Prize for her play The Sugar Syndrome, *London, 2004:*

I don't have to do jobbing television writing at the moment, because I was lucky enough to win the George Devine Award, which has ten thousand pounds attached to it. But I will have to at some point. Even if I wrote three plays a year, the money I'd receive would be very difficult to live on. So I'm trying to take advantage of the moment. I spend most of my time with people whom I've been friends with for years, and I try to keep grounded about how silly the world of theater can be sometimes, as well as how wonderful. I talk with other writers, and that's why I've developed a cynical attitude toward television. I keep hearing about bad experiences: writers' phone calls never being returned after they'd been told they were "the new thing" just a few months earlier. The reviews were not that great for their last play, so the television people just disappeared. When writers talk to each other, you realize, "God, I'm not alone. Everyone has really bad times, and plays that don't work so well."

An Interview with Sarah Ruhl

Sarah Ruhl's plays include Passion Play *(1997–2004),* Orlando *(1998),* Euridyce *(2000),* Melancholy Play *(2001),* Late: A Cowboy Song *(2001), and* The Clean House *(2002), which won the Susan Smith Blackburn Prize in 2003–2004. This interview took place in New York City in June 2004.*

AG: Where were you born?

SARAH RUHL: I was born outside of Chicago, in Evanston. I think I was born in Evanston. But I grew up in Wilmette, another little town near Chicago. Grew up there in the same house until I went to college.

AG: What did your parents do?

SR: My father was a businessman; he was in marketing. He probably should have been a history professor. My parents both came from Iowa, and my father had that strong, midwestern sensibility. My mother was an actor and then got a Ph.D. in English.

AG: Is that how you first became interested in theater?

SR: I grew up going to rehearsals with her. She claimed recently that, before I could write, I would go to rehearsals with her and say, "Mom, can you write down this note I have for you?" I was mentally taking notes before I could read or write.

AG: Do you remember seeing her act?

Sarah Ruhl, winner of the twenty-sixth Susan Smith Blackburn Prize for The Clean House. *(Photograph: Anthony Charuvastra)*

SR: I have strong memories of watching her in plays. She had done interesting work in Chicago during the 1960s, but by the time I was born she had moved to the suburbs and was doing community theater. She taught at a Catholic high school and directed plays there, so sometimes I saw her directing. She recently played Virginia in a reading of *The Clean House* at the Piven Theater Workshop in Evanston. We sat around the kitchen table working on the script.

AG: Have you ever written a play for your mother?

SR: She's tried to get me to write a play for her, but I'm not sure I can do that, because it's difficult to imagine your mother and be imaginatively free at the same time. Your parents come into your imagination anyway, in a subterranean way. But being conscious of them as players—that's hard.

AG: When do you remember writing something for the first time?

SR: I remember, very early, writing these dictations with my mom. I remember that I wanted to write stories, but I couldn't write yet, so she would write them out for me. I have a little interview from kindergarten: "What would you like to be?" "I would like to be a writer and an artist and a teacher." Very clearly delineated. So I had some sense that writing was important for me. In the fourth grade I wrote my first play, which was a drama about landmasses. I think I wrote it partly because I loved the new words. "Peninsula." The landmasses were characters, and there was a dispute about who owned what land, and then there was a trial, and the sun came down and settled it. Mr. Spangenberger, my fourth-grade teacher, didn't put it on—I don't know why. Maybe it wasn't very good. But he was a very good teacher. He had a missing finger, and he told us that a fish had bitten it off when he was canoeing, but I always thought it was probably something much more domestic or sad.

AG: You've written poetry.

SR: I wrote a lot of poetry from when I was eighteen until I was around twenty-two. I published a little chapbook, which shall remain nameless. But I was very serious about writing poetry. Then I switched over to playwriting when I met Paula Vogel at Brown University. And playwriting made sense, because I had grown up around theater. But it just had never occurred to me to write plays until college. I took a class with Paula—junior year, I think. My father had just died—he had had bone cancer—and I came back to Brown and was really unable to write. I remember being unable to read, too. I would keep putting down the book, unable to concentrate. And Paula said, "You need a distancing mechanism. Write a play in which a dog is a protagonist." So I wrote this short play about my father through the eyes of a dog. It unlocked the floodgates.

AG: In your plays, is there a connection with poetry?

SR: When I first started writing plays, I would steal little snippets of what I'd been working on in a poem, or I'd have an idea poetically and would try to translate it into a play. But the more I've been writing plays, the more I feel as if I've found my own idiom, which fulfills that impulse to write poetry. I don't write poetry as much as I used to.

AG: There's such leanness to your playwriting.

SR: I don't like extra words.

AG: The language of *The Clean House* is honed in the way poets hone their verse.

SR: If you're spare in a certain poetic way, you don't have to deal with subtext so much, because there's space around things. Then there's a subtext in the same way that there's poetic subtext when you read a poem, and there doesn't have to be the psychological subtext of realistic speech. David Mamet's language, "Are we talking? Are we fucking talking?" really isn't mimetic on one level. It's poetic. It's as if he's interested in how words create a kind of poetic speech. And I tend to like it when there are not so many fussy, contemporary, extra words. I could imagine liking that at another point in my life: "Oh, that's interesting, how people have these verbal ticks, and how we overarticulate ourselves." But that's not the first thing I love.

AG: Do you see *The Clean House* as a turning point in your playwriting?

SR: I don't know. I didn't see it as a turning point when I wrote it. It just seemed like I was writing another play. I don't think you can look at your process that way. You'd go crazy if you thought too much about it. I think about process within the play, but I don't think of it as a trajectory.

AG: How did *The Clean House* emerge?

SR: It came out of a true story. About three or four years ago, I was at a party full of doctors, in Providence, Rhode Island. I always seem to be surrounded by doctors; my partner's a doctor, my sister's a doctor. Two uncles are doctors. So I was at this party of doctors, and a woman came in, and I said, "How are you?" and she said, "It has been such a hard month. My cleaning lady from Brazil decided she was depressed one day and wouldn't clean. So I had her medicated, and she still won't clean."

I couldn't stop thinking about this. Not only about what she said, but the transparency with which she said it, as though there were nothing wrong with her statement. As though her cleaning woman were just for cleaning. It was a view of the universe where things are only valued for their utilitarian purpose. Politically it freaked me out, and the assumptions about race and gender freaked me out. And class: "I took her to the hospital and had her medicated, and she still wouldn't clean. And I did not go to medical school to clean my own house." Telling this to a group of people at a cocktail party. I thought, "Ah, 'I did not go to medical school to clean my own house.' What does that mean? Does class get us beyond the obligation to clean for ourselves, to care for our own dirt in a daily way? Does medical school supersede our gender? As women are we supposed to clean up after other people?"

Anyway, I was thinking about this woman and this maid, and McCarter Theatre commissioned a one-act, so I decided to write about a woman whose maid won't clean. It was hard to write, actually. The first ten pages were easy, but the rest of it was murder. I kept going down the wrong garden path and having to go back. It took me a year to write one act. Then I took time off, took six months off, and I very quickly wrote the second act. I knew what I wanted that to be by the time I was writing it. The second act also comes from a true story, about a man, a surgeon, who left his wife for a woman on whom he had performed a mastectomy. When my father had cancer, wit and humor were a saving grace. That was part of what was animating the play.

AG: Do you consider it a comedy?

SR: I suppose I would. I don't think of my work in that way. I am very concerned about genre in a sense; I'm concerned about what a farce is, what a Greek tragedy is. But I'm only interested in it if there's some redefinition of the genre. Still, when I began to write this play, I wasn't thinking about genre, I was actually thinking about cleaning.

I do think about form and structure obsessively, but there has to be some distinction between caring about form as an architectural entity and caring about form as some kind of preconceived determination: "I'm writing a two-act comedy." Every play is a new formal challenge. You have no idea what the form will be until you know what the play is, and you have no idea what the play is until you know what the form is. It's always happening. It's always in a dynamic.

Something in the play that fascinated me when writing it was the relationship between cleaning and death. We deal with entropy on a daily basis: dust accumulates, vegetables rot. Even if we took no action in the world with our little paltry wills, entropy would still happen, and how do we keep that at bay? How do we react to it? Do we care? Do we want other people to do something about it? Do we not want to think about it? Something about the body being in decay, the house being in decay. They're both formal structures in that sense.

AG: On the page and in performance, the play seems to be a mingling of comedy and pathos, light and dark.

SR: The image I get when you make that comment is painterly. There are paintings that are suffused with light, or a Renaissance painting that uses chiaro-scuro, or a Rembrandt painting that's very dark but has one tiny source of light. It seems that for the most part, things are interesting in relief. That's why I, for no other visceral reason, would write a dark comedy rather than a comedy, or a tragedy with some humor. I don't think I could find tragedy bearable unless it had some sense of life in it. Similarly, I couldn't bear only laughing and not thinking for two hours. I'd want some contrast, because that's how we live.

AG: You studied playwriting at Brown University. What was the most valuable lesson you learned about your work?

SR: To do it. To do the work. That's why Paula [Vogel] is so inspiring. She makes you think, "I could do this work. I could do it for my life." Not many people make you think that. It would never have occurred to me that this was some-thing I could make a life of. I thought I would write, but I thought I would have a job and write on the side. I thought I would be a scholar, an academic. The idea that I could do something as decadent as write plays for my life? Just absurd. But Paula says, "This is how you would do it. Here are these tools, and here is my example." With total generosity.

AG: Currently you live in California. Are you writing for film or television?

SR: No, I'm not. I moved out to California for love, not for work. I would like to write some beautiful little film, if the right director came along. But I have no interest in turning out scripts for money. Maybe at some point I'll need the money and I'll be less snooty about it.

AG: Do you find a difference between writing in a northeastern city and writing in southern California?

SR: I haven't written enough plays in California yet to know. The quality of light is different; the air, the space. I'm happier in New York City than anywhere in the world, but I get less writing done in New York than anywhere else, too, because I'm too happy to be writing. In L.A., I'm not happy consuming the culture, so I just hole up and write.

AG: Are there advantages or disadvantages to being a woman writing in the American theater?

SR: One of the only advantages to being a woman or being a historical outsider is that you have a sense of distance, and a sense of the hoops you have to jump through before you can speak in the world. There is a breed of men: "I love talking and I love my voice, and everybody's always told me I am smart and interesting, and I'm going to talk some more and oh, my God, my plays are all being produced and I'm only twenty-one." I think the only thing you can say, looking at that as a woman playwright, or as a woman director who sees that the male directors are young and hip at twenty-six and that a woman at twenty-six is considered unseasoned and not worth trusting—which I see all the time—is that it is an advantage. Your work is more thoughtful, and by the time it gets out the door you've suffered slightly more and are less facile. I personally have never experienced any particular discrimination. I can remember Paula Vogel saying, "If you're a woman writing for the theater, you are a feminist." And I think that's right.

❦

The British playwright Joanna Laurens, who received the Special Commendation of the Susan Smith Blackburn Prize in 2000–2001 for her play The Three Birds, *New York, 2004:*

The *Guardian* ran a story about the top fifty women in their fields, and they asked me if I'd do it, and I said, "Yes." But then afterward, I did think, "Wouldn't it be nice if we reached the stage where we didn't feel the need to have this only about women?" Because the fact that this is fifty "women" and not fifty "people" means that we still identify women as a minority, and we still feel the need to exclude men in order to empower women. When we've passed the point where we need to do that, then we'll know that we've reached an equal, just society. We're not there yet, which is a little depressing.

An Interview with Rukhsana Ahmad

Rukhsana Ahmad is a playwright, short story writer, novelist, and translator. She was born in Karachi, where she studied English literature and later taught at Kara-chi University. She moved to London with her husband in 1973. Her plays include Song for a Sanctuary *(1991), an adaptation of S. H. Manto's story* Black Shalwar *(1997);* River on Fire *(1997), which was a finalist for the Susan Smith Blackburn Prize in 2001–2002; and* The Man Who Refused to Be God *(2001). This interview took place in London in June 2004.*

AG: Would you talk about your background?

RUKHSANA AHMAD: My father was an engineer. He was a very dynamic and powerful, energetic man. They were complete opposites, my father and mother. He was much more rural in his culture than my mother was; my mother was from Delhi. She was very inhibited, very graceful, very elegant. A beautiful woman. And my father was a right womanizer. He remarried when my youngest brothers were due to be born. His marriage with my mother was very unhappy.

AG: Did they divorce?

RA: No, because she could not. She kept going back to her family to say, "I

Rukhsana Ahmad, a finalist for the twenty-fourth Susan Smith Blackburn Prize for River on Fire. *(Photograph: Linda Brownlee. Courtesy of renaissance one, 2004)*

want to take a divorce," and they would say, "Who's going to support seven kids?" There was no way she could support us and manage, because all of us were under ten years old. It was an impossible situation. There were four girls and three boys, and then one of my brothers died in a flying accident at the age of twenty. A short story I wrote recently, "First Love" (2004), is based on his story. That was the first time I dealt with it, thirty years on. He was the guy who was going to salvage life for the family, especially my mother — it had a terrible impact on her.

My political knowledge and intelligence comes partly from those early experiences. Here was a country that was at war with itself — the Bangladesh War of Independence. My brother was the only person in the family who kept saying, "The Bengalis are right, we should be giving them more autonomy." And ironically, he was the one whose plane got hijacked, and he had to crash himself to not suffer the disgrace of becoming the guy who got hijacked. It was his first solo flight. That short story is a retelling of his story, and it was the first time I had written something so directly autobiographical. It was very painful to write. As in the story, I had been antiwar, and my brother and I used to have arguments. My sister and I, we'd both pick on him, and he'd defend his militarism, which came from the army people in the family.

My eldest sister never got on with my father. She would defy him and invite a beating. My father was quite abusive verbally and occasionally physically abusive; he would get violent. I never remembered all of this very clearly, and when I wrote *Song for a Sanctuary,* which takes place in a refuge for women who have been abused, I thought, "Why the hell did I do this play?" But every play you do, you're exploring something for yourself, and I think that play was revisiting the trauma of domestic violence, what it does to you. I believe that feminism for women is an experiential thing.

AG: When did you first realize you were a writer?

RA: I really wanted to be a writer at nine or ten. I started writing a novel then — a very romantic novel, too, it was. Fortunately for humanity it wasn't saved. The interesting thing about it is that it was in Urdu, and I do feel the biggest loss in my writing has been the loss of language, because so many of my characters think in a different language. I'm able to convey that, but only partially. There is a silence that is enclosed by language or the absence of it. If I could write a completely bilingual play, which would be understood in Pakistan, that play would be much more powerful, because both languages would be understood there. But because I'm in England, and my audience is white and largely without Urdu, I cannot do that.

Language is a very complex subject. In Pakistan, as elsewhere, language and power are so connected. That I went to a convent meant that Urdu was taken away quite early—and Urdu was not my mother tongue anyway; my parents were Punjabi. But Urdu is the language of the powerful elite, and there is a great sense of inferiority about Punjabi among Punjabis. So my parents had never taught us Punjabi; we grew up speaking Urdu, and I only acquired my Punjabi after I married into a Punjabi household based in Lahore. I can speak decent Punjabi now, but I can't write in it, and I can just about read it. With Urdu, my style is not evolved enough to write in it now, but I think I could write scripts. I could manage dialogue quite easily.

AG: When did you learn to speak English?

RA: Very early, because it was the medium of education in the convents where I studied (it was a privileged education). I am very comfortable in English; I think in it and dream in it. But I am also very divided in my consciousness of the world. You know how you have an understanding of certain concepts and notions in one language, and you don't know the exact equivalents in another? In that sense, I feel language is an inhibition here.

I didn't start writing in English formally until I studied English literature at university in Pakistan, and even so, I thought, "Well, to be able to write you must be in London." There was this idea of "I'm not good enough" for a very long time. I started teaching literature before my marriage, but my mother said, "You have to get married now." And actually, life had come to a kind of cul-de-sac. I'd never have the money to move out of my mother's house if I remained teaching at the university, which paid something like five hundred rupees, which would not get you a week's living anywhere. So I decided to get married, and I lost my job in 1973 because my husband was based in London.

I couldn't get even a school-teaching job here. I did my master's again here in England, and I remember going to a job agency and them telling me, "The only job we can offer you is charring." So I thought, "Well, I might as well find out about this motherhood lark," and decided to have the kids, and had them very quickly. All three of them by the end of the seventies. I thought, "I'll take five years to raise them," which was a completely foolish idea. I had them very close together and was completely overwhelmed. That was the time I got very politicized, because I realized how disempowered I'd become in that process. I'd also gotten totally de-skilled by being in a country that did not recognize my qualifications. I started writing in order to survive. I started writing about the status of women in Pakistan, and then I was invited by Ravi Randhawa to join the Asian Women Writers Workshop, later the Asian Women Writers Collective. Suddenly I was with a group of women who were of Asian extraction, knew the languages, knew the culture, knew what I was talking about, and the first story I wrote went down very well and got me a theater job.

AG: Do you consider yourself a feminist?

RA: Yes. I do. I have no embarrassment about saying that anywhere. I'm less rigid a feminist than I was. I used to be austere. But the Women's Movement was like that.

AG: You write in your introductory notes to the published version of *Song for a Sanctuary* that you based the play on an actual incident, which in turn reminded you of personal events.

RA: That's right. The play didn't start with a personal story at all, but the emotion came from a memory of mine. Actually, two incidents inspired the play. There was a murder of a Sikh woman in a refuge for abused women, and a friend of mine, Rahila Gupta, wrote a poem in response, and we all went on a march protesting violence against women. I felt quite envious of her being able to write something, but I just couldn't think of what to write. Then I heard about a dispute at a refuge where the workers got locked out by the residents, and I started researching that story and the class and culture differences. The first version of that play had the lock-out in it, but I worked with a director who said the lock-out had to go—it didn't work dramatically—so I took it out. The cultural conflict stayed.

AG: There's a great deal in that play: abuse of women, the faults of the refuge system, the racism of one of the women who runs the refuge.

RA: That character is very politically driven. I was satirizing that feminism of the eighties which saw everything in black and white, which believed that if ideas were not pure enough, they had to be thrown out. I see the extremism of that position, its dangers, and the character is based on that type of person. You see that kind of person always in a refuge, the kind who is completely driven by political motives and can never see the humanity of other, more complex positions.

AG: The play is quite disturbing, and the ending is brutal—bleak and shocking. You cannot help but draw the conclusion that no matter how painful a woman's position in relation to her abuser, if her only alternative is poverty she really has no choice.

RA: Well, my mother's position was similar, and the character of the woman who is eventually killed by her husband is quite closely based on my mother.

AG: What has it been like as a woman of Pakistani birth living in London and working in the theater here?

RA: Things have evolved hugely in the last fifteen or eighteen years. But it's not been easy. I don't want to complain about it, because on the whole I haven't done badly. I don't feel unsuccessful. I feel unacknowledged at times, and I feel marginalized at times, because I'm not integrated into the theater culture enough: circles of actors and writers, and drama parties, where people hang out. People do all their socializing in pubs here, their networking happens in pubs. And a pub is not necessarily a charming place to meet. I don't drink enough to be interested in hanging out there. I think my age was probably not a good thing, and I made a political decision to continue to wear the *kameez shalwar,* which I think held me back. If I had appeared to be more integrated than I seemed to be on the surface, then I might have done better.

It might also have to do with the fact that my work is not easy. I am very politically motivated as a writer, my ideas are usually quite layered and complex, and I try to say too many things in one piece of writing. So I'm not my best friend as a playwright, probably. Others are better at offering a product that fulfills expectations. In *River on Fire,* for example, I was writing a more complex piece of theater than I was ready to write at that time. Not having a visible audience has been a problem. After three or four years of writing and rewriting and struggle, I finally put the play on myself with the Kali Theatre Company, which Rita Wolf and I had formed to produce *Song for a Sanctuary.* I did not want to do that; I did not want to be the producer for *River on Fire.* But I found it very difficult to place the play. Nobody would touch it — they didn't know what it was saying. Fortunately, Kali Theatre colleagues wanted it. Helena Uren, the director, was wonderfully supportive. And when it was finally put on, it was perfectly accessible; audiences loved it.

In *River on Fire* the theme is minorities and the treatment of minorities. It's a very big issue for me. You judge a society by its treatment of its minorities. And the worse the treatment is, the more primitive a society is in my mind. Sometimes a society is able to change its government and it won't, and sometimes it can't. I'm not entirely a believer in the dictum "You get the government you deserve," because it doesn't apply to totalitarian government. You get somebody like Saddam Hussein, and you're stuck with him for thirty years. You get him out, and what do you have? A mess. But I know that our treatment of minorities in Pakistan has been horrible, too, and I feel very ashamed of that. And we should be ashamed. Every time I see a horrible racist thing happen here and I think, "I wish we weren't here," I then think, "My God, if I was in Pakistan, I would hate things much more."

I recognized finally that actually I have the audience that I want. I would know how to raise an audience for a play of mine, and that audience would come — not in such vast numbers as they do for *Bombay Dreams,* but then I wouldn't want to write *Bombay Dreams,* so I'm not worried. There is now a reasonably large Asian audience. I think this is the trap actually. The fact that you're perceived as Asian, that in itself is a problem for Asian writers. People assume that you can only write for Asian audiences. Once they recognize that your work can sell to a larger audience, then there won't be a problem. Once you're successful, your Asianness is less of a problem. I think people are beginning to recognize this though, as the brown pound is getting more powerful.

Rita Wolf eventually got married and moved to New York, and I was left with the Kali company, and I ended up leading writing workshops, feeling very much that there weren't enough Asians in the theater. That has been a problem, that I am a bit of an activist and a bit of a do-gooder. Why I'm guilty of that altruism, I don't know. It comes from a Puritan streak in my mother, I think. It's as if everything has to be justified. Your time needs to be justified, in terms of the good value it has produced. Everything you do has to be worthy. Unfortunately, my work suffers from that sense of worthiness. I hope this will change, as I have recently started enjoying telling stories much more, and realizing that telling stories is a valuable thing to do per se. You should be allowed to tell them for pleasure, too.

AG: It's an ancient mechanism.

RA: My grandmother was a great storyteller. She had no education, so she remembered each and every story she ever heard. She was a repository of stories from the Bible to the Koran, of stories from all over the world. They used to go to storytellers in the marketplace; people would have sessions of storytelling. I think that instinct in me, the ability to tell a story, was the first skill I recognized as a writer, but I also have this problem of wanting to have something of value in the story, something that justifies it. Also, I think my writing suffers from my literariness. When I first produce a draft, it is elaborate and suffers from an excess of writing. Which is the problem of a literary background; you come with a lot of verbiage.

Kali soaked up a lot of time and ended up being a whole lot of educational training and workshops for people. But in the end the Arts Council gave us Revenue Funding, and at that point I had to make a decision: do I want to be a writer and prioritize my life in that direction? So I resigned.

You haven't asked much about theatrical influences. I'm very much a theater person; I go to see plays a great deal. My training was in literature, but my theater influences are people like Arthur Miller, people whose politics might be different from mine in some ways but in some ways not. I love Alice Childress's *Wine in the Wilderness* (1969). I admire August Wilson's work. I love *Ma Rainey's Black Bottom* (1984). That's the kind of writing I like.

AG: You spoke earlier about the theme of minorities in *River on Fire*. Another theme in your work, which I particularly noticed in *Black Shalwar,* is the contrast between materialism and spirituality.

RA: In *Black Shalwar*, the prostitute's materialism becomes emblematic of survival. It's actually about selfhood. *Black Shalwar* is about selfhood. But I don't argue for spiritualism, which is the direction of the man with whom the prostitute moves to Delhi. I argue for a kind of rounded humanity that includes love, sexual love, and that's one of the things that I hope emerges in my play *The Man Who Refused to Be God,* about the Indian philosophical teacher Jiddu Krishnamurti. The search for God in a sterile way is not a useful route. If there is going to be a kind of godliness, it is going to be a godliness about loving other human beings. If there is a kind of religion that I ever might return to, it would be that mystical notion that there is a god in other human beings. I would hope that would be my message: of extreme humanism rather than any extreme form of religion.

❦

The Irish-born playwright Lin Coglan, a finalist for the 2003–2004 Susan Smith Blackburn Prize for her drama Mercy, London, 2004:

In the last ten years or so, I've become very intrigued with the connection between storytelling and healing, and how we use stories to empower ourselves, heal ourselves, communicate in order not to feel isolated. I see writing as a healing tool. When I trained at college, the most important question I was ever asked was, "What is your writing for? What is the purpose of your work?" It was not simply good enough to indulge yourself by writing stories and throwing them at an audience because you thought they were interesting. The stories had to serve a purpose, in terms of what you were passionate about, and why and who that audience was, and why that work would be of value to an audience.

SIXTEEN

Prescriptions for a Playwriting Life

Dear Emily: On Being a Playwright

TIMBERLAKE WERTENBAKER

❦

Dear Emily,

When you asked for advice on becoming a playwright, I thought it would be quite easy to give you some tips, and I rashly promised to write them out. As I started writing, I realized how difficult and even presumptuous it is to give advice. So, my first advice to you is never to listen to other people's advice. When I announced I wanted to be a playwright, everyone advised me not to. That would be my general advice to anyone who wants to be a playwright: Don't. Now, if you are determined to ignore this first very sensible piece of advice, then you must ask yourself the following questions.

Do you really want to write plays?

Can this cock-pit hold
The vasty fields of France? or may we cram
Within this wooden O the very casques
That did affright the air at Agincourt?
　　　　　—SHAKESPEARE, *Henry V*, Act 1, Scene 1

To answer that, you must ask yourself if you wouldn't prefer to write film scripts, poetry, novels. Many playwrights go on to film, and if you want to do that, that's fine, but then you don't need to read any further. Writing plays—writing more than a handful of plays—requires a real love of theater and a belief in the value of theater. All of these are constantly under threat—by the media, the critics themselves, by our society, which likes fast food for the mind. Plays tend to be two- to three-course meals, even if you make them light. Can you accept the limitations of time and space when you write? Plays function through depth rather than expanse. Can you accept that discipline? Finally, are you intrigued by and attracted to the physical mystery of the stage?

Do you love actors?

Good my lord, will you see the players well bestowed? Do you hear, let them be well used, for they are the abstract and brief chronicles of the time. After your death you were better have a bad epitaph than their ill report while you live.

— SHAKESPEARE, *Hamlet,* Act 2, Scene 2

You will have to work closely with actors on your plays. If you don't like them, don't trust them, or despise them, you will have a hard time. One of the most rewarding aspects of playwriting is the work between actors and writers, the understanding that takes place. But it can also be fraught, when actors ask you to change your carefully crafted lines or claim their characters make no sense. I have a general policy: I ignore what actors say for the first two weeks of rehearsals, when they are struggling with their own fears and prejudices, and I listen to everything they say in the last two weeks. I do, however, discriminate between the actors who have earned my trust and those who haven't. If an actor struggles for weeks with a line or a scene, and it still doesn't work, it's probably the fault of the play. If the actor simply isn't trying and is determined to make you change something, then it's probably the actor. A good director will negotiate between these conflicting demands. But we come to a crucial point: choosing your director.

Do you have good judgment?

This is certain: only good judgment secures good fortune.

— SOPHOCLES, *Antigone* (trans. T. Wertenbaker)

You need good judgment for many reasons, but mostly in your choice of directors. Of course, sometimes the director chooses you, but even then, you must use your judgment. Don't go with the reputation but with the work. Do you like their work? Do you feel safe with them? I think your instinct must operate there; it is time to leave the head behind. A famous director may not be the best for your work, women don't necessarily direct women's plays better, even if, for political reasons, you wish this were so. Ask yourself as well why they are coming to you. Do they genuinely like your play, or are they coming to you on the back of a previous success?

This is one of the most fraught and important areas in theater, because most new plays are judged by their first production.

Do you have a life?

Everything in life exerts a tremendous attraction on the artist. . . . [N]o artist can exist if he is expected to renounce life like a monk.
— STANISLAVSKY, *Stanislavsky on the Art of the Stage*
(trans. David Magarshack)

If you don't have a life, get one.
There are many reasons for this. The first is that however wonderful and intoxicating the theater is, it is also fickle and difficult. You will have fallow periods, difficult times, moments of discouragement. This is when family and friends and other interests will come to your rescue. The other reason is that life feeds plays. You can write one or two plays on an empty life, no more.

How thick-skinned are you?

I can't stand a naked light bulb, any more than I can a rude remark or a vulgar action.
— TENNESSEE WILLIAMS, *A Streetcar Named Desire*

I say this as someone who gets deeply depressed after bad reviews. But it is impossible to survive without a certain thickness of skin. I know no playwrights who have got through without attacks from peers and critics. If this is going to be unbearable, it's best not to start. I wish I could advise you on how to acquire a thick skin. Philosophy helps; a certain detachment. Read the Roman stoics, try Buddhism, or study accounts of expeditions to the North Pole . . .

Do you have a sport or a hobby?

ESTRAGON: What do we do now?
VLADIMIR: While waiting.
ESTRAGON: While waiting.
  Silence.
VLADIMIR: We could do our exercises.
ESTRAGON: Our movements.
VLADIMIR: Our elevations.
ESTRAGON: Our relaxations.

VLADIMIR: Our elongations.
ESTRAGON: Our relaxations.
VLADIMIR: To warm us up.
ESTRAGON: To calm us down.
—SAMUEL BECKETT, *Waiting for Godot*

This may seem odd, but I believe it is very important. A sport will give you relief, and at the very least you can work out your aggressions against actors, directors, or critics. It will also bring oxygen to your brain when you need it. Keep one up or develop one. Long walks in a city will do, or even, as in *Waiting for Godot,* hopping from one foot to another. I also think it's best to keep your competitive feelings for a sport rather than for the theater. People will always try to place you and make you feel competitive; the award system does that, too (however nice it is to get awards). But try to rise above that. A writer is an individual, not part of an Olympic team.

Are you courageous?

The people who succeed and do not push on to a greater failure are the spiritual middle classers. Their stopping at success is the proof of their compromising insignificance. How petty their dreams must have been!
—EUGENE O'NEILL, "Damn the Optimist," *New York Herald Tribune,*
February 13, 1921

Theater is a place for the bold.
There is nothing more exposed than a first night. There is nothing scarier than starting a new play. The first read-through is agony. But more than that, through your writing career, you'll be asked or be tempted to make compromises, with fashion, with opinion, with peer pressure. Have you the courage to resist? All new playwriting must be an exploration. Have you the courage to find a new route even through well-known territory? Have you the courage to explore unmapped areas? Have you the courage to stand still before the full mystery of human beings?

Are you an optimist?

All the same, you won't disappear, you won't be without influence. After you will come maybe six people of your sort, then twelve, and so on, until

in the end people like you are in the majority. In two, three hundred years
life on earth will be astonishingly, unimaginably beautiful.
—ANTON CHEKHOV, *The Three Sisters* (trans. T. Wertenbaker)

It's my belief no one can write unless they are optimists. Beckett is considered a pessimist, but I would call him the greatest optimist. You have to believe
in humanity. It is that belief which will give you the compassion needed to write
plays. You also need to be an optimist to keep going in the teeth of initial dis-
couragements or later ones. But more than anything, you need to believe in the
future. You cannot write for present success, you must hope that your work will
resonate down the generations.

Are you curious?

Plays are not journalism.
—PHYLLIS NAGY, *State of Play: Playwrights on Playwriting*

Real curiosity goes beyond the events and tries to find causes, a common
human ground, a trigger. Call it interest, depth. You can hear a conversation
in a bus and report the conversation, or you can try to find out who is speaking and why; let your curiosity hover. Curiosity leads beyond the self and the
superficial interpretation of events.

Are you true?

This above all: to thine own self be true,
And it must follow as night the day
Thou canst not then be false to any man.
—SHAKESPEARE, *Hamlet,* Act 1, Scene 3

As you put on a play or come to write many more, there will be many people
telling you how to do things. Beware of people who ask for a happy ending
instead of a sad one (yes, this doesn't happen only in film); beware of those
who are afraid something of yours might offend; of those driving you to more
conventional content.

Beware of the temptation of accepting something just because it pays well.
This can lead to much misery, if your heart is not in your work. You do need to
live (although I'd advise any playwright to have another source of income—advice I didn't take myself and wish I had), but you must try not to compromise.

This does not mean refusing to listen to people. Some directors are marvelous editors and will help you make your play more clear. The danger is when someone wants you to write to express something in *them*. You'll know the difference, because with one, you'll feel what they say is right and do it immediately, with the other, you'll find yourself struggling to please someone and it won't work. In other words, if someone is trying to help you make your play better *on its own terms,* then listen to them; if they are trying to meddle with the *content,* then beware.

If you want to write historical plays when journalistic plays are the fashion, or a tragedy when whimsy is in demand (or vice versa), you will have to possess nerves of steel to remain true to yourself, but you must. Some playwrights lead a trend, some are simply lone voices whose sound eases our isolation, but no playwright worth anything is a follower. This advice may not bring you success, but it will bring you a certain happiness or at least contentment.

Finally, cultivate a broad circle of friends and accept any help on offer. I know I have survived thanks to help that came in all sorts of surprising ways. Early on, I was regularly fed by a dear family friend who was an Italian Catholic. When I told her I was determined to become a playwright, she shook her head in dismay, but then perked up. "I know," she said, "I'll light candles to the Patron Saint of Hopeless Causes." And she did.

Good luck!
Timberlake

Afterword

BILL BLACKBURN

❦

During the past three decades, we've seen a steady rise in mastery and thematic scope in plays by women, now rivaling the level in women's fiction writing. It's a source of deep satisfaction that the Susan Smith Blackburn Prize's encouragement and recognition appear to have been important factors in this progress, as shown in testimonies of the finalists.

As this book demonstrates, the battle for parity is not over. It is still too great a problem for women's work to be brought to production and often for even the most brilliant writers to find the time to create.

But women will continue to deal boldly, in their own ways, with the problems now so terrifying and fascinating in our lives. Given the application of enough imagination, skill, sanity, and sense of humor, anything can be investigated dramatically between humans onstage, however profound or however esoteric the issue.

Against certain politically correct conventions, I feel that women writers have a gender-specific muse and sensibility, as do men, and that they are the stronger for it. I find support for this view in the previous pages, as well as in the plays. These dimensions can bring distinctive ability to observe and to affect while maintaining universality.

Therefore, I look forward to more plays from women on issues that seem destined to persist and grow: the dumbing-down of society, experts versus anti-elitism, the erosion of art, religion in politics, autocracy within democracy, the demands of fundamentalism, assaults on the environment, limits on scientific enquiry, suppression of women globally, tolerance of poverty.

The theater, while it entertains and enthralls, makes it possible to confront these issues, to understand and cope with them. The voices of women, their creative insight, their ideas and talents, have never seemed so necessary.

Appendix: The Susan Smith Blackburn Prize

❧

Winners, Commendations, and Finalists, by Author

* = Winner
† = Special Commendation
§ = Joint top finalist (1994–1995 only)
§ No first prize awarded; three top finalists honored

Adams, Judith	1997–1998, 1998–1999†, 2000–2001
Adshead, Kay	1987–1988, 2001–2002
Ahmad, Rukhsana	2001–2002
Allen, Claudia	2002–2003
al-Shaykh, Hanan	1996–1997
Anderson, Jane	1990–1991, 1991–1992, 1992–1993†
Ayvazian, Leslie	1995–1996†, 2004–2005
Baldwin, Nicola	1993–1994, 1999–2000
Barry, Lynda	1991–1992
Beber, Neena	2003–2004
Bell, Hilary	1998–1999
Betts, Jean	2003–2004
Bhatti, Gurpreet	2004–2005*
Bovasso, Julie	1980–1981
Brown, Tina	1978–1979
Bruce, Lesley	1993–1994†
Buffini, Moira	1992–1993, 1997–1998*
Burger, Katherine	1996–1997
Burke-Kennedy, Mary Elizabeth	1984–1985
Cahill, Kathleen	1984–1985
Carpenter, Bridget	1999–2000*

Carr, Marina	1996–1997*
Carson, Jo	1989–1990
Cho, Julia	2001–2002
Churchill, Caryl	1979–1980, 1982–1983†, 1983–1984*, 1987–1988*
Cizmar, Paula	1981–1982†, 1982–1983
Clark, Kathleen	1987–1988
Cleage, Pearl	1983–1984, 1993–1994, 1995–1996
Clifford, Sara	1998–1999
Coghlan, Lin	2003–2004†
Coles, Jane	1993–1994*
Collins, Kathleen	1982–1983, 1986–1987
Coman, Sherry	1990–1991
Commire, Anne	1988–1989
Congdon, Constance	1985–1986, 1995–1996
Conger, Trista	1988–1989
Cooper, Helen	1984–1985, 1986–1987, 2002–2003
Corthron, Kia	1997–1998
Cruz, Migdalia	1990–1991†, 1996–1997
Cunningham, Alexandra	2000–2001
Curran, Leigh	1978–1979
Damashek, Barbara	1987–1988
de Lancie, Christian	1993–1994
de Matteo, Donna	1982–1983
Dee, Ruby	1993–1994
Devlin, Anne	1985–1986*
Dhingra, Dolly	1999–2000
Di Mambro, Ann Marie	1994–1995
Diggs, Elizabeth	1981–1982, 1987–1988†
Donohue, Nancy	1979–1980
Drexler, Rosalyn	1983–1984
Duffy, Carol Ann	1982–1983
Dunn, Nell	1981–1982*
Dworkin, Susan	1980–1981
Edmundson, Helen	1993–1994
Edson, Margaret	1993–1994
Egloff, Elizabeth	1995–1996, 1996–1997
Eilenberg, Charlotte	2002–2003
Ensler, Eve	1998–1999, 2000–2001
Ewing, Nancy	2000–2001
Field, Barbara	1982–1983, 1988–1989
Flakes, Susan	1996–1997
Fodor, Kate	2002–2003
Fornés, Maria Irene	1985–1986, 1987–1988

Franceschild, Donna	1989–1990
Franklin, J.e.	1981–1982, 1989–1990, 1992–1993
Freed, Amy	1993–1994, 2001–2002
Gallagher, Mary	1979–1980, 1986–1987*, 1989–1990
Gannon, Lucy	1988–1989, 1989–1990*
Garrett, Lillian	1989–1990
Garrett, Nancy Fales	1982–1983
GeBauer, Judy	1987–1988
Gee, Shirley	1983–1984, 1984–1985*, 1989–1990
Gems, Pam	1978–1979, 1985–1986, 1996–1997†
Gersten, Alexandra	2002–2003
Gilman, Rebecca	1998–1999, 1999–2000, 2004–2005
Gionfriddo, Gina	2001–2002*
Glass, Joanna	1978–1979, 1980–1981†, 1983–1984, 2004–2005
Glover, Sue	1991–1992
Goldberg, Jessica	1998–1999*
Green, Debbie Tucker	2002–2003
Groff, Rinne	2002–2003
Harmon, Nikki	1988–1989
Harris, Valerie	1978–1979
Harris, Zinnie	2000–2001†, 2003–2004
Hayes, Catherine	1981–1982
Hébert, Julie	1998–1999†
Henley, Beth	1979–1980†, 1987–1988
Holborough, Jacqueline	1987–1988
Holland, Endesha Ida Mae	1992–1993
Horsfield, Debbie	1984–1985
Houston, Velina Hasu	1985–1986
Howe, Tina	1979–1980, 1983–1984, 1997–1998
Iizuka, Naomi	2000–2001
Janaczewska, Noelle	1997–1998
Janiurek, Lenka	1978–1979
Jellicoe, Ann	1980–1981
Johnson, Catherine	1991–1992
Johnson, Cindy Lou	1984–1985, 1986–1987
Johnston, Jennifer	1996–1997
Jones, Charlotte	2000–2001*
Jones, Marie	1999–2000
Jordan, Julia	1996–1997, 2001–2002†
Judd, Yazmine	1998–1999
Kaplan, Shirley	1981–1982
Kearsley, Julia	1980–1981, 1982–1983
Keilstrup, Margaret	1981–1982

Kennedy, Adrienne	1990–1991
Kesselman, Wendy	1980–1981*, 1989–1990
Kreitzer, Carson	2003–2004
Kriegel, Gail	1983–1984
Kurtti, Casey	1987–1988
Kuti, Elizabeth	1999–2000†
Lathrop, Mary	1991–1992
Laurens, Joanna	2000–2001†
Lauro, Shirley	1980–1981, 1991–1992
Lavery, Bryony	1980–1981, 2002–2003†, 2004–2005
Lawrence, Maureen	1990–1991, 1994–1995
Lebow, Barbara	1985–1986, 1994–1995, 1995–1996, 1997–1998
Lenkiewicz, Rebecca	2004–2005
Lochhead, Liz	1998–1999
Logan, Rosie	1986–1987
Loomer, Lisa	1993–1994†, 2003–2004
Luckham, Claire	1991–1992
Ludlum, Anne	2002–2003
MacDonald, Sharman	1984–1985†, 1990–1991, 1995–1996
Mack, Carol	1982–1983
Mann, Emily	1981–1982, 1984–1985, 1996–1997, 1999–2000
Marnich, Melanie	2004–2005
McCartney, Nicola	1997–1998
McCullough, Mia	2004–2005
McDonald, Heather	2002–2003
McGravie, Anne	1984–1985
McKeaney, Grace	1981–1982
McLaughlin, Ellen	1986–1987*, 1989–1990
McLeod, Jenny	1999–2000
McIntyre, Clare	1992–1993
Medley, Cassandra	1988–1989
Meredith, Lois	1993–1994
Meyer, Marlane	1986–1987, 1988–1989, 1989–1990, 1992–1993*
Miller, Susan	1979–1980, 1988–1989, 1994–1995§, 2001–2002*
Mitchell, Ann	1981–1982
Morgan, Abi	2003–2004
Moss, Chloe	2004–2005†
Mueller, Lavonne	1980–1981, 1986–1987
Muinzer, Philomena	1979–1980
Munro, Rona	1990–1991*
Murray, Melissa	1985–1986, 1986–1987
Nagy, Phyllis	1995–1996†
Nemeth, Sally	1994–1995

Noble, Ann	2003–2004
Norman, Marsha	1978–1979†, 1982–1983*, 1983–1984
Nottage, Lynn	1997–1998
Oakes, Meredith	2000–2001
Obolensky, Kira	1998–1999
O'Brien, Edna	1979–1980
Oglesby, Tamsin	1995–1996
O'Malley, Mary	1978–1979*, 1985–1986†
Orlandersmith, Dael	1999–2000†, 2002–2003*
Page, Louise	1982–1983, 1984–1985
Parks, Suzan-Lori	1996–1997, 1999–2000
Pearson, Sybille	1980–1981
Perloff, Carey	2001–2002
Pinnock, Winsome	1989–1990†, 1991–1992
Prebble, Lucy	2003–2004
Quang, Nu	1992–1993
Raffo, Heather	2004–2005†
Rahman, Aishah	1985–1986
Rebeck, Theresa	1994–1995, 2002–2003
Reid, Christina	1984–1985
Reingold, Jacquelyn	1994–1995
Reynolds, Anna	1992–1993
Richmond, Gillian	1990–1991
Rivers, Susan	1984–1985
Ruhl, Sarah	2003–2004*
Ryan, Kate Moira	1996–1997
Sanchez-Scott, Milcha	1986–1987
Schneider, Barbara	1979–1980*, 1980–1981
Schofield, Julia	1987–1988
Scollard, Rose	1995–1996
Shank, Adele Edling	1981–1982, 1982–1983
Siefert, Lynn	1983–1984†, 1991–1992†
Smith, Anna Deavere	1992–1993, 1993–1994
Son, Diana	1998–1999
Sontag, Susan	1992–1993
Stephenson, Shelagh	1997–1998†
Stuart, Kelly	2001–2002
Sturges, Karen Duke	1979–1980
Swados, Elizabeth	1991–1992
Teale, Polly	2003–2004
Thatcher, Kristine	1985–1986, 1994–1995§
Thomas, Freyda	1999–2000
Thompson, Judith	2002–2003

Thomson, Katherine	2004–2005
Thornton, Jane	1985–1986
Thuna, Leonora	1986–1987†
Todd, Susan	1981–1982
Tolan, Kathleen	1997–1998
Trainor, Kay	1992–1993
Vogel, Paula	1991–1992, 1992–1993, 1994–1995, 1995–1996, 1997–1998*
Wagener, Terri	1978–1979, 1983–1984
Walker, Celeste Bedford	1999–2000
Wallace, Naomi	1994–1995§, 1995–1996*
Wasserstein, Wendy	1978–1979, 1981–1982, 1988–1989*, 1992–1993
Watson, Alison	1980–1981
Weisman, Annie	2000–2001
Wertenbaker, Timberlake	1988–1989†, 1991–1992*
West, Cheryl L.	1990–1991*
Wettig, Patricia	2004–2005
Wilson, Erin Cressida	1995–1996
Wilson, Tracey Scott	2001–2002
Wood, Victoria	1979–1980
Woods, Sarah	2000–2001
Wyatt, Elizabeth	1988–1989
Wymark, Olwen	1978–1979, 1979–1980
Yeger, Sheila	1988–1989, 1990–1991
Youngblood, Shay	1989–1990
Zacarias, Karen	2003–2004

Winners, Commendations, Finalists, Judges, and Presenters, by Year
I. 1978–1979 (FEBRUARY 6, 1979, LONDON)

Winner: Mary O'Malley, *Once a Catholic*
Special Commendation: Marsha Norman, *Getting Out*
Finalists:

Tina Brown, *Happy Yellow*
Leigh Curran, *The Lunch Girls*
Pam Gems, *Queen Christina*
Joanna Glass, *Artichoke*
Valerie Harris, *Nights Alone*
Lenka Janiurek, *In the Blood*
Terri Wagener, *Renascence*
Wendy Wasserstein, *Uncommon Women and Others*
Olwen Wymark, *Loved*

Judges:
  Walter Clemons
  Harold Clurman
  Michael Codron
  Joan Plowright
  Michael Rudman
  Tom Stoppard
  Nina Vance
Presenter: Joan Plowright

II. 1979–1980 (FEBRUARY 13, 1980, NEW YORK)

Winner: Barbara Schneider, *Details without a Map*
Special Commendation: Beth Henley, *Crimes of the Heart*
Finalists:
  Caryl Churchill, *Cloud Nine*
  Nancy Donohue, *The Beach House*
  Mary Gallagher, *Father Dreams*
  Tina Howe, *The Art of Dining*
  Susan Miller, *Nasty Rumors and Final Remarks*
  Philomena Muinzer, *We're on the One Road*
  Edna O'Brien, *Virginia*
  Karen Duke Sturges, *Ysabelle*
  Victoria Wood, *Talent*
  Olwen Wymark, *Find Me*
Judges:
  Peggy Ashcroft
  Michael Billington
  Howard Davies
  André Gregory
  Jack Kroll
  Nina Vance
Presenter: Irene Worth

III. 1980–1981 (FEBRUARY 10, 1981, NEW YORK)

Winner: Wendy Kesselman, *My Sister in This House*
Special Commendation: Joanna Glass, *To Grandmother's House We Go*
Finalists:
  Julie Bovasso, *Angelo's Wedding*
  Part 1 of *the Lorenzo Trilogy*
  Susan Dworkin, *Deli's Fable*

Ann Jellicoe, *The Tide*
Julia Kearsley, *Wednesday*
Shirley Lauro, *Margaret and Kit*
Bryony Lavery, *The Family Album*
Lavonne Mueller, *Killings on the Last Line*
Sybille Pearson, *Sally and Marsha*
Barbara Schneider, *Turtles*
Alison Watson, *Moving In*
Judges:
Anne Barton
Robert Cushman
Geraldine Fitzgerald
Brendan Gill
Joyce Carol Oates
Michael Rudman
Presenter: Geraldine Fitzgerald

IV. 1981–1982 (FEBRUARY 22, 1982, LONDON)

Winner: Nell Dunn, *Steaming*
Special Commendation: Paula Cizmar, *Death of a Miner*
Finalists:
Elizabeth Diggs, *Close Ties*
J. e. Franklin, *Under Heaven's Eye . . . 'Til Cock Crow*
Catherine Hayes, *Skirmishes*
Shirley Kaplan, *A Connecticut Cowboy*
Margaret Keilstrup, *Wonderland*
Emily Mann, *Still Life*
Grace McKeaney, *Last Looks*
Adele Edling Shank, *Stuck*
Susan Todd & Ann Mitchell, *Kiss and Kill*
Wendy Wasserstein, *Isn't It Romantic*
Judges:
Elizabeth Hardwick
Nancy Meckler
Marina Warner
Arnold Wesker
Edwin Wilson
Joanne Woodward
Presenter: Ronald Harwood

V. 1982–1983 (FEBRUARY 22, 1983, NEW YORK)

Winner: Marsha Norman, *'night, Mother*
Special Commendation: Caryl Churchill, *Top Girls*
Finalists:
    Paula Cizmar, *Madonna of the Powder Room*
    Kathleen Collins, *The Brothers*
    Donna de Matteo, *The Flip Side*
    Carol Ann Duffy, *Take My Husband*
    Barbara Field, *Neutral Countries*
    Nancy Fales Garrett, *Playing in Local Bands*
    Julia Kearsley, *Waiting*
    Carol Mack, *Territorial Rites*
    Louise Page, *Salonika*
    Adele Edling Shank, *Sand Castles*
Judges:
    Maria Aitken
    Zoe Caldwell
    James Fenton
    Francine du Plessix Gray
    Mel Gussow
    Jonathan Lynn
Presenter: Zoe Caldwell

VI. 1983–1984 (FEBRUARY 24, 1984, NEW YORK)

Winner: Caryl Churchill, *Fen*
Special Commendation: Lynn Siefert, *Coyote Ugly*
Finalists:, Pearl Cleage, *Hospice*
    Rosalyn Drexler, *Dear*
    Shirley Gee, *Typhoid Mary*
    Joanna Glass, *Play Memory*
    Tina Howe, *Painting Churches*
    Gail Kriegel, *On the Home Front*
    Marsha Norman, *Traveler in the Dark*
    Terri Wagener, *Ladies in Waiting*
Judges:
    Edward Albee
    Howard Davies
    Christopher Hampton
    Ann Holmes
    Hilary Spurling
    Meryl Streep
Presenter: Meryl Streep

VII. 1984–1985 (FEBRUARY 25, 1985, LONDON)

Winner: Shirley Gee, *Never in My Lifetime*
Special Commendation: Sharman MacDonald, *When I Was a Girl I Used to Scream and Shout*
Finalists:
   Mary Elizabeth Burke-Kennedy, *Women in Arms*
   Kathleen Cahill, *Permission from Children*
   Helen Cooper, *Mrs. Gauguin*
   Debbie Horsfield, *Touch and Go*
   Cindy Lou Johnson, *Moonya*
   Emily Mann, *Execution of Justice*
   Anne McGravie, *Wrens*
   Louise Page, *Golden Girls*
   Christina Reid, *Tea in a China Cup*
   Susan Rivers, *Under Statements*
Judges:
   Beryl Bainbridge
   Robert Brustein
   Colleen Dewhurst
   John Guare
   Benedict Nightingale
   Jules Wright
Presenter: Peggy Ashcroft

VIII. 1985–1986 (FEBRUARY 24, 1986, LONDON)

Winner: Anne Devlin, *Ourselves Alone*
Special Commendation: Mary O'Malley, *Talk of the Devil*
Finalists:
   Constance Congdon, *No Mercy*
   Maria Irene Fornés, *The Conduct of Life*
   Pam Gems, *Camille*
   Velina Hasu Houston, *Tea*
   Barbara Lebow, *A Shayna Maidel*
   Melissa Murray, *Coming Apart*
   Aishah Rahman, *Windhawk!*
   Kristine Thatcher, *Niedecker*
   Jane Thornton, *Amid the Standing Corn*
Judges:
   Gordon Davidson
   Jane Howell
   Julian Mitchell

John Peter
Maureen Stapleton
George White
Presenter: Janet Suzman

IX. 1986–1987 (FEBRUARY 23, 1987, NEW YORK)

Winners:
  Mary Gallagher, *How to Say Goodbye*
  Ellen McLaughlin, *A Narrow Bed*
Special Commendation: Leonora Thuna, *Fugue*
Finalists:
  Kathleen Collins, *While Older Men Speak*
  Helen Cooper, *Mrs. Vershinin*
  Cindy Lou Johnson, *Blessé*
  Rosie Logan, *Queer Folk*
  Marlane G. Meyer, *Etta Jenks*
  Lavonne Mueller, *Five in the Killing Zone*
  Melissa Murray, *Body Cell*
  Milcha Sanchez-Scott, *Roosters*
Judges:
  Sara Pia Anderson
  Francis King
  Kenneth Koch
  Jane Lapotaire
  Maria Tucci
  Linda Winer
Presenter: Marsha Norman

X. 1987–1988 (FEBRUARY 22, 1988, LONDON)

Winner: Caryl Churchill, *Serious Money*
Special Commendation: Elizabeth Diggs, *Saint Florence*
Finalists:
  Kay Adshead, *Thatcher's Women*
  Kathleen Clark, *Southern Comforts*
  Barbara Damashek, *Whereabouts Unknown*
  Maria Irene Fornés, *Abingdon Square*
  Judy GeBauer, *Reclaimed*
  Beth Henley, *The Lucky Spot*
  Jacqueline Holborough, *Dreams of San Francisco*
  Casey Kurtti, *Three Ways Home*
  Julia Schofield, *Love on the Plastic*

Judges:
  Arvin Brown
  David Hare
  Julie Harris
  Stanley Kauffmann
  Anna Massey
  Claire Tomalin
Presenter: Anna Massey

XI. 1988–1989 (FEBRUARY 27, 1989, NEW YORK)

Winner: Wendy Wasserstein, *The Heidi Chronicles*
Special Commendation: Timberlake Wertenbaker, *Our Country's Good*
Finalists:
  Anne Commire, *Starting Monday*
  Trista Conger, *The Stones Cry Out*
  Barbara Field, *Playing with Fire*
  Lucy Gannon, *Raping the Gold*
  Nikki Harmon, *A Kind of Madness*
  Cassandra Medley, *Ma Rose*
  Marlane Meyer, *Kingfish*
  Susan Miller, *For Dear Life*
  Elizabeth Wyatt, *Angela*
  Sheila Yeger, *Self-Portrait*
Judges:
  Michael Attenborough
  Michael Coveney
  Jon Jory
  Fidelis Morgan
  Edith Oliver
  Jessica Tandy
Presenter: Jessica Tandy

XII. 1989–1990 (FEBRUARY 19, 1990, LONDON)

Winner: Lucy Gannon, *Keeping Tom Nice*
Special Commendation: Winsome Pinnock, *A Hero's Welcome*
Finalists:
  Jo Carson, *Daytrips*
  Donna Franceschild, *The Cow Jumped over the Moon*
  J. e. Franklin, *Christchild*
  Mary Gallagher, *¿De Donde?*
  Lillian Garrett, *The Ladies of the Camellias*

Shirley Gee, *Warrior*
Wendy Kesselman, *Olympe and the Executioner*
Ellen McLaughlin, *Infinity's House*
Marlane Meyer, *The Geography of Luck*
Shay Youngblood, *Shakin' the Mess Outta Misery*
Judges:
Claire Bloom
Zelda Fichandler
John Gross
Elliot Norton
Juliet Stevenson
Nicholas Wright
Presenter: Juliet Stevenson

XIII. 1990–1991 (FEBRUARY 26, 1991, NEW YORK)

Winners:
Rona Munro, *Bold Girls*
Cheryl L. West, *Before It Hits Home*
Special Commendation: Migdalia Cruz, *The Have-Little*
Finalists:
Jane Anderson, *The Baby Dance*
Sherry Coman, *Say Zebra*
Adrienne Kennedy, *The Ohio State Murders*
Maureen Lawrence, *Tokens of Affection*
Sharman MacDonald, *Shades*
Gillian Richmond, *The Legacy*
Sheila Yeger, *Variations*
Judges:
Simon Curtis
John Dillon
Christopher Logue
Alison Lurie
Imogen Stubbs
August Wilson
Presenter: John Guare

XIV. 1991–1992 (FEBRUARY 24, 1992, LONDON)

Winner: Timberlake Wertenbaker, *Three Birds Alighting on a Field*
Special Commendation: Lynn Siefert, *Little Egypt*
Finalists:
Jane Anderson, *Defying Gravity*

Lynda Barry, *The Good Times Are Killing Me*
Sue Glover, *Bondagers*
Catherine Johnson, *Dead Sheep*
Mary Lathrop, *The Urn of Drew*
Shirley Lauro, *A Piece of My Heart*
Claire Luckham, *The Dramatic Attitudes of Miss Fanny Kemble*
Winsome Pinnock, *Talking in Tongues*
Elizabeth Swados, *Groundhog*
Paula Vogel, *The Baltimore Waltz*

Judges:
Gregory Boyd
Arthur Kopit
Genista McIntosh
Julia Miles
Prunella Scales
Max Stafford-Clark

Presenter: Prunella Scales

XV. 1992–1993 (FEBRUARY 24, 1993, NEW YORK)

Winner: Marlane Meyer, *Moe's Lucky Seven*
Special Commendation: Jane Anderson, *Hotel Oubliette*
Finalists:
J. e. Franklin, *Whistling Girls and Crowing Hens*
Endesha Ida Mae Holland, *Parader without a Permit*
Clare Mclntyre, *No Warning for Life*
Nu Quang, *Where Is My Daughter?*
Anna Reynolds and Moira Buffini, *Jordan*
Anna Deavere Smith, *Fires in the Mirror*
Susan Sontag, *Alice in Bed*
Kay Trainor, *Bad Girl*
Paula Vogel, *And Baby Makes Seven*
Wendy Wasserstein, *The Sisters Rosensweig*

Judges:
Rosemary Harris
Ronald Hayman
Mark Lamos
Nicky Pallot
Diana Rigg
Lanford Wilson

Presenter: Julia Miles

XVI. 1993–1994 (FEBRUARY 13, 1994, LONDON)

Winner: Jane Coles, *Backstroke in a Crowded Pool*
Special Commendation:
  Lesley Bruce, *Keyboard Skills*
  Lisa Loomer, *The Waiting Room*
Finalists:
  Nicola Baldwin, *Confetti*
  Pearl Cleage, *Flyin' West*
  Christian de Lancie, *F-64*
  Ruby Dee, *The Disappearance*
  Helen Edmundson, *The Clearing*
  Margaret Edson, *Wit*
  Amy Freed, *Poetomachia*
  Lois Meredith, *Professional Misconduct*
  Anna Deavere Smith, *Twilight: Los Angeles, 1992*
Judges:
  Mel Gussow
  Garry Hynes
  David Suchet
  Irving Wardle
  Wendy Wasserstein
  Stan Wojewodski
Presenter: Diana Rigg

XVII. 1994–1995 (FEBRUARY 8, 1995, NEW YORK)

Joint Top Finalists (No first prize awarded; three top finalists):
  Susan Miller, *My Left Breast*
  Kristine Thatcher, *Emma's Child*
  Naomi Wallace, *In the Heart of America*
Finalists:
  Ann Marie Di Mambro, *Brothers of Thunder*
  Maureen Lawrence, *Father's Day*
  Barbara Lebow, *The Keepers*
  Sally Nemeth, *Egg House*
  Theresa Rebeck, *The Family of Mann*
  Jacquelyn Reingold, *Girl Gone*
  Paula Vogel, *Hot 'n' Throbbing*
Judges:
  André Bishop
  Sebastian Born
  Colin Chambers

Jane Edwardes
John Lahr
Marsha Norman
Presenter: Marsha Norman

XVIII. 1995–1996 (FEBRUARY 26, 1996, NEW YORK)

Winner: Naomi Wallace, *One Flea Spare*
Special Commendation:
Leslie Ayvazian, *Nine Armenians*
Phyllis Nagy, *Disappeared*
Finalists:
Pearl Cleage, *Blues for an Alabama Sky*
Constance Congdon, *Dog Opera*
Elizabeth Egloff, *The Lover*
Barbara Lebow, *The Empress of Eden*
Sharman MacDonald, *The Winter Guest*
Tamsin Oglesby, *Two Lips Indifferent Red*
Rose Scollard, *Shea of the White Hands*
Paula Vogel, *The Mineola Twins*
Erin Cressida Wilson, *Hurricane*
Judges:
Richard Coe
Heidi Landesman
James MacDonald
Sharon Ott
Fiona Shaw
Charles Spencer
Presenter: Sharon Ott

XIX. 1996–1997 (FEBRUARY 2, 1997, LONDON)

Winner: Marina Carr, *Portia Coughlan*
Special Commendation: Pam Gems, *Stanley*
Finalists:
Hanan al-Shaykh, *The Paper Husband*
Katherine Burger, *Morphic Resonance*
Migdalia Cruz, *Salt*
Elizabeth Egloff, *The Devils*
Susan Flakes, *To Take Arms*
Jennifer Johnston, *The Desert Lullaby*
Julia Jordan, *Tatjana in Color*
Emily Mann, *Greensboro, a Requiem*

Suzan-Lori Parks, *Venus*
Kate Moira Ryan, *Hadley's Mistake*
Judges:
  Joanne Akalaitis
  Jude Kelly
  Sian Thomas
  Michael White
  Robert Whitehead
  George Wolfe
Presenter: Diana Rigg

XX. 1997–1998 (FEBRUARY 23, 1998, HOUSTON)

Winners:
  Moira Buffini, *Silence*
  Paula Vogel, *How I Learned to Drive*
Special Commendation: Shelagh Stephenson, *An Experiment with an Air-Pump*
Finalists:
  Judith Adams, *Burdalane*
  Kia Corthron, *Splash Hatch on the E Train Going Down*
  Tina Howe, *Pride's Crossing*
  Noelle Janaczewska, *Cold Harvest*
  Barbara Lebow, *The Left Hand Singing*
  Nicola McCartney, *The Hanging Tree*
  Lynn Nottage, *Mud, River, Stone*
  Kathleen Tolan, *A Girl's Life*
Judges:
  Sebastian Barry
  Eric Bentley
  Kate Duchene
  Simon Reade
  Marian Seldes
  Daniel Sullivan
Presenter: Edward Albee

XXI. 1998–1999 (FEBRUARY 22, 1999, NEW YORK)

Winner: Jessica Goldberg, *Refuge*
Special Commendation:
  Judith Adams, *The Bone Room*
  Julie Hébert, *The Knee Desires the Dirt*
Finalists:
  Hilary Bell, *Shot While Dancing*

Sara Clifford, *A Thousand Days*
Eve Ensler, *Lemonade*
Rebecca Gilman, *Spinning into Butter*
Yazmine Judd, *Unfinished Business*
Liz Lochhead, *Perfect Days*
Kira Obolensky, *Lobster Alice*
Diana Son, *Stop Kiss*
Judges:
Edward Albee
Jane Alexander
Eileen Atkins
Michael Bogdanov
Carey Perloff
Jenny Topper
Presenter: Robert Whitehead

XXII. 1999–2000 (FEBRUARY 27, 2000, LONDON)

Winner: Bridget Carpenter, *Fall*
Special Commendation:
Elizabeth Kuti, *Tree Houses*
Dael Orlandersmith, *The Gimmick*
Finalists:
Nicola Baldwin, *"23.59"*
Dolly Dhingra, *The Main Course*
Rebecca Gilman, *Boy Gets Girl*
Marie Jones, *Stones in His Pockets*
Emily Mann, *Meshugah*
Jenny McLeod, *Poison*
Suzan-Lori Parks, *Topdog/Underdog*
Freyda Thomas, *The Gamester*
Celeste Bedford Walker, *Distant Voices*
Judges:
Kathleen Chalfant
Susannah Clapp
Ralph Fiennes
A. R. Gurney
Nicolas Kent
Irene Lewis
Presenter: Fiona Shaw

XXIII. 2000–2001 (FEBRUARY 25, 2001, LONDON)

Winner: Charlotte Jones, *Humble Boy*
Special Commendation:
   Zinnie Harris, *Further than the Furthest Thing*
   Naomi Iizuka, *36 Views*
   Joanna Laurens, *The Three Birds*
Finalists:
   Judith Adams, *Queueing for Everest*
   Alexandra Cunningham, *No. 11 (Blue and White)*
   Eve Ensler, *Conviction*
   Nancy Ewing, *Leaving Watermaine*
   Meredith Oakes, *Her Mother and Bartok*
   Annie Weisman, *Be Aggressive*
   Sarah Woods, *Antigone*
Judges:
   Simon Russell Beale
   Richard Christiansen
   Robert Falls
   Lyn Gardner
   Caro Newling
   Paula Vogel
Presenter: Simon Russell Beale

XXIV. 2001–2002 (FEBRUARY 11, 2002, NEW YORK)

Winners:
   Gina Gionfriddo, *U.S. Drag*
   Susan Miller, *A Map of Doubt and Rescue*
Special Commendation: Julia Jordan, *Boy*
Finalists:
   Kay Adshead, *The Bogus Woman*
   Rukhsana Ahmad, *River on Fire*
   Julia Cho, *99 Histories*
   Amy Freed, *The Beard of Avon*
   Carey Perloff, *The Colossus of Rhodes*
   Kelly Stuart, *Mayhem*
   Tracey Scott Wilson, *The Story*
Judges:
   Glenn Close
   Michael Colgan
   Christopher Durang
   Philip Franks

Brigid Larmour
Molly Smith
Presenter: Glenn Close

XXV. 2002–2003 (FEBRUARY 24, 2003, HOUSTON)

Winner: Dael Orlandersmith, *Yellowman*
Special Commendation: Bryony Lavery, *Frozen*
Finalists:
  Claudia Allen, *Unspoken Prayers*
  Helen Cooper, *Three Women and a Piano Tuner*
  Charlotte Eilenberg, *The Lucky Ones*
  Kate Fodor, *Hannah and Martin*
  Debbie Tucker Green, *Born Bad*
  Rinne Groff, *Orange Lemon Egg Canary*
  Anne Ludlum, *Cover Shot*
  Heather McDonald, *When Grace Comes In*
  Theresa Rebeck and Alexandra Gersten, *Omnium Gatherum*
  Judith Thompson, *Habitat*
Judges:
  Ellen Burstyn
  Felix Cross
  Peter Eyre
  Sue Higginson
  Tony Kushner
  Carole Rothman
Presenter: Gregory Boyd

XXVI. 2003–2004 (FEBRUARY 23, 2004, NEW YORK)

Winner: Sarah Ruhl, *The Clean House*
Finalists:
  Neena Beber, *Jump/Cut*
  Jean Betts, *The Collective*
  Lin Coghlan, *Mercy*
  Zinnie Harris, *Midwinter*
  Carson Kreitzer, *The Love Song of Robert Oppenheimer*
  Lisa Loomer, *Living Out*
  Abi Morgan, *27*
  Ann Noble, *Ariadne's Thread*
  Lucy Prebble, *The Sugar Syndrome*
  Polly Teale, *After Mrs. Rochester*
  Karen Zacarias, *Mariela in the Desert*

Judges:
Mike Bradwell
Blair Brown
James Houghton
Charles Isherwood
Janet McTeer
Samuel West
Presenter: Blair Brown

XXVII. 2004–2005 (MARCH 7, 2005, LONDON)

Winner: Gurpreet Kaur Bhatti, *Behzti (Dishonour)*
Special Commendation:
Chloe Moss, *How Love Is Spelt*
Heather Raffo, *Nine Parts of Desire*
Finalists:
Leslie Ayvazian, *Rosemary and I*
Rebecca Gilman, *The Sweetest Swing in Baseball*
Joanna McClelland Glass, *Trying*
Bryony Lavery, *Last Easter*
Rebecca Lenkiewicz, *The Night Season*
Melanie Marnich, *Cradle of Man*
Mia McCullough, *Since Africa*
Katherine Thomson, *Harbour*
Patricia Wettig, *My Andy*
Judges:
Stockard Channing
Sara Garonzik
Paulette Randall
Corin Redgrave
Carole Woddis
Matt Wolf
Presenter: Paulette Randall

XXVIII 2005–2006 (FEBRUARY 24, 2006, LONDON)

Winners:
Amelia Bullmore, *Mammals*
Elizabeth Kuti, *The Sugar Wife*
Finalists:
Kay Adshead, *Bites*
April De Angelis, *Wild East*
Bathsheba Doran, *Living Room in Africa*

Melissa James Gibson, *Current Nobody*
Debbie Tucker Green, *Stoning Mary*
Linda Marshall Griffiths, *Pomegranate*
Beth Henley, *Ridiculous Fraud*
Oni Faida Lampley, *Tough Titty*
Kira Obolensky, *Modern House*

Judges:
Jack Bradley
Blair Brown
Anne Cattaneo
Lindsay Duncan
Tim Sanford
Erica Whyman

Presenter: Lindsay Duncan

U.S. Judges

Akalaitis, Joanne	1996–1997
Albee, Edward	1983–1984, 1998–1999
Alexander, Jane	1998–1999
Bentley, Eric	1997–1998
Bishop, André	1994–1995
Bloom, Claire	1989–1990
Boyd, Gregory	1991–1992
Brown, Arvin	1987–1988
Brown, Blair	2003–2004
Brustein, Robert	1984–1985
Burstyn, Ellen	2002–2003
Caldwell, Zoe	1982–1983
Chalfant, Kathleen	1999–2000
Channing, Stockard	2004–2005
Christiansen, Richard	2000–2001
Clemons, Walter	1978–1979
Close, Glenn	2001–2002
Clurman, Harold	1978–1979
Coe, Richard	1995–1996
Davidson, Gordon	1985–1986
Dewhurst, Colleen	1984–1985
Dillon, John	1990–1991
Durang, Christopher	2001–2002
Falls, Robert	2000–2001
Fichandler, Zelda	1989–1990
Fitzgerald, Geraldine	1980–1981
Garonzik, Sara	2004–2005

Gill, Brendan	1980–1981
Gray, Francine du Plessix	1982–1983
Gregory, André	1979–1980
Guare, John	1984–1985
Gurney, A. R.	1999–2000
Gussow, Mel	1982–1983, 1993–1994
Hardwick, Elizabeth	1981–1982
Harris, Julie	1987–1988
Harris, Rosemary	1992–1993
Holmes, Ann	1983–1984
Houghton, James	2003–2004
Isherwood, Charles	2003–2004
Jory, Jon	1988–1989
Kauffmann, Stanley	1987–1988
Koch, Kenneth	1986–1987
Kopit, Arthur	1991–1992
Kroll, Jack	1979–1980
Kushner, Tony	2002–2003
Lahr, John	1994–1995
Lamos, Mark	1992–1993
Landesman, Heidi	1995–1996
Lewis, Irene	1999–2000
Lurie, Alison	1990–1991
Miles, Julia	1991–1992
Norman, Marsha	1994–1995
Norton, Elliot	1989–1990
Oates, Joyce Carol	1980–1981
Oliver, Edith	1988–1989
Ott, Sharon	1995–1996
Perloff, Carey	1998–1999
Rothman, Carole	2002–2003
Seldes, Marian	1997–1998
Smith, Molly	2001–2002
Stapleton, Maureen	1985–1986
Streep, Meryl	1983–1984
Sullivan, Daniel	1997–1998
Tandy, Jessica	1988–1989
Tucci, Maria	1986–1987
Vance, Nina	1978–1979, 1979–1980
Vogel, Paula	2000–2001
Wasserstein, Wendy	1993–1994
White, George	1985–1986
Whitehead, Robert	1996–1997
Wilson, August	1990–1991

Wilson, Edwin	1981–1982
Wilson, Lanford	1992–1993
Winer, Linda	1986–1987
Wojewodski, Stan	1993–1994
Wolf, Matt	2004–2005
Wolfe, George	1996–1997
Woodward, Joanne	1981–1982

U.K. Judges

Aitken, Maria	1982–1983
Anderson, Sara Pia	1986–1987
Ashcroft, Peggy	1979–1980
Atkins, Eileen	1998–1999
Attenborough, Michael	1988–1989
Bainbridge, Beryl	1984–1985
Barry, Sebastian	1997–1998
Barton, Anne	1980–1981
Beale, Simon Russell	2000–2001
Billington, Michael	1979–1980
Bogdanov, Michael	1998–1999
Born, Sebastian	1994–1995
Bradwell, Mike	2003–2004
Chambers, Colin	1994–1995
Clapp, Susannah	1999–2000
Codron, Michael	1978–1979
Colgan, Michael	2001–2002
Coveney, Michael	1988–1989
Cross, Felix	2002–2003
Curtis, Simon	1990–1991
Cushman, Robert	1980–1981
Davies, Howard	1979–1980, 1983–1984
Duchene, Kate	1997–1998
Edwardes, Jane	1994–1995
Eyre, Peter	2002–2003
Fenton, James	1982–1983
Fiennes, Ralph	1999–2000
Franks, Philip	2001–2002
Gardner, Lyn	2000–2001
Gross, John	1989–1990
Hampton, Christopher	1983–1984
Hare, David	1987–1988
Hayman, Ronald	1992–1993
Higginson, Sue	2002–2003

Howell, Jane	1985–1986
Hynes, Garry	1993–1994
Kelly, Jude	1996–1997
Kent, Nicolas	1999–2000
King, Francis	1986–1987
Lapotaire, Jane	1986–1987
Larmour, Brigid	2001–2002
Logue, Christopher	1990–1991
Lynn, Jonathan	1982–1983
MacDonald, James	1995–1996
Massey, Anna	1987–1988
McIntosh, Genista	1991–1992
McTeer, Janet	2003–2004
Meckler, Nancy	1981–1982
Mitchell, Julian	1985–1986
Morgan, Fidelis	1988–1989
Newling, Caro	2000–2001
Nightingale, Benedict	1984–1985
Pallot, Nicky	1992–1993
Peter, John	1985–1986
Plowright, Joan	1978–1979
Randall, Paulette	2004–2005
Reade, Simon	1997–1998
Redgrave, Corin	2004–2005
Rigg, Diana	1992–1993
Rudman, Michael	1978–1979, 1980–1981
Scales, Prunella	1991–1992
Shaw, Fiona	1995–1996
Spencer, Charles	1995–1996
Spurling, Hilary	1983–1984
Stafford-Clark, Max	1991–1992
Stevenson, Juliet	1989–1990
Stoppard, Tom	1978–1979
Stubbs, Imogen	1990–1991
Suchet, David	1993–1994
Thomas, Sian	1996–1997
Tomalin, Claire	1987–1988
Topper, Jenny	1998–1999
Wardle, Irving	1993–1994
Warner, Marina	1981–1982
Wesker, Arnold	1981–1982
West, Samuel	2003–2004
White, Michael	1996–1997
Woddis, Carole	2004–2005

Wright, Jules	1984–1985
Wright, Nicholas	1989–1990

Presenters

Albee, Edward	1997–1998
Ashcroft, Peggy	1984–1985
Beale, Simon Russell	2000–2001
Boyd, Gregory	2002–2003
Brown, Blair	2003–2004
Caldwell, Zoe	1982–1983
Close, Glenn	2001–2002
Fitzgerald, Geraldine	1980–1981
Guare, John	1990–1991
Harwood, Ronald	1981–1982
Massey, Anna	1987–1988
Miles, Julia	1992–1993
Norman, Marsha	1986–1987, 1994–1995
Ott, Sharon	1995–1996
Plowright, Joan	1978–1979
Randall, Paulette	2004–2005
Rigg, Diana	1993–1994, 1996–1997
Scales, Prunella	1991–1992
Shaw, Fiona	1999–2000
Stevenson, Juliet	1989–1990
Streep, Meryl	1983–1984
Suzman, Janet	1985–1986
Tandy, Jessica	1988–1989
Whitehead, Robert	1998–1999
Worth, Irene	1979–1980

Board of Directors

Emilie S. Kilgore and William Blackburn (Co-Presidents)

Michael Attenborough	Julia O'Faolain
Adam Blackburn	Charles Perlitz
Bertrand Davezac	Meg Poole
Cabanné Gilbreath	Lucy Reid
John Guare	Amber Rudd
Lady Hale	Wendy Wasserstein
Alexander Kilgore	Edwin Wilson
Marsha Norman	Matt Wolf

About the Contributors

❧

Rukhsana Ahmad has written and adapted plays both for the stage and for BBC Radio. She was a finalist for the Susan Smith Blackburn Prize and has been nominated for awards from the Writers' Guild, CRE, and SONY. Her stage plays include *Song for a Sanctuary, River on Fire*, The Gate-Keeper's Wife, Black Shalwar, The Man Who Refused to Be God, Last Chance,* and *Partners in Crime.* Radio plays and adaptations include *Song for a Sanctuary, An Urnful of Ashes, The Errant Gene, Woman at Point Zero, Wide Sargasso Sea,* and *The Guide.* She has written a novel, *The Hope Chest* (Virago), and is working on her second novel, *Strangers and Kin.*

Jean Betts is a founder and member of Circa and Taki Rua Theatres; of Playmarket, a playwrights' agency; and the Women's Play Press and the Play Press, all in Wellington, New Zealand. A graduate of the Drama School/Toi Whakaari and of Canterbury University, she is an actor, director, designer, dramaturg, and playwright. Her plays include *Ophelia Thinks Harder, Revenge of the Amazons, Camelot School, The Misandrist,* and *The Collective*,* which is based on John Fuegi's book, *Brecht and Company.* A number of Ms. Betts's plays have been published by the Women's Play Press and performed at universities, and *Ophelia Thinks Harder* has been performed in South Africa, Australia, the United States, Italy, and Canada.

Gurpreet Kaur Bhatti's first play, *Behsharam (Shameless),* was produced at Soho Theatre and the Birmingham Repertory Theatre in 2001. In 2004, Birmingham Repertory Theatre also produced *Behzti (Dishonour),* which won the 2005 Susan Smith Blackburn Prize. Recent work by Ms. Bhatti includes *The Cleaner,* an hourlong film for BBC1, and her first feature film, *Pound Shop Boys* (commissioned by October Films/Film Council and developed through PAL). Other credits include the half-hour film *Dead Meat* (Channel 4); *Mera Des (My Coun-*

try) for Radio 3; the serials *Pile Up* and *The Bride* (Carlton Television); over thirty episodes of *Westway,* the BBC World Services Drama Serial; and nine episodes of *Eastenders.*

Michael Billington has been drama critic of the *Guardian* since 1971. He is also the author of biographies of Harold Pinter and Peggy Ashcroft; studies of Tom Stoppard and Alan Ayckbourn; and a collected volume of criticism, *One Night Stands.* He broadcasts frequently on the arts in Britain and is a visiting professor at King's College, London, where he conducts a course on theater with students from the University of Pennsylvania.

Bill Blackburn moved to London from New York with Susan and infant son, Adam, in 1962. He continued his work in advertising and later in manufacturing food and drink. Their daughter, Lucy, was born a few years later. After Susan died, he coestablished the Susan Smith Blackburn Prize and managed its development in the United Kingdom. He was remarried in 1985 to Perri Thompson, a fashion designer, and now lives in London and Dorset with their daughter, Christabel.

Moira Buffini trained as an actor, and one of her first jobs was teaching drama in England's Holloway Prison. She cowrote the monologue *Jordan** with Anna Reynolds and went on to perform it; it won the Writers Guild Award for the Best Fringe Play of 1992. She produced and directed her second play, *Blavatsky's Tower,* on the London Fringe. Other plays include *Gabriel,* which she wrote for Soho Theatre in 1997; *Silence,* which was commissioned by the National Theatre Studio, eventually produced at the Plymouth Theatre Royal, and won the Susan Smith Blackburn Prize; and *Loveplay,* which was produced by the Royal Shakespeare Company. In 2002, her play *Dinner* was produced at the National Theatre Loft and subsequently nominated for an Olivier Award for Best Comedy. It transferred to Wyndhams Theatre in the West End the following year. She has recently written and directed a short play, *The Teacher,* for the National Theatre, for their National Headlines series. Her writing for television and film includes *Melissa Malone* for BBC Wales, *Presence* for Prospect Entertainment and the Film Council, and the screenplay of *Gabriel* for Channel 4 and Passion Pictures.

Charlotte Canning is a professor of theater at the University of Texas at Austin. She is the author of *Feminist Theaters in the U.S.A.: Staging Women's Experience* (Routledge) and *The Most American Thing in America: Performance and the Circuit Chatauquas* (Iowa University Press).

Bridget Carpenter most recently was a playwright-in-residence at the Royal National Theatre in London. In 2003, her play *The Faculty Room,* which had its premiere at the Humana Festival of the Actors Theatre of Louisville, was awarded the Kesselring Prize, and a London production is planned. Ms. Carpenter received a Guggenheim Fellowship in 2002, and in 2000 she was the recipient of the Susan Smith Blackburn Prize for her play *Fall.* She has taught playwriting in elementary and high schools, to college students, and at a prison. She holds an M.F.A. from Brown University and is a member of New Dramatists. She considers the Susan Smith Blackburn Prize one of her most cherished accomplishments.

Pearl Cleage is an Atlanta-based writer of a dozen plays, including *Flyin' West, Blues for an Alabama Sky,* and *Hospice,* all of which were finalists for the Susan Smith Blackburn Prize. She has collaborated with her husband, Zaron W. Burnett Jr., on the "Live at Club Zebra!" performance series, which was featured at the National Black Arts Festival and the National Black Theatre Festival. She has also published four novels: *What Looks Like Crazy on an Ordinary Day, I Wish I Had a Red Dress, Some Things I Never Thought I'd Do,* and *Babylon Sisters.*

Fatima Dike is a playwright, poet, raconteur, director, teacher, and political activist. Her plays include *The Sacrifice of Kreli,* written in English and Xhosa; *The First South African; The Crafty Tortoise,* a children's play based on African folklore; *Glass House; What's New?;* and the urban drama *Street Walking and Company Valet Service.* Often hailed as "the mother of South African Theatre," she received the South African Women for Women Award in 1997. In 2000, the Cape Tercentenary Foundation granted her an award for lifetime service to the performing arts.

Christopher Durang's plays include *A History of the American Film* (Tony nomination), *Sister Mary Ignatius Explains It All for You* (Obie Award), *Beyond Therapy, Baby with the Bathwater, The Marriage of Bette and Boo* (Obie Award), *Laughing Wild, Durang/Durang,* and *Betty's Summer Vacation* (Obie Award). His most recent works are *Mrs. Bob Cratchit's Wild Christmas Binge;* a musical, *Adrift in Macao;* and a play, *Miss Witherspoon,* a commission from McCarter Theatre Center. Since 1994, he and Marsha Norman have been co-chairs of the playwriting program at the Juilliard School, for which he and Ms. Norman were honored in 2004 with the Margo Jones Medal. Mr. Durang is a member of the Dramatists Guild Council.

Gina Gionfriddo received the Susan Smith Blackburn Prize for her play *U.S. Drag,* which has been produced by Connecticut Repertory Company and by Clubbed Thumb in New York. It is published in *Women Playwrights: The Best Plays of 2002* (Smith & Kraus) and *Seven Different Plays,* volume 2 (Broadway Play Publishing). Her other plays include *After Ashley,* produced at the Humana Festival of the Actors Theatre of Louisville and the Vineyard Theatre in New York and published in *Humana Festival 2004: The Complete Plays* (Smith & Kraus) and by

Dramatists Play Service; and *Guinevere,* presented at the National Playwrights Conference of the Eugene O'Neill Memorial Center. In 2002, she received the Helen Merrill Award for Emerging Playwrights.

Amy S. Green is associate professor of speech, theater, and media studies at John Jay College of Criminal Justice in New York and immediate past chair of its Women's Studies Committee. Professor Green is the author of *The Revisionist Stage: American Directors Reinvent the Classics* (Cambridge University Press) and two original testimonial dramas: *Girls in Blue,* about female officers of the New York Police Department; and *What Happened: The September 11th Testimony Project.* She holds citations for directing from the Kennedy Center/American College Theatre Festival and is regional chair of the National Critics Institute. She earned her B.F.A. in theater arts at Hofstra University and her M.A. and Ph.D. in theater at the Graduate School of the City University of New York.

Alexis Greene is an author, theater critic, and teacher. Her books on theater include *The Lion King: Pride Rock on Broadway,* with Julie Taymor (Hyperion); *Women Who Write Plays: Interviews with Twenty-Three American Dramatists* (Smith & Kraus); and the biography *Lucille Lortel: The Queen of Off Broadway* (Limelight Editions). Ms. Greene is cofounder of Literary Managers and Dramaturgs of the Americas (LMDA), and she has taught theater at Hunter College, Vassar College, and New York University. She holds a Ph.D. in theater from the Graduate Center of the City University of New York.

Mandy Greenfield serves as the director of artistic operation at Manhattan Theater Club (MTC), where she develops new plays and line-produces shows on and off Broadway. At MTC, Ms. Greenfield's credits include new work by Daniel Goldfarb, Jeffrey Hatcher, Craig Lucas, Donald Margulies, Rona Munro, John Patrick Shanley, and Regina Taylor; she has worked with the directors Mark Brokaw, Doug Hughes, Lynne Meadow, Anna D. Shapiro, and Daniel Sullivan. Before joining MTC, Ms. Greenfield produced several Off-Broadway premieres, including *Betty Rules,* and new plays by Helen Edmundson, Jessica Goldberg, and Daniel Goldfarb. Ms. Greenfield is a graduate of Yale University.

Mel Gussow was a cultural writer for the *New York Times* and the author of the biography *Edward Albee: A Singular Journey.* He wrote books on Harold Pinter, Tom Stoppard, Samuel Beckett, and Arthur Miller. His most recent book was *Gambon: A Life in Acting.* He was the author of *Theater on the Edge: New Visions, New Voices,* a collection of theater reviews and essays, and he was a coeditor of the Library of America two-volume edition of the plays of Tennessee Williams. He was a past winner of the Margo Jones Medal, the George Jean Nathan Award for Dramatic Criticism, and a Guggenheim Fellowship.

Emilie S. Kilgore is president of the Susan Smith Blackburn Prize, which she co-founded as a memorial to her sister. She graduated Magna Cum Laude in art history from Smith College and received an M.A. from Goddard College. She worked at the Frick Collection in New York before moving to Houston, where she is currently the curator of the Fayez Sarofim Collection. Ms. Kilgore edited *Contemporary Plays by Women* (Prentice Hall), published in England as *Landmarks of Contemporary Women's Drama, 1992* (Methuen Press); and *The Susan Smith Blackburn Prize: Six Important New Plays by Women* (Smith & Kraus). She has been a trustee of the Alley Theatre, Stages Repertory Theatre, and the Houston Museum of Fine Arts, among others. In 1995, Smith College awarded her its alumnae medal, and in 2003, she was the recipient of the Margo Jones Medal.

Gwynn MacDonald has directed and produced theater, television, film, and radio. She is the artistic director of the New York City–based Juggernaut Theatre Company, which produced the First 100 Years of the Professional Female Playwright, a project exploring the lives and work of women dramatists from the seventeenth and eighteenth centuries. As artistic director of Juggernaut, Ms. MacDonald has also directed the world premiere of Joe Pintauro's *Rosen's Son* and Cathy Caplan's *Silver Nitrate,* and she produced Caplan's *Lapis Blue Blood Red* in conjunction with the Metropolitan Museum's retrospective of Artemisia Gentileschi's paintings. She is a member of the Lincoln Center Theater Directors Lab and a 2005 panelist on the New York State Council of the Arts Theatre Program Artists Panel. Ms. MacDonald studied theater and theory at Princeton University.

Sharman MacDonald is a playwright and screenwriter whose work includes *When I Was a Girl I Used to Scream and Shout,* which received the Special Commendation of the Susan Smith Blackburn Prize. Other plays by Ms. MacDonald include *The Brave, When We Were Women, All Things Nice, Shades*, The Winter Guest, Borders of Paradise, Sea Urchins,* and *After Juliet.* She has also written the libretto for an opera, *Hey Persephone!* for the Almeida Opera/Aldeburgh Festival, and a film, *The Music Lesson.*

Emily Mann is artistic director of McCarter Theatre Center in Princeton, New Jersey. Ms. Mann wrote and directed *Having Our Say,* adapted from the autobiography of Sarah L. Delany and A. Elizabeth Delany with Amy Hill Hearth (three Tony Award nominations, including Best Play and Best Director), as well as the screenplay (Peabody and Christopher Awards). Her other stage plays include *Annulla: An Autobiography; Still Life** (six Obie Awards); *Execution of Justice*,* for which she made her Broadway debut as both playwright and director; and *Greensboro, a Requiem.* Her recent directing credits include a revival of Edward Albee's *All Over* (Obie Award); Nilo Cruz's Pulitzer Prize–winning drama *Anna in the Tropics* (two Tony Award nominations); and Steven Dietz's *Last of the*

Boys. Four of Ms. Mann's plays have been finalists for the Susan Smith Blackburn Prize, and she is a winner of the Dramatists Guild/Hull-Warriner Award. She is a member of the Dramatists Guild and serves on its council.

Susan Miller won the Susan Smith Blackburn Prize and the Pinter Review Prize in Drama for her play *A Map of Doubt and Rescue.* She has received a Guggenheim Fellowship in playwriting and two Obie Awards for *Nasty Rumors and Final Remarks** and for her acclaimed one-person play, *My Left Breast**, which premiered in the Humana Festival of the Actors Theatre of Louisville. Other plays by Ms. Miller include *For Dear Life**, *Flux, Cross Country, Confessions of a Female Disorder, It's Our Town, Arts and Leisure,* and *The Grand Design.* Her plays have been produced by Second Stage, the Public Theater, Naked Angels, and the Mark Taper Forum, among others. Ms. Miller was a consulting producer on the first season of the Showtime series *The L Word.* She is a member of the Dramatists Guild.

Marsha Norman won the 1983 Pulitzer Prize in drama, the Susan Smith Blackburn Prize, and a Drama Desk Award for *'night, Mother.* She also won Tony and Drama Desk Awards for her book to the Broadway musical *The Secret Garden.* Most recently, Ms. Norman has written the book for the musical *The Color Purple.* She is vice president of the Dramatists Guild; a member of the Fellowship of Southern writers; and cochair with Christopher Durang of the playwriting department of the Juilliard School. In 2004, in honor of their work at Juilliard, Ms. Norman and Mr. Durang together received the Margo Jones Medal.

Lynn Nottage's most recent plays include *A Stone's Throw/The Antigone Project* (Women's Project and Productions), *Fabulation or, the Re-Education* (Playwrights Horizons), and *Intimate Apparel* (Roundabout Theatre Company, Mark Taper Forum, South Coast Repertory, and Center Stage). *Intimate Apparel* was a winner of the New York Drama Critics Circle Award, Outer Critics Circle Award for Best Play, the John Gassner Award, the American Theatre Critics/Steinberg 2004 New Play Award, and the 2004 Francesca Primus Award. Ms. Nottage's play *Mud, River, Stone* was a finalist for the Susan Smith Blackburn Prize, and she is the recipient of the 2004 PEN/Laura Pels Award for an emerging playwright. An anthology of Ms. Nottage's work, *Crumbs from the Table of Joy and Other Plays,* is available through Theatre Communications Group (TCG). She is a graduate of Brown University and the Yale School of Drama, where she is a visiting lecturer, and she is a member of New Dramatists.

Dael Orlandersmith is a playwright and actor. Her plays include *Yellowman,* which won the Susan Smith Blackburn Prize, *The Gimmick**, *Beauty's Daughter* (Obie Award), and *Monster. Yellowman* and a collection of earlier work have been published by Vintage Books. Ms. Orlandersmith has toured extensively with the

Nuyorican Poets Café (now Real Live Poetry) and, in addition to performing her own plays and poetry, has appeared on television and in films, notably in Hal Hartley's *Amateur* and *Get Well Soon* with Courteney Cox. She is the recipient of a Guggenheim Fellowship, a grant from the New York Foundation for the Arts, and the Helen Merrill Award for Emerging Playwrights.

Sarah Ruhl's plays include *The Clean House* (Susan Smith Blackburn Prize), *Melancholy Play, Eurydice, Late: A Cowboy Song, Orlando,* and *Passion Play.* Her work has been produced at Yale Repertory Theater, Berkeley Repertory Theater, South Coast Repertory, and Woolly Mammoth. Ms. Ruhl is the recipient of the Whiting Writers' Award and the Helen Merrill Award for Emerging Playwrights. She received her M.F.A. from Brown University and is a member of New Dramatists.

Diana Son's plays include *Stop Kiss* (GLAAD 1999 Media Award, Susan Smith Blackburn Prize finalist), which has been produced at over one hundred theaters throughout the world and has been published by Overlook Press; *Fishes; BOY; 2000 Miles;* and *R.A.W. ('Cause I'm a Woman).* She is a recipient of the Berilla Kerr Award for Playwriting, and in the United States her work has been produced at the Public Theater, La Jolla Playhouse, Seattle Rep, Oregon Shakespeare Festival, New Georges, and the Delaware Theatre Company, among others. She is a member of the Dramatists Guild and an alumna of New Dramatists.

Max Stafford-Clark founded the Joint Stock Theatre in 1974, following his tenure as artistic director of the Traverse Theatre in Edinburgh. From 1979 to 1993, he was artistic director of the Royal Court Theatre, and in 1993 he founded the touring company Out of Joint. Mr. Stafford-Clark's work as a director has been involved overwhelmingly with new writing, and he has commissioned and directed first productions by many of Britain's leading playwrights. For Out of Joint, these have included *The Queen and I,* by Sue Townsend; *The Libertine,* by Stephen Jeffreys; *The Break of Day,* by Timberlake Wertenbaker; *The Steward of Christendom,* by Sebastian Barry; *Shopping and Fucking,* by Mark Ravenhill; *Blue Heart,* by Caryl Churchill; *Our Country's Good*,* by Timberlake Wertenbaker; and *The Permanent Way,* by David Hare. At Joint Stock and for the Royal Court, he directed several plays by Caryl Churchill, including *Cloud Nine*, Top Girls*,* and *Serious Money*,* as well as plays by other notable British dramatists. His book, *Letters to George,* was published in 1989 (Nick Hern Books). He has an honorary doctorate from Oxford Brookes University and holds a visiting professorship at the University of Hertfordshire.

Elizabeth Swain is a director, actor, and professor of theater at Marymount Manhattan College in New York City. Her directing credits include the plays of Shakespeare, Aphra Behn, Susanna Centlivre, Mishima, Timberlake Wertenbaker, Wendy Kesselman, and Tom Stoppard, whose *Arcadia* she staged in 2004.

She has directed Rob Ackerman's play *Airborn* at the New York State Theatre Institute and Biyi Bandele's adaptation of Aphra Behn's novel *Orinoco* for the National Black Theatre. In 1998, she was the Brown Foundation Fellow at the University of the South at Sewanee. She has appeared on Broadway, Off Broadway, in regional theater, and on television. Her publications include numerous critical articles on British and American theater, and she is the author of *David Edgar: Playwright and Politician* (Peter Lang).

Peta Tait is a professor of theater and drama at La Trobe University in Australia. In addition to cowriting *Mesmerized* and *Breath by Breath,* her recent performance works include *Appearing in Pieces,* the award-winning *700 Positions,* and *Whet Flesh.* She is the author of *Performing Emotions: Gender, Bodies, Spaces in Chekhov's Drama and Stanislavski's Theatre* (Ashgate) and *Converging Realities: Feminism in Australian Theatre* (Currency Press). She is coeditor with Elizabeth Schafer of *Australian Women's Drama* (Currency Press) and editor of *Body Show/s: Australian Viewings of Live Performance* (Rodopi Press). Currently Ms. Tait is writing a history of trapeze performance.

Judith Thompson is a playwright, screenwriter, director, actor, and professor of theater at the University of Guelph in Canada. Her plays include *The Crackwalker, White Biting Dog, I Am Yours, Women in the Streets, Sled, Perfect Pie, Habitat*, Capture Me,* and *Enoch Arden on Sauraurin.* She has also written feature films, television movies, numerous radio plays, and adaptations of Shakespeare for children. She has twice won the Governor General's Award, as well as the Prix Italia, the Chalmers Award, the Canadian Author's Association Award, the Toronto Arts Award, the Nellie Award for Radio, and the B'nai B'rith Award.

Wendy Wasserstein's plays include *Uncommon Women and Others*, Isn't It Romantic*, The Heidi Chronicles** (1989 Pulitzer Prize in drama, Tony Award, Susan Smith Blackburn Prize), *The Sisters Rosensweig*, An American Daughter, Old Money,* and *Third.* Her books include *Bachelor Girls* (Random House), *Shiksa Goddess; or, How I Spent My Forties* (Vintage Books), *Pamela's First Musical* (Hyperion), and *Sloth.*

Timberlake Wertenbaker was resident writer with Shared Experience in Britain in 1983 and at the Royal Court during 1984–1985. Her plays include *New Anatomies; The Grace of Mary Traverse; Our Country's Good** (winner of the Laurence Olivier Play of the Year Award in 1988 and the New York Drama Critics Circle Award for Best New Foreign Play in 1991); *The Love of the Nightingale* (winner of the Eileen Anderson Central TV Drama Award); *Three Birds Alighting on a Field* (Susan Smith Blackburn Prize, Writers' Guild Award, and London Critics Circle Award); *The Break of Day; After Darwin; Dianeira; The Ash Girl; Credible Witness;* and *Galileo's Daughter.* Her films include *The Children,* based on

Edith Wharton's novel (Isolde Films), and *Do Not Disturb* (BBC2). Ms. Wertenbaker's many translations include Marivaux's *False Admissions, Successful Strategies,* and *La Dispute;* Ariane Mnouchkine's *Mephisto;* Eduardo De Filippo's *Filumena,* and, most recently, Jean Anouilh's *Wild Orchids* for the Chichester Festival Theatre. She has translated and adapted Sophocles' *Oedipus Tyrannos, Oedipus at Kolonos,* and *Antigone* and Euripides' *Hecuba,* as well as *The Way You Want Me* by Luigi Pirandello. She is a fellow of the Royal Society of Literature and a member of PEN.

Carole Woddis has been a theater journalist and critic for over thirty years; for the past twelve years, she has been London theater critic and feature writer for the Glasgow-based *Herald.* Previously, she was a press officer for the Royal Shakespeare Company, the National Theatre, the Roundhouse, and the Royal Ballet. She is coeditor with Trevor R. Griffiths of two editions of the *Bloomsbury Theatre Guide* (known as *Back Stage* in the United States), and in 1991 she published a collection of interviews with actors, *Sheer Bloody Magic* (Virago). With Stephen Unwin, she is coauthor of *A Pocket Guide to Twentieth-Century Drama* (Faber and Faber). For the past nine years she has been a visiting tutor at Goldsmiths College, University of London, where she also teaches journalism.

Permissions and Credits

Speeches and Excerpts

Speech by Michael Attenborough, reproduced by permission of Mr. Attenborough.
Speech by Cheryl L. West, reproduced by permission of Ms. West.
Speech by Lyn Gardner, reproduced by permission of Ms. Gardner.
Speech by Christopher Durang, reproduced by permission of Mr. Durang.
Speech by Gina Gionfriddo, reproduced by permission of Ms. Gionfriddo.
Speech by Meryl Streep, reproduced by permission of Ms. Streep.
Excerpt from interview with Julia Cho, reproduced by permission of Ms. Cho.
Excerpt from interview with Lucy Prebble, reproduced by permission of Ms. Prebble.
Excerpt from interview with Joanna Laurens, reproduced by permission of Ms. Laurens.
Excerpt from *Sweeping the Nation* reproduced by permission of Susan Miller. Copyright © 2005 Susan Miller.

Chapter 1

Quoted material from the *Feminist Memoir Project,* Random House, reproduced by permission of Ann Snitow.
Elizabeth Goodman interview with Pam Gems from *Feminist Stages: Interviews with Women in Contemporary British Theatre.* Harwood Academic Publishers, 1996, p. 27. Reproduced by permission.
Carry On Understudies by Michelene Wandor. Routledge, 1986, p. 34; originally published by Eyre Methuen, 1981. Reproduced by permission.
Plays by Women, vol. 1, ed. Michelene Wandor. Methuen, [1982], p. 34. Reproduced by permission.

Plays by Women, vol. 5, ed. Michelene Wandor. Methuen, [1986], p. 44. Reproduced by permission.

Chapter 5

Quoted material from *Still Life* by Emily Mann. Copyright © Emily Mann. Reproduced by permission of Emily Mann.

Chapter 7

Quoted material from *Steaming* by Nell Dunn, published by Amber Lane Press Ltd. Copyright © Nell Dunn, 1981. Reproduced by permission.

Quoted material from *Before It Hits Home* by Cheryl L. West. Copyright © 1993, Cheryl L. West. CAUTION: The quotes from BEFORE IT HITS HOME included in this volume are reprinted by permission of Dramatists Play Service, Inc. The English language stock and amateur stage performance rights in this Play are controlled exclusively by Dramatists Play Service, Inc., 440 Park Avenue South, New York, NY 10016. No professional or nonprofessional performance of the Play may be given without obtaining, in advance, the written permission of Dramatists Play Service, Inc., and paying the requisite fee. Inquiries concerning all other rights should be addressed to Joyce Ketay Agency, 630 Ninth Avenue, Suite 706, New York, NY 10036. Attn: Carl Mulert.

Quoted material from *Boy Gets Girl* by Rebecca Gilman reproduced by permission of Rebecca Gilman.

Chapter 9

Material quoted from *Hot 'n' Throbbing* by Paula Vogel, copyright © 2005 Paula Vogel, by permission of Paula Vogel.

Material quoted from *Stop Kiss* by Diana Son, *BOY* by Diana Son, and *R.A.W.* by Diana Son reproduced by permission of Diana Son.

Excerpts from *The Baltimore Waltz and Other Plays* by Paula Vogel, copyright © 1996 by the author.

The Mammary Plays by Paula Vogel, copyright © 1998 by the author.

The America Play and Other Works by Suzan-Lori Parks, copyright © 1995. *The Red Letter Plays* by Suzan-Lori Parks, copyright © 2001 by the author.

Topdog/Underdog by Suzan-Lori Parks, copyright © 1991, 2001 by the author. Published by Theatre Communications Group. Used by permission.

Chapter 10

Material quoted from Susan Miller and from *My Left Breast* by Susan Miller, reproduced by permission of Susan Miller.

Material quoted from Anna Deavere Smith by permission of Anna Deavere Smith.
Material quoted from *Fires in the Mirror* by Anna Deavere Smith, published by Random House, Inc., p. 135. Reproduced by permission of Random House, Inc.
Material quoted from Lisa Kron by permission of Lisa Kron.
Unpublished material quoted from *Jordan* by Anna Reynolds and Moira Buffini, reproduced by permission of Anna Reynolds and Moira Buffini.
Quoted material from Dael Orlandersmith copyright © Dale Orlandersmith. Reproduced by permission of Dael Orlandersmith.

Chapter 11

Quoted material from *A Wedding Story* by Bryony Lavery, published by Faber & Faber Ltd., 2001. Reproduced by permission of Faber & Faber Ltd.
Quoted material from *Origin of the Species* by Bryony Lavery. Reproduced by permission of Bryony Lavery.
Quoted material from interviews with Bryony Lavery reproduced by permission of Bryony Lavery.
Quoted material from *Feminist Views on the English Stage: Women Playwrights, 1990–2000,* by Elaine Aston. Reproduced by permission of Elaine Aston.
Quoted material from *Rage and Reason: Women Playwrights on Playwriting,* by Heidi Stephenson and Natasha Langridge, Methuen, 1997. Reproduced by permission of Methuen.

Chapter 16

Material quoted from *Waiting for Godot, Nine Plays of the Modern Theater.* New York: Grove Press, 1981, p. 179. Reproduced by permission of Grove/Atlantic, Inc.

Index

❧

Bold page numbers refer to photographs.

Wagner, Jane, 158

Waiting for Godot (Beckett), 19, 243–244

Wa-Lehulere, Itumeleng, 202–203

Walker, Alice, 52

Walker, Keith, 85

Wallace, Naomi, 50, 84, 86, 87–88, 91, **133**

Wandor, Michelene, 31–32, 33

Warehouse, 36

Warren, Mercy Otis, 106

Wasserstein, Wendy: and comedy, 46, 51, 141, 181, 182, 184, 185–188, 189; exposure to women playwrights, 1; and mainstream success, 15, 45, 46, 49, 50–51, 52; and Susan Smith Blackburn Prize, **130**

Weaver, Lois, 25

Webb, Daniel, **38**

Wedding Story, A (Lavery), 174, 175

Welty, Eudora, 48

Wertenbaker, Timberlake: as established playwright, 15; interview with, 54–68; themes of, 43; and Women's Theatre Group, 32; on writing, 55, 60, 61, 65, 196, 241–246

West, Cheryl L., 70–71, **70**, 73, 110–112, **131, 132**

West, Mae, 13

When I Was a Girl I Used to Scream and Shout (MacDonald), 73, 93, 95, 96

Whistling Girls and Crowing Hens (Franklin), 132

White, Joe, 59

White, Maureen, 218

White Biting Dog (Thompson), 217

Wibberley, Jane, 31

Widow Ranter, The (Behn), 83, 105

Williams, Robin, 185

Williams, Tennessee, 45, 48, 243

Wilson, August, 52, 239

Wilson, Tracy Scott, **134**

Wine in the Wilderness (Childress), 239

Winter, Resnais, 21

Wiseman, Jane, 12

Wit (Edson), **76**

Woddis, Carole, **135,** 141, 170–180

Wolf, Matt, **135**

Wolf, Rita, 74, 238, 239

Wollstonecraft, Mary, 179

Woman in the Window, The (De Groen), 205

Woman Keeps a Secret, A (Centlivre), 83

Women's Experimental Theater (WET), 22, 25

Women's Interart, 22

Women's Movement: and assumed truths, 72, 77; austerity of, 235; conferences of, 28, 29; and consciousness-raising, 14, 23, 24, 25, 26, 31, 33, 72; and female gaze, 72, 76, 77–78; and Fornés, 19; and grassroots theater movement, 21–22; and identity of women playwrights, 74; momentum of, 72, 74, 195; and mother-daughter relationships, 25–26; and opportunities, 18; and phases of feminist theatre, 31–32; political activism of, 29–30, 31, 33, 72, 73, 100, 107–108, 210; and representation of women's experiences, 21, 23–24, 26–27, 72, 208; as source of inspiration, 195; as white woman's movement, 24–25, 72; and women as central characters of plays, 72, 204; and women's authority, 159; and women's experience of war, 84; and women's freedom, 195; and women's playwriting, 14–15, 100–101, 204, 208. *See also* Feminism

Women's Playhouse Trust, 34

Women's Project, 22

Women's Project and Productions, 22, 50

Women's Street Theatre Group, 30

Women's Theater Council, 45

Women's Theatre Festival, 31, 32, 33

Women's Theatre Group (WTG), 31, 32, 34

Women's Theatre Season, 34

Wonder, The (Centlivre), 83

Woolf, Virginia, 12

Work to Role (Women's Theatre Group), 32

Worth, Irene, 9, **127**